CLINICAL PAPERS AND ESSAYS ON PSYCHO-ANALYSIS

by

Karl Abraham, M.D.

With a Preface by Ernest Jones, M.D.

Edited by Hilda C. Abraham, M.D., Translated by Hilda C. Abraham, M.D. and D. R. Ellison, M.A., with the assistance of Hilda Maas, M.D. and Anna Hackel, B.SC.

MARESFIELD REPRINTS
LONDON

PREFACE

Our judgement at the time of Karl Abraham's premature death that it was by far the most severe blow that had befallen the young science of psycho-analysis in the first thirty years of its development still holds good. Abraham was the most mature of the first generation of those who accepted Freud's discoveries and theories. His rich clinical experience, both in psychopathology and in clinical psychiatry, combined with his keen powers of observation and his cool critical judgement give to his contributions a quite special value in a field where such qualities are of the highest importance. His work has far more than a purely historical interest. The fundamental significance of his clinical observations, and the clarity and precision with which he recorded them, give them a rank of permanent scientific worth.

The present volume fills what has been a crying need ever since the first selected collection of Abraham's writings were published in the present Library series so long ago as 1927; it is gratifying to know that those parts of it that had previously appeared elsewhere in English have now found a thoroughly trustworthy re-translation. It will belong to the small group of the indispensable psycho-analytical classics.

ERNEST JONES

CONTENTS

CONTENTS

PART II

PART III: ESSAYS

ILLUSTRATIONS

INTRODUCTION

THE publication in English of a second volume of the works of Dr. Karl Abraham was first planned soon after the end of the recent war. At that time, however, practical considerations made the project impossible and it had to be postponed. It was taken up again three years ago, about twenty-seven years after the author's death.

The original plan was to translate such of Dr. Abraham's papers as had not previously been translated into English and to publish them together with those of his works which, although already translated, either had not been published in England or had not been collected in book form.

When all the papers which had already been translated were assembled, however, it was seen that they differed so widely in style, and varied so considerably in accuracy, that they would never make a harmonious or satisfactory collection.

It was therefore decided to start afresh from the original German text and to re-translate it. Apart from one paper which was read by the author in English at the International Congress of Psychology held at Oxford in 1923, the present volume is an entirely new translation. It is hoped that its arrangement will show the growth of the author's maturity and the development in his style.

In the present translation an attempt has been made to retain the flavour of the original work. To this end, and also because of its historical interest, psychiatric and psycho-analytical terms which were in current use at the time of the original work but which have since fallen into disuse, like 'dementia praecox', and terms which have since acquired a more limited application, like 'complex' and 'censorship', have been retained. Here and there, a footnote draws attention to a change in nomenclature or word-usage. The use of italicising, underlining and inverted commas, so frequently resorted to in the German scientific literature of the period, however, has been discarded. Where the author quoted from Freud's works, the quotations were from the earliest editions; in the present volume relevant references to the Standard Edition are given wherever possible.

My grateful thanks are due to Mr. Donald Ellison for his collaboration in the work of translating and editing, to Dr. Hilde Maas for her painstaking care in checking the accuracy of the translation and for her advice on points connected with editing the work, and to Mrs. Anna Hackel for her valuable assistance in preparing the work for publication, and particularly for her careful checking of references. To my mother my thanks are due for compiling the index, and also for encouraging me to undertake this work, which I dedicate to the memory of my father.

HILDA C. ABRAHAM

March, 1955

Part One

CLINICAL PAPERS

I

ON THE SIGNIFICANCE OF SEXUAL TRAUMA IN CHILDHOOD FOR THE SYMPTOMATOLOGY OF DEMENTIA PRAECOX[1]

(1907)

ACCORDING to Freud's theory, the symptoms of hysteria are based upon emotionally charged memories which mainly belong to the sphere of sexuality, and which can be traced back to the earliest infancy of the individual. Unfulfilled wishes and unpleasant experiences which the ego is unable to tolerate are repressed from consciousness. They remain active in the unconscious, and may subsequently emerge again under special circumstances as hysterical symptoms. The mechanisms of these psychological processes, namely repression and conversion into hysterical symptoms, have also become known to us through Freud's work. More recent investigations, among them those published by Bleuler[2] and Jung,[3] have shown that Freud's theories are also of great value for the understanding of dementia praecox. In the symptoms of dementia praecox we find the same material used as in hysteria; in both cases sexuality plays a dominant role, in both the same psychic mechanisms are at work. There are, therefore, far-reaching analogies between hysteria and dementia praecox. It seems to me of great interest to find out whether the infantile sexuality of the individual is expressed in the symptoms of a subsequent outbreak of dementia praecox in the same way as Freud has demonstrated in cases of hysteria; in other words, whether the analogy between the two illnesses extends this far. I have found in a number of cases confirmation of my suspicion that this is so. I shall first of all take from one of my case histories an extract which is relevant to our subject.

[1] Psychiatric Clinic of Zurich University. From a paper read at the annual meeting of the Deutsche Verein für Psychiatrie at Frankfurt on 27th April, 1907. First published in *Zentralblatt für Nervenheilkunde und Psychiatrie*, **24** Jahrgang, Nr. 238, 1907.

[2] Bleuler: 'Freudsche Mechanismen in der Symptomatologie von Psychosen. *Psychiatr.-neurol.*' *Wochenschrift* 1906.

[3] Jung: *Die Psychologie der Dementia Praecox*. Halle 1907.

In the patient's home—she is now fifty-seven years old—her mother's young brother (the patient's uncle) was brought up with the other children. He was often punished by the patient's father, with the result that one day he ran away. Years later he returned, threatened to take revenge for his former ill-treatment, and loafed about in the neighbouring inns. One day he took the patient, who was then ten years of age, to a barn adjoining the house and there raped her. He threatened her that if she told her parents what had happened he would set the house on fire. As he was often drunk, and also very brutal to her brother, she feared that he might carry out this threat. She therefore said nothing and submitted to her uncle on several subsequent occasions. Later the uncle disappeared again, but the girl continued to keep her secret. Some time after this episode the patient had frequent feelings in her genitalia which were similar to those she had experienced during the uncle's assault, and which caused her to masturbate. She then began to feel insecure and felt as if everyone knew what had happened and despised her for it. She always felt as though people were laughing at her, that they did not acknowledge her in the street, and that they were talking about her. She herself stated that after her uncle's attack she became melancholy and mad. For a long time she was very depressed and filled with thoughts of suicide. Throughout her life she remained shy and withdrawn. She also suffered for many years from nightly visions in which, in particular, she saw the barn on fire. This vision was obviously doubly determined: the uncle had threatened arson, and had raped her in the barn. She also had terrifying dreams. Once a flight of owls appeared, looked sharply at her, flew towards her, tore away the bedclothes and her nightgown and screamed: 'Shame on you, you're naked!' This is an obvious reminiscence of the attack. At a later time she had visions of hell whilst she was awake. The scenes she saw had a strong sexual tinge. She saw transformed creatures, half human-being, half animal: snake, tiger or owl. Drunkards also appeared, changing into tigers and attacking the female animals. Here again is a memory of the drunken uncle. The wish for sexual satisfaction is probably hidden behind the feeling of anxiety. The patient has had very little pleasure during her life, but has had much trouble with her family and has often suffered privation. At the age of thirty-seven she went through a particularly difficult period. At that time she heard the voice of another uncle whom she had liked since her childhood. He had been unhappily married. Affection and sympathy made her feel close to this uncle, who was in every respect the antithesis of the bad uncle. At the time she heard his voice, this good uncle was already dead. His voice came from heaven; it was the voice of an angel. It forbade her to commit suicide, and prophesied that she would outlive all her siblings, inherit the farm, marry a neighbour's son, and bear two children. In this hallucination a clear wish-fulfilment is apparent, like those which, according to Freud's investigations, are contained, though in a more concealed form, in dreams. Such an hallucination in her thirty-eighth year is a simple acceptance of life, as though to say: there is no need to abandon all hope yet. The hope, however, has not been fulfilled. Some years ago the patient was tricked out of her small fortune by a swindler. She was no longer fully able to earn her living, had to be supported by public funds, and led a miserable existence. Another severe depression set in, and the patient, at the age of fifty-seven, has now little left to expect from life. Once more she begins to plan suicide, and becomes hallucinated. This time, however, the voice comes from hell, and belongs to the bad uncle. It rouses the patient's fear of the future and advises her to kill herself. It was because of this depressive state that she was admitted to hospital.

These are the relevant features of the case history. In this case it is particularly clear that a childhood experience charged with strong emotion, or as Freud would say, a trauma occurring in pre-puberty, has determined the content of the patient's hallucinations and delusions; the impact of this event upon the infantile psyche determines the symptoms of the patient's psychosis in her fifty-eighth year. I do not go so far as to say that without this sexual trauma the patient would have remained mentally healthy, having regard to the fact that two of her siblings have also suffered from dementia praecox. Besides, many children undergo a similar trauma without becoming psychotic. For the moment I will merely say that in this case the manifest signs of psychosis followed directly upon the sexual trauma. I will now mention some further observations, and return to the significance of sexual trauma later.

Another patient was lured into the woods by a neighbour at the age of nine. He tried to rape her, but she managed to escape. She said nothing at home about the incident. At the time she got over her shock without noticeable consequences. After her first menstruation her phantasy began to revolve more around sexual matters, and she had to think often of her experience. She herself says that she relived it over and over again. Gradually, however, she regained her cheerfulness and zest for life.

At the age of twenty-three she wanted to marry, but her father prevented the marriage for selfish motives. The patient was in a state of strong sexual excitement. When she was not permitted to marry the man she loved, she had an attack for the first time in her life in which she screamed and breathed heavily, without losing consciousness. During analysis it was discovered that at that time the patient was working in the vineyards. She walked towards her lover's house, anxiously wondering if she would see him. Suddenly she had to breathe heavily, and then the first attack broke out. When I cautiously enquired about these attacks the patient said that she felt they were connected with the neighbour's assault. It came to light that he also had breathed heavily whilst she, screaming with fear, had tried to free herself. This is the origin of the screaming and of the heavy breathing. The strong sexual excitement at the age of twenty-three reawakened the memory of the patient's first sexual experience. The attacks may be regarded as an expression of her desire for sexual satisfaction. The patient imagines herself, as it were, in the sexual situation which had left such a strong impression upon her in childhood. The attack is an expression of the patient's unconscious desire for a man to put her again into the same situation. For a time she suffered frequently from these attacks. Then followed a period of years during which she was free from them. When the patient was thirty-three years old another marriage project came to nothing, whilst her younger brother married shortly afterwards. She reacted to this with more attacks like the earlier ones. At the same time she developed a persecutory delusion against her brother's wife. As time went on more and more people were drawn into this delusional system. The remarks which she imagines she hears made by people around her all refer to the fact that she has not married. She was again free from attacks for a number of years. In her phantasy she was constantly preoccupied with marriage projects, even when she was well into middle age. She sought medical advice because of her sexual excitement. External circumstances have recently deprived her of the last hopes of the future, whereupon the attacks recurred. She had to be admitted to the mental hospital at the age of forty-three because of her violent outbursts against her supposed persecutors.

The attacks closely resembled hysteria; the diagnosis of dementia praecox, however, was fully established for a variety of reasons which I cannot discuss here in detail. In this case, as in the one described first, there is a connection between sexual trauma and the symptoms of the psychosis. In the latter case, however, the symptoms did not appear until many years after the incident. An experience, which brought with it a similar sexual excitement to that connected with the assault, had a precipitating effect. Whilst in the first case the illness followed directly upon the trauma, in the second a subsequent experience similar to the traumatic one was the precipitating factor. I have had the opportunity of observing other cases which followed one or other of these two courses. I will mention briefly the case of a woman who, from her early childhood, had been subjected to constant sexual importuning on the part of her father and her elder brother. When she was grown up she was seduced by a man whom she later married. He offended her by his brutal treatment, so that she felt a strong revulsion against him. During her first pregnancy she developed a psychosis in which she was frightened by visions. A bull, which resembled her father, came menacingly towards her; at other times she saw the devil, bearing her husband's features and carrying a spear, with which he thrust at her. Those who are familiar with the symbolism of dreams will have no doubt as to the meaning of this vision. The patient's entire thinking was bound up in this transparently sexual symbolism. Her husband's brutality and complete lack of consideration reawakened in her the memory of her father's similar behaviour, and in her psychosis both found expression in the manner described.

Freud originally taught that every case of hysteria can be traced to a psycho-sexual trauma in pre-puberty. He has recently modified this theory.[1] He now lays the main stress on the manner in which the individual reacts, in accordance with his innate disposition, to sexual impressions. In people who later develop hysteria, signs of abnormal sexuality are to be found in childhood. The deepest root of hysteria still lies, therefore, in infantile sexuality, but the trauma is not now considered an essential pre-requisite; it has a more secondary significance. My experiences with dementia praecox show similar results, although I have only been able to analyse a relatively small number of such cases. Some of these cases had a history of sexual trauma, like those described above. Others showed evidence of sexual abnormality in childhood, but without any serious sexual interference. In my experience, the abnormal sexuality of these patients shows itself in a premature appearance of libido and also in pathological phantasies, which are prematurely engaged with sexual matters to the exclusion of all other conscious

[1] Freud: *My views on the Part Played by Sexuality in the Aetiology of the Neuroses*, 1906, Standard edn., 7.

thoughts. If in later life dementia praecox breaks out, these phantasies entirely gain the upper hand. I should like to illustrate my views with a typical example.

A boy was from early childhood excited by the sight of women and showed other signs of sexual precocity. He had a strong passion for his grown-up sister, who loved him tenderly. The sister formed the focal point of his subsequent psychosis. The patient, who is now twenty-four years old, after initial marked hesitation, eagerly recounts a scene from his childhood. One morning his sister, who attracted him by her comely form, came into his bedroom and put her arms tenderly around him. She died soon afterwards, but even after her death the patient continued to love her passionately. He was ten years old at the time of her death. From puberty onwards he made no progress at school, and was unable to study for any profession. He has since shown the characteristic picture of catatonia. I can mention only a few features of this very complicated case. In the patient's visual hallucinations his sister plays the main role. She appears to him, for instance, as Christ, and for this reason he calls her the girl-Christ. This, incidentally, is impressive evidence of the close connection between religious and sexual ecstasy in psychopathic states. On other occasions the patient sees a beautiful youth taking possession of a lovely maiden. They are Apollo and Diana, who in the Greek myth are brother and sister. Diana bears the features of his dead sister, whilst Apollo resembles the patient himself.

These and many other of the patient's hallucinations reveal the sexual attraction which his sister had for him from childhood, and represent sexual union between them as having been accomplished. We know from Freud's dream investigations how infantile wishes return in the dreams of adults. The same holds good for the hallucinations of dementia praecox.

In a hebephrenic patient I was able to trace the delusions, whose sexual nature was apparent, back to an event in her sixth year. At that time she had observed her mother's menstrual period, and this impression had continuously occupied her phantasy ever since.

Because of the limited time at my disposal, it is unfortunately impossible for me to give more than these few fragments from case histories.

It remains an open question whether such pathological phantasies as those already referred to are in themselves an early manifestation of dementia praecox, or whether a dementia praecox which develops at a later age merely makes use of infantile sexual phantasies and experiences. Personally I consider that the individual predisposition is the primary factor. Experiences of a sexual nature, whether they have the true value of a trauma, or produce a less severe impression upon infantile sexuality, are not the causes of illness, but merely determine its symptoms. They are not the cause of delusions and hallucinations; they merely give them their particular content. They are not responsible for the appearance of stereotyped words and postures; they merely determine the form which such manifestations take in an individual case. It is difficult to decide whether every case of dementia praecox contains infantile sexual material, or whether this is only true for a limited number of cases. Investigations on this point are difficult, and often fail completely.

In the various cases which I have quoted here, and also in a number of others, I ascertained that the patients had kept this sexual experience to themselves in childhood and also in later life. Breuer and Freud have emphasised, in their *Studies on Hysteria*, the great importance of this fact in cases of hysteria. They based the psycho-analytical treatment of hysteria on the 'abreaction' of memories repressed into the unconscious. I would mention in passing that a number of patients connect their delusion of guilt with the fact that they had been secretive in their childhood and had not told their relatives of their experience. I am unfortunately unable to consider here the psychological effect of abreaction in cases of dementia praecox.

In dementia praecox the phantasy systems revolving around sexuality are predominantly symbolical. Those states in which disturbances of concentration occur are particularly prone to symbol-formation. Recent investigations have shown that in cases of dementia praecox the disturbance of concentration is of basic importance. The same is true for neuroses and for dreams, in both of which we find the same tendency to symbol-formation. Freud's works have demonstrated the importance of infantile psychic activity for the dream and for hysteria. I can confirm that the same holds good for cases of dementia praecox, and so establish a new analogy between the dream, hysteria, and dementia praecox.

In conclusion, I should like to meet the possible objection that stories of sexual experiences may have been put into the minds of patients. During investigation anything in the nature of suggestion was strictly avoided. In a number of cases patients were only too ready to relate such experiences. The possibility cannot be ruled out that psychotics project their sexual phantasies back into childhood, but in none of the cases to which I have referred is there any cause for such a suspicion. Moreover, in cases of dementia praecox we can easily distinguish between delusional and factual reports.

From the analysis of the symptoms of dementia praecox we learn that the same significance is attributable to the infantile phantasy material in the psychology of this illness as in hysteria and in the dream. For this reason the psychological investigation of dementia praecox will have to be based on Freud's theories. From those theories much powerful assistance can be derived.

II

THE SIGNIFICANCE OF INTERMARRIAGE
BETWEEN CLOSE RELATIVES IN THE
PSYCHOLOGY OF THE NEUROSES [1]
(1909)

IT has long been assumed that marriage between near relatives is harmful to the offspring of such a union. Medical literature, as well as popular belief, attributes a variety of nervous and mental disorders to parental consanguinity. There can be no doubt that in many families inbreeding and mental or nervous disorders go together. It does not necessarily follow, however, that the inbreeding and the disorders are cause and effect. The question is rather whether the incidence of intermarriages in certain families is not due to a specific cause, whether such neuropathic families are not compelled to intermarry by a peculiar tendency prevailing among their members. If we regard intermarriage as a psychopathological phenomenon, we observe that it cannot be viewed apart from a series of other psychological phenomena to which it is fundamentally related.

I do not claim that the views on the psychology of inter-marriage put forward here are of general validity. Such marriages between relatives may, of course, like any other marriages, be contracted for purely practical reasons. In other cases, external reasons such as being cut off from general social life may prevent mixing with people outside the family. More-over the tendency towards inbreeding may vary among different peoples and at different social levels. In cases, however, where relatives are led to marry solely by reason of individual desire I would infer that the capacity for transferring love on to persons outside the family is deficient, attachment to members within the family being at the same time excessive.

Such behaviour has its origin in the sexual abnormalities to be found in neurotics. These abnormalities already exist in their childhood. Neuropathic children make excessive erotic demands at an early age. These excessive demands for love are

[1] Incorporating a paper read at a session of the Berlin Society for Psychiatry and Nervous Diseases on November 9th, 1908.

but an intensification of the demands made by normal children.[1] The normal child naturally gives his affection in the first place to persons in his immediate environment. There can be no doubt that this love is a sexual manifestation being mainly directed, in the case of a boy towards his mother or sister, and in the case of a girl, towards her father or brother.[2] In the second phase of childhood, the manifestations of such love often admit of no doubt as to their true nature. Neurotic children show intense jealousy of the person they love and whom they want to possess exclusively, regarding the other members of the family merely as rivals. In this respect their behaviour closely resembles that of adults in love. It should be mentioned that such behaviour in neurotic children is often encouraged by their parents. The parents over-indulge them and so intensify their demands for proofs of love, sometimes stimulating premature sexual feelings in them.

Under normal conditions infantile sexual feelings for the parent of the opposite sex or for siblings of the opposite sex undergo sublimation. That is to say, these feelings are transformed into feelings of veneration and piety. By means of this process, as Freud explains, the love of parents and siblings is divested of conscious sexuality. It is only in certain dreams that infantile incestuous phantasies survive.[3]

The changes of puberty lead to a detachment of the child from parental authority. The degree of this detachment varies with different children. Libido is set free so that it can be transferred on to persons of the opposite sex outside the family. The nearest relatives are thenceforth excluded from the object-choice. In the unconscious, however, the repressed infantile leanings continue to exert an important influence. It is often clearly noticeable, for instance, that a man is attracted by women in whom he discerns characteristics possessed by his mother or sisters.

[1] Cf. Freud: *Three Contributions to the Theory of Sex*, 1905. Editor's footnote: Now known under the title: *Three Essays on the Theory of Sexuality*.

[2] Among those authors who on the whole reject Freud's ideas, Oppenheim (*Lehrbuch der Nervenkrankheiten*, Fifth edn., p. 1256) draws attention to the particular tenderness, the excessive love of hysterical children. He does not, however, admit these to be manifestations of infantile sexuality. Cf. Report on the Meeting of the Berlin Society for Psychiatry and Nervous Diseases on November 9th, 1908 in the *Neurolog. Zbl.* 1908, Part XXIII.

[3] With regard to the 'Oedipus motive' in the dream, see Freud, *Interpretation of Dreams*, Second edn., 1909, p. 185.

In neuropathic individuals the course of this important process of development is disturbed. The abnormal strength of infantile sexual attachment prevents the complete repression of incestuous phantasies. It also makes liberation from parental authority more difficult to achieve. That is why many neurotics remain childishly dependent. If in puberty the child is still fully under the influence of his parents, and if his libido is still attached to his infantile sexual object then two consequences will ensue. First, normal transference on to women outside the family will be always difficult and may for many years be impossible for him. Secondly, attachment to so close a relative is condemned by prevailing morality. Hence instinctual repression occurs. The neurotic will always oscillate between abnormal libidinal strength and libidinal deficiency resulting from repression. This causes a far-reaching repression of instincts. This process is exemplified in the model sons and daughters so often met with in neuropathic families. The love of such children for their parents retains its infantile character even after puberty.[1]

This particular psycho-sexual development may produce a variety of possible consequences in the life of the neurotic. We are here especially concerned with one of these possible consequences, namely intermarriage between relatives. In enumerating those manifestations which are psycho-genetically closely related to these intermarriages I must mention at the outset one phenomenon which does not strictly belong to them, that is, true incest. If incestuous intercourse actually takes place, then instinctual repression is lacking. A brief reference to such cases should here be interpolated. The case-histories of nervous patients include accounts of sexual episodes between siblings, occurring during childhood. Among patients suffering from dementia praecox, however, the tendency towards incest is remarkably strong. I have seen a number of cases of dementia praecox where incest between siblings and between father and daughter had undoubtedly been practised.

I will not go more closely into the problem of true incest. Instead I will turn to those neuropathic persons whose unconscious attachment remains fixated on to their infantile sexual objects, and for whom, therefore, hetero-sexual attachments outside the family are difficult. Two possibilities are open to

[1] Cf. Freud: 'Die kulturelle Sexualmoral', etc. in the *Zeitschrift Sexualprobleme*, 1908, p. 123.

Editor's footnote: Now known under the title: *Civilised Sexual Ethics and Modern Nervous Sickness.*

such a man: he may remain unmarried or he may marry a close relative.[1] It is impossible to consider these two possibilities separately because they both happen surprisingly often in one and the same family. Families in which intermarriages between close relatives are frequent, often also have many unmarried members.[2] I would like to cite as an example a family where intermarriages between close relatives occurred in several generations. In one generation most of the siblings remained single and of the two brothers who did marry, one chose a relative.[3]

Such families clearly show diminished sexual activity. The choice of a relative demands less initiative than is needed to face the difficulty of approaching a stranger. A girl of one's own family is either well known from childhood days or is at least much easier to get to know. What seems to me to be more important, however, is the fact that a relative will be most likely to show certain traits, especially beloved in mother or sister. Thus a cousin in particular becomes a substitute for the sister. I know of two cases where a man married his cousin in the firm conviction that he could choose none other than a relative. One of these two men, who was under treatment with me for nervous symptoms, had gone abroad to study. There he visited relatives whom he had never seen before. Although normally shy and reserved, he at once fell in love with his cousin and married her.

Some men of this type marry late in life. In such cases they often choose a niece. I have come across a few examples of such marriages. They all show a strange similarity, in that the man is invariably under the complete domination of the wife. In all such cases I have known the men were very dependent and entered into marriage as the weaker partner because their possibility of marriage was restricted to one particular woman.

The frequent occurrence of intermarriage between relatives in one family obviously indicates a peculiar predisposition. I know of families where strangely persistent inbreeding occurred throughout several generations. In one case, for instance, three brothers married three cousins who were also sisters. This

[1] I am here mainly referring to men because the choice is usually in their hands.

[2] This observation was also confirmed by Professor Oppenheim among others.

[3] Editor's note: There is no doubt that the author is here referring to his own family.

family showed such a degree of inbreeding that their family tree can hardly be disentangled.[1]

In some families the tendency to inbreeding is less prominent than celibacy. The few observations at my disposal show such celibates to be very neuropathic eccentrics, who live in total seclusion from the outside world. I recall in this connection one family where all eight brothers remained unmarried. I cannot be certain whether other psycho-sexual abnormalities also played their part.[2]

Closely related to such neuropaths is another group comprising those who are unable to choose their own marriage partner. It is interesting to note that such men often leave it to their mother or sister to choose a wife for them. Such degree of dependence illustrates the extraordinary strength of infantile transference. One famous example of this kind will be mentioned later.

Among neuropathic men there are those who may marry a woman outside their family but one considerably older than themselves. It has been proved that a mother-substitute was sought.

All these groups, however, have one psycho-sexual characteristic in common which I should like to call a monogamous trait. The attachments formed in adolescence are normally not lasting, but are transferred to a succession of people without a final choice being made. Close relationships are formed, only to be dissolved again. Many members of families which show a tendency to inbreeding undergo a development along different lines. They show no polygamous tendencies. They are not prone to flirt or to make easy attachments or rapid changes in their personal relationships. Just as they found it difficult to detach the earliest fixation of their libido, so they encounter a recurrence of this difficulty in later life. Once they transfer their affection on to a person of the opposite sex, this affection usually endures throughout life. Even where such people do not marry relatives their restricted choice is apparent.

We have so far dealt with manifestations of neurotic libido which are not usually regarded as pathological, but which nonetheless constitute a deviation from the normal. There is,

[1] I am indebted to Dr. Magnus Hirschfeld for the very interesting communication that men with homosexual tendencies often marry their cousins. As with such men sexual activity with women is minimal, the choice of a relative is specially convenient.

[2] Of course it is not to be inferred that such causes as those described here are to be found in every case of celibacy.

however, a series of manifestations which, whilst having the same psychological basis, appear to be definitely pathological. It must be stressed that in these latter cases other equally important psychological and possibly also somatic factors are at work. To this category belong cases of psychological impotency in men. Their abnormal libidinal fixation on to mother or sister, that is to say a repressed incestuous phantasy, is at the basis of their disturbance. Other contributory factors are involved. I here refer mainly to the analyses published by Stekel.[1] I myself have observed several cases of this kind in which this factor proved very important. I cite as an example a case of two brothers, both suffering from psychological impotency and both in love with their sister to an abnormal extent.

Women whose affection for their father or brother is excessive are often frigid in marriage. Their infantile sexual fixation combined with other factors makes them incapable in later life of transferring libido successfully. Other patients strive strenuously to suppress their incestuous phantasies. In trying to avoid these phantasies they are easily driven into the paths of homosexuality. They turn away from the mother towards the father. Here, too, contributing factors are invariably found to be at work. According to the observations of experienced authors many homosexuals who otherwise show no interest in women are attached to their mother with a spiritual, sublimated love.[2]

In cases of fully developed neurosis, there are other noteworthy modes of expressing sexual infantilism. I will indicate them briefly. Hysterical symptoms often serve to express the patient's wish for identification with a particular beloved person. One patient, under treatment with me for his psychological impotency, and whose abnormal love for his mother is apparent, copies her in many of his symptoms.[3]

In chronic mental diseases of the dementia praecox group, two ways of expressing infantile incestuous phantasies particularly attracted my attention. Some of these patients developed a delusion representing the accomplished union with the person loved in infancy. I give here a short example from one of my

[1] *Nervöse Angstzustände und ihre Behandlung*. Berlin and Vienna, 1908.

[2] Other connections may also exist between consanguinity and homosexuality. Dr. Hirschfeld told me of a valuable observation he made: a son, the product of an incestuous union between father and daughter, is himself a homosexual.

[3] Cf. specially Freud: *Bruchstück einer Hysterieanalyse. Fragment of an Analysis of a Case of Hysteria*, Standard edn., 7.

earlier publications.[1] A patient's delusions centred around a sister who had died when he was ten years old. She constantly appeared in his hallucinations also. Once I found this patient completely absorbed in a vision. He saw, as he told me, how a very beautiful youth tried to take possession of a comely maiden. They were Apollo and Diana. Diana bore the features of the patient's deceased sister, whilst Apollo resembled the patient himself. In the myth Apollo and Diana are brother and sister. Thus the infantile fixation of his libido found expression even in the hallucinations of the grown man.

Another possible outcome in cases of dementia praecox is the reversal of excessive transference into negativism, and into persecutory delusions against the formerly beloved person. I have dealt in detail with this process in an earlier paper.[2]

In conclusion I should like to quote some famous examples which seem to bear out my views. They could easily be multiplied. A few instances may suffice, however, to show that my assumptions are not based upon artificial attempts at interpretation.

One example of true incest is that of Lord Byron. He could never free himself of his love for his sister. That is why his marriage to a woman outside the family ended unhappily. The poet Konrad Ferdinand Meyer was abnormally attached to his mother and sister.[3] At an advanced age he married a girl his sister had chosen for him. Möhrike, who was excessively attached to his sister, did not marry until he had reached the age of forty-seven years.

The traditional theory that marriage between close relatives gives rise to nervous and mental diseases in the offspring does not give due weight to the complexity of the whole problem.

The peculiar psycho-sexual constitution which, according to Freud, forms the basis of the neuroses, is in itself the most important cause of intermarriage between close relatives. Only secondarily does such intermarriage constitute a detrimental

[1] Abraham: 'Über die Bedeutung Sexueller Jugendtraumen'. ('On the Significance of Sexual Trauma in Childhood for the Symptomatology of Dementia Praecox.' See this Vol.)

[2] Abraham: 'Die Psycho-sexuellen Differenzen.' ('The Psychosexual Differences Between Hysteria and Dementia Praecox.' *Selected Papers on Psycho-analysis*, Hogarth Press, 1927.)

[3] Cf. Sadger, Konrad Ferdinand Meyer: In *Grenzfragen des Nerven und Seelenlebens*, Wiesbaden 1908.

In this paper the homosexual component is also given due consideration.

factor by reinforcing the existing neurotic disposition. Such intermarriages are therefore primarily a consequence of a neuropathic predisposition and only secondarily a factor increasing it.

To put intermarriages between close relatives into proper perspective in relation to the phenomena met with in a study of the psychology of the neuroses, one has to consider them along with a number of other manifestations. Taken together they show the extraordinary importance of infantile sexual wishes in the psychic life of the adult.

III

OBSERVATIONS OF THE CULT OF THE MOTHER AND ITS SYMBOLISM IN INDIVIDUAL AND FOLK PSYCHOLOGY
(1911)

WE know from the analysis of dreams and of neuroses that the mother's body is often represented by certain recurrent symbols. Two representations are most frequently met with: one is the lonely house in a garden or in a wood where one feels one has lived in former times. The other is a secret room with a narrow portal in which one would like to take refuge from danger. I will mention a few examples, but for the sake of brevity will omit the full analytical material for my interpretation. These psychological phenomena are, incidentally, familiar to every psycho-analyst.

(1) A. reports a very vivid phantasy, recurring since childhood. He imagines a magnificent house situated in a large, tropical garden. At the same time he has the feeling that he lived there as a little boy.

(2) B., who suffers from severe anxiety states, withdraws in his daydreams to a secret hiding place. Deep in the forest and underground lies a recess known only to himself. His greatest wish is to live there alone with his phantasies.

(3) C. dreams on one occasion that he finds himself in a desolate, eerie place amidst rocks. Suddenly stones begin to rain down on him until they become a raging torrent. Overwhelmed by the most intense anxiety, he still feels there must somewhere be an opening in the ground into which he only has to slip to be completely safe. 'At the same time I had a blissful feeling of something warm and motherly.' As a boy the patient was often violently beaten by his tyrannical father (the torrent of stones raining down on him). These scenes were for the child associated with the most intense anxiety. In the phantasy he escapes from this anxiety by taking refuge inside his mother's body.

These examples represent more or less easily recognisable 'womb phantasies'. They are quoted, however, not for the purpose of swelling the numbers of such phantasies, but in order to compare them with corresponding phenomena to be found in folk psychology. In the first place there are the biblical myths about the birth and rebirth of mankind. The first of these myths contains the symbolical Garden of Eden, the second the house, that is to say, the 'ark'. There Noah lived for a time exactly corresponding to the period of human gestation.

I would particularly refer, in this connection, to a little known religious cult of the mother's body. In a certain part of Russia there is a religious sect whose followers are called Дыромолъи, that is to say, the worshippers of the hole. Inside their houses they drill a hole in the wall in front of which they perform the rites of their cult. Their prayer is: Изба моя, дыра моя, спаси меия which means: 'My house, my hole save me'. The rhythm of this prayer is unfortunately lost in the translation.

We thus find in this cult the same symbolism which we have already come across in the previously mentioned phantasy formations.

IV

ON THE DETERMINING POWER OF NAMES
(1911)

In his paper on 'The Implications of Names' [1] Stekel has drawn attention to hidden relations between names and occupations as well as between names and neuroses. As the author proves by an abundance of examples, the bearer of a particular name often feels that he has a duty to it; in other cases a name may arouse certain psychological reactions such as obstinacy, pride and shame. The question advanced by Stekel certainly deserves our attention. I will here attempt a contribution towards its clarification.

From experience with my neurotic patients I can confirm Stekel's observation. By way of illustration I may mention that in two cases of obsessional neurosis I found a correspondence between the meaning of the patient's name and the content of his obsessional ideas, and that I am now treating a homosexual whose name fully corresponds to his feminine character traits. I should like to add that in some families a certain character-trait expressed in a particular name is handed down. I know, for instance, a family whose members are especially characterised by their pride, and whose name is in full accordance with their personalities. In such cases an ancestor may have assumed, or have been given, such a name because such a quality was particularly evident. This trait would be handed down even without the support of the name. The latter, however, imposes a duty on the descendants to make a particular display of their special characteristic.

A classic example of the determining effect of names is to be found in Goethe's *Wahlverwandtschaften* (Part 1, Chapter 2): '... Mittler speaks of his present deeds and ambitions. This strange man had previously been a priest, and had been outstanding in his unceasing activities in his profession, especially in his ability to resolve all quarrels between members of a family as well as between neighbours, and extending from disputes between individuals to those involving whole villages and several landed proprietors. Throughout the time of his ministry

[1] *Zeitschrift für Psychotherapie und medizinische Psychologie*, **3**, Part II 1911.

no married couple had been separated and the courts were not troubled with disputes and lawsuits. He had early become aware of his need for a knowledge of law. He had concentrated all his efforts in this direction, and soon felt himself able to be a match for the ablest lawyer. The circle of his activities increased to an astonishing extent and he was just about to be promoted so that he might carry on in a more exalted sphere the work he had previously done in a humbler sphere, when he won a considerable sum of money in a lottery. He bought himself a fair-sized estate, which he let to farming tenants. This he made the centre of his activities, firmly resolved, in accordance with his old habits and inclinations, not to live in a house where there were no disputes to settle, and no one to whose aid he could go. Those who are superstitious about the meaning of names assert that his being called Mittler had induced him to take up this oddest of all vocations.' [1]

Certainly one often finds that a boy who has the same first name as a famous man tries to emulate him, or shows an interest in him in some other way. The first name of Alexander, for instance, may cause its bearer to take a special interest in Alexander the Great and to identify himself with him in his phantasies. A notable example is that of the historian Ottokar Lorenz, who wrote a history of King Ottokar of Bohemia.

I also agree with Stekel when he says that in the choice of a love-object the determining influence of the name is often apparent. I refrain, however, from mentioning the examples known to me.

The reference to the custom some people have of amusing themselves by transforming their name is also interesting. In this connection Stekel mentions Stendhal. German literature contains a particularly curious case of this kind, that of Johann Fischart, who made the strangest changes in his name, using it to develop the most peculiar associative references.

The only objection I have is to Stekel's choice of a term. He calls it the 'Verpflichtung des Namens' (the obligation towards the name). This does not appear to me sufficiently clear, nor is it formally accurate. I should therefore recommend the term which I have used in the title of this contribution.

[1] Editor's note: the name Mittler means go-between, middle-man or meddler.

V

SHOULD PATIENTS WRITE DOWN THEIR DREAMS?

(1913)

In a short paper entitled 'The Handling of Dream Interpretation in Psycho-analysis'[1] Freud briefly considered the question whether or not it was of advantage to let patients write down their dreams immediately on waking. He came to the conclusion that such a procedure was superfluous. 'Even if the text of a dream is thus laboriously preserved instead of being swallowed by oblivion one is soon convinced that the patient gains nothing by it. No associations are evoked by the text, and the result is the same as if the dream had not been preserved.'[2]

My own experience fully confirms this view. The question, however, seems to me to be of considerable interest to the psycho-analyst who makes daily use of dream-interpretation. For this reason I will mention some instances from my own practice. These arose with precisely those patients who had already been told of the futility of immediately writing down their dreams.

Case 1. A patient had a very elaborate and eventful dream associated with strong emotion. On waking he drowsily reached for his writing materials which, contrary to the physician's instructions, he had put at his bedside. Next morning he brought me two large pages covered with notes. It at once became obvious, however, that what he had written was entirely illegible. The desire to rescue the dream from oblivion is in this case obviously countered by the opposite striving towards repression. The result is a compromise in that the dream is written down, but the writing is illegible, disclosing nothing.

Case 2. A patient who asked me about writing down his dreams and who I had advised against doing so, produced a whole series of dreams a few nights later. Waking in the middle of the night, he ingeniously tried to rescue from repression the dreams he considered most important. He owned a dictaphone and spoke his dreams into the machine. Characteristically he

---

[1] Editor's note: This is the title under which this paper appears in the Standard edn. First published in 1912.

[2] Editor's translation.

ignored the fact that it had not been working properly for some days. The record was therefore not clear, and had to be largely supplemented from the dreamer's memory. The analysis of the dream was accomplished without very much resistance, so it can be assumed that it would have been preserved equally well without being recorded.

The patient remained unconvinced by this experience, and renewed the attempt once more. The dictaphone, which had in the meantime been repaired, gave on the morning after the dream a clearly audible reproduction. But, as the patient himself admitted, the content was so confused that he had difficulty in putting it into proper sequence. The succeeding nights produced abundant dream-material dealing with the same complexes. As this material could be adequately reproduced without any mechanical help this case, too, proved the futility of the immediate recording of dreams.

Case 3 proves most strikingly how useless it is to oppose by such means a powerful tendency to repress. The patient complained for several weeks of being unable to remember a particular dream. She related that the same dream had recently recurred every night. Starting suddenly in fright, she resolved to tell me the dream on the following morning, but on each occasion she forgot it. One day she told me she would keep writing material in readiness that night in order to note the dream immediately on waking. I advised against this, remarking that an impulse which gave rise to dreams night after night would find its way into consciousness without such aid; for the time being, her resistance might still be too strong. She saw the point and gave up her intention. When she went to bed, however, the wish to record the night's dream returned again. The patient left pencil and paper ready. She awoke with a start from the same dream, turned on the light, and wrote something down. She went to sleep again, reassured by the belief that the dream could not now escape her. Next morning she overslept and arrived late for her treatment—a sign of resistance. She handed me a sheet of paper, remarking that in her hurry she had not looked at it closely in the morning.

As in Case 1 it was somewhat difficult to decipher the few words she had scribbled, owing to the indistinct writing. The words were these: 'Write down dream despite agreement'. Her resistance had won. The patient had written down, not the dream, but only her intention of doing so. Then she had contentedly gone back to sleep.

About a week after this unsuccessful attempt she was able to relate the dream, which had recurred several more times. Its content derived from a powerful transference. The patient dreamed that I was approaching her, and the dream ended every time by her waking in fright. After other transference symptoms had made a detailed analysis of this incident necessary, the reason for concealing the dream had disappeared.

I should like to mention briefly the motives which lead patients to attach such importance to an immediate writing-down of their dreams. It is in many cases a transference-phenomenon. The patient who brings to the analytical hour notes of a dream unconsciously desires to show the physician that the dream particularly relates to him. In some cases a dream set down in writing and handed to the analyst is in effect a gift to him, as though the patient were to say: 'Here is my most precious possession'. Obviously neurotic vanity here plays its part. Many patients showing marked narcissism are actually in love with the beauty of their dreams. They preserve them from oblivion because they consider them precious.

Just as the neurotic with auto-erotic tendencies wants to retain the products of his body and is anxiously concerned to lose as little as possible of his bodily substance, so also he guards against the loss of his mental products.

VI

A SCREEN-MEMORY CONCERNING A CHILD-HOOD EVENT OF APPARENTLY AETIOLOGICAL SIGNIFICANCE

(1913)

The following communication is taken from a case which, for external reasons, I was able to observe for a very short period only and which therefore could not be properly analysed. The analysis of the patient's screen-memory is therefore of a fragmentary character; in the few available sessions it was not possible to analyse all his associations. In some instances I had to draw the inferences for myself—though to the experienced eye they were perfectly obvious. Wherever I have made such interpolations, I shall expressly say so.

The patient, a man of forty-seven, had suffered since his youth from an obsession. He had to look at and examine all objects in the most painstaking manner and especially had to make their back fully accessible to his view. Once he had carefully scrutinised an object he had further to ruminate over its origin and make. From his childhood onwards there also existed a compulsion to pray and to brood upon religious questions. These obsessive symptoms were of such intensity that the patient became endlessly involved with each object. He could no longer follow his profession and finally could not even leave the house as every object in the street held his attention for long periods. His wife had to go everywhere with him and had to drag him along to prevent his stopping whenever his attention was arrested; otherwise he would stay for an indefinite period, meditating and talking to himself. His behaviour on the occasion of his first interview with me illustrates this.

The house in which I lived at the time had a front garden. My nameplate was affixed to the gate. The patient was not content to read this, but after entering the garden he lit a match to examine the back of the plate. Then, as his wife told me, he spent some time ruminating and talking to himself about the way such nameplates are made. When his wife had at long last got him into my consulting-room, a small bronze figure caught his eye. He took it off the table, turned it round, looking with particular attention at the back of the statue. Only with difficulty was it possible to divert his attention from the train of thought upon which he had embarked.

It was not until the second interview, during which his wife was not present, that the patient became more communicative. He at once related a childhood event which he vividly remembered. Spontaneously and with great conviction he asserted that this event was the starting-point of his whole illness.

The patient told me that one day when he was seven years old he was walking along a street near his parents' home. He passed a house in the basement of which there was a small shop. He noticed that the woman who kept it was involved in an altercation with some other people. Suddenly he saw her turn her back on her opponents, lift her skirts and show them her bare buttocks. The patient then went home and related his adventure to the housemaid, a trusted, elderly person. She reprimanded him, saying he had been indecent and ought not to have looked, and that now the policeman would take him away. The patient vividly described how these words had terrified him: he had felt sick with anxiety. Then, he continued, in order to comfort himself, he had begun to pray. This soon became an obsession he was powerless to resist. He had to pray over and over again that God would make him into a good, tall, handsome, virtuous man. In order to make sure that he never omitted a single word of his ever-increasing prayers, he wrote down a whole litany on a sheet of paper which he read many times a day.

The reported memory referred to an event which may have made a strong impression on the boy's scopophilic instinct. Yet its pathogenic importance must be doubted from the outset despite the patient's emphatic assertion that his self-reproaches and compulsive praying followed immediately upon the event described. First of all, it was striking that the patient related the story fluently and without inhibition. Usually, recollections closely connected with this illness can only be brought to the knowledge of the physician after the overcoming of considerable resistances. The causal connection between the remembered event and the obsessional neurosis, emphasised so strongly by the patient is, however, inherently improbable. A threat such as that made by the housemaid in our case does not usually disturb a boy so deeply. A boy in his eighth year, growing up in a middle-class home in which apprentices and servants are living alongside the family, would normally be expected to react to such an incident and the subsequent threat by being amused or by remaining indifferent. Further, it is in no way clear how a single and rather trivial incident should have caused such an unusually severe and increasingly extensive neurosis. One had therefore to assume from the outset the fact of a recollection which derived its 'memory value' from other memories, repressed into the unconsciousness. Everything pointed to this being a so-called screen- or cover-memory.[1]

On going further into the history of his childhood, the patient assured me that he had had no other experience of a sexual character during that period. He laid great stress on the fact that he and his siblings were 'brought up very strictly'. No sexual incidents ever occurred with any of the servants. During a more detailed account of his parents' home-life I asked him with whom he had shared his bedroom during his boyhood. The patient at once showed a noticeable uncertainty. He then said that he had slept in a room with his sisters, but that 'nothing had ever happened'. Here he began to show marked resistance. His next association was a memory of having once had to pat the back of his elder sister's neck 'because she had a pain or something'.[2] Then another situation emerged from his memory. The wet-nurse who had fed him, and whom he described as a beautiful woman, stayed on in his parents' house after he had been weaned. He remembered that in his fifth year he shared a bed with this nurse. Again he followed this up with the stereotyped assurance that 'nothing had happened there either'. Immediately afterwards another association forced him to correct himself: he had always liked pressing his abdomen against the nurse's body, particularly against her buttocks. Now he remembered having sometimes slipped her nightdress up so as to touch this part of her body more closely.[3]

Finally another memory followed. The patient related how,

[1] See Freud: *Über Deckerinnerungen*, *Monatsschrift für Psychiatrie*, 6, 1899. Editor's note: Freud: Standard edn. 3, *Screen Memories*.

[2] This association obviously covers other repressed material. Unfortunately it was not possible to follow this clue further. It may be pointed out that the back of the head and neck in phantasies frequently represent the buttocks (displacement upwards). See Sadger: 'Die sexual-symbolische Verwertung des Kopfschmerzes.' *Zentralblatt für Psychoanalyse.* 2, 1912.

[3] Well established psycho-analytical experience justifies us in assuming further that the wet-nurse's buttocks attained for the patient's sexuality only secondarily the significance, appertaining primarily to her breasts. But the analysis did not get far enough to confirm this sequence of events.

also at the age of seven, he had been ill, and that during this illness his mother had taken him into bed with her. During that period he used to lift his mother's nightdress. In this way the earlier events with the wet-nurse were continued.

The patient transferred this last memory into the same period of his life as the scene he first described.

This fragmentary material does not in any way give us a complete picture of the origin of this illness. It does, however, enable us to recognise in the patient's childhood those phenomena of the instinctual life which, according to Freud,[1] give rise to a form of obsessional neurosis called compulsive rumination. The strongly developed sexual scopophilia deserves special mention. The boy is not content merely to look at what his eyes chance to alight upon, but he actively seeks to reveal that part of the body which excites him.

Insofar as these memories could be reawakened in a few sessions, they showed that he acted in a similar fashion at the age of four with his wet-nurse and at the age of seven with his mother. It is to be noted that these memories emerged only gradually, whereas the patient reported much more fully another childhood scene which from the start he had clearly tended to put into the foreground.

It is not too rash to assume the following sequence of events. The boy had satisfied his overpowering scopophilic instinct with his mother. As the psycho-analysis of obsessional neurosis has taught us, such incestuous actions tend to lead to the most severe self-reproaches and to the most complicated acts of expiation. Our patient suffered very greatly from self-reproaches, but he linked them with a relatively harmless scene. Here we are in the presence of an obvious displacement, the motives for which are easily recognisable. The patient had actively touched his mother. The scene in the basement shop, however, he had witnessed inadvertently and as a passive spectator. He had repressed the first fact into the unconscious and thus banished the memory most painful to him. Yet he had retained with the greatest exactness a relatively harmless memory and had linked it with strong feelings of self-reproach. The gain derived by the patient from this displacement need hardly be stressed. The intensity with which he had repressed into the unconscious the original painful memory is revealed by the way in which he vividly remembered the basement-shop

---

[1] 'Bemerkungen über einen Fall von Zwangsneurose.' *Jahrbuch für Psychoanalytische Forschungen*. **1**. 1909. Editor's note: *Observations on a Case of Obsessional Neurosis*, Standard edn. **10**.

scene for many years, whilst far more important childhood events reappeared only during his analysis.

The external impetus for the assumed displacement is not unknown. When the boy had told the housemaid of his adventure, she had scolded him for his impropriety and had warned him of the consequences of his behaviour. The effect of her words could only be so powerful because they awakened in him the memory of deeds he regarded as far more serious. The sudden recognition of these misdeeds could then be directly followed by self-reproaches, compulsive praying and so forth; to all appearances they were the after-effects of the unimportant basement-shop scene.

This scene thus proves to be a screen-memory corresponding in every detail to the description given by Freud in 1899. According to Freud, screen-memories are those which in spite of their unimportant content can claim great memory-value. They owe this memory-value, however, not to their inherent content, but to its connection with other, repressed material. The screen-memory may thus be said to be a detached fragment of an important memory or it may represent such a memory symbolically. Freud further explains how material of painful content which plays a part in the actual life of the neurotic tries to hide behind a harmless childhood scene. At the time when the patient was seen, he was undoubtedly still completely dominated by his scopophilia, directed to the 'backside'. The self-reproaches caused by this scopophilia were partially diverted, that is to say displaced, on to the apparently pathogenic childhood scene.

The interpretation of the basement-shop scene as a screen-memory found an interesting confirmation from another source.

The patient produced further memories, mainly concerning puberty and the years immediately following it. He came to describe a phase during which his neurotic symptoms, present since childhood, became very much worse. The new exacerbation, it was now discovered, had followed upon a sexual incident very similar to that analysed in detail above. Our patient reported that when he was eighteen years of age his mother had, on one occasion, for some reason passed through his bedroom during the night. She must have thought him asleep. He saw her lifting the back of her nightgown, so that her buttocks were exposed. It is striking that, according to his description, the patient was once more an accidental spectator, seeing a woman exposing herself. One may assume that his scopophilia was at that time particularly alert and that it was showing an incestuous trend. Whether in this instance he was in any way actively concerned, cannot be ascertained. It seems clear, however, that the self-reproaches accompanying his incestuous instinctual impulses were displaced on to the scene of that night. We may therefore assume this to be another screen-memory.

The description given by the patient, however, leads us to make one criticism. It gives the impression of purposeful elaboration. It is not clear why the mother should have exposed herself in the way described, whilst passing through his room. The true circumstances cannot, of course, be ascertained. Undoubtedly, however, the patient's desire to see his mother naked may have served to falsify his perception at the moment when she passed through his room that night. He may have imagined that he saw at that moment what he desired to see. A clear wish-fulfilment would then be contained in his erroneous perception or recollection.

This paper is primarily intended to be a contribution to the psychology of memory disturbances. It may also serve to remind practitioners of the necessity for scepticism towards such of the patient's statements as concern the aetiology of his neurosis. Screen-memories of the type here described, so eagerly pushed into the foreground by the patient, always serve to lead the physician astray and to divert his attention from the deeper layers of the mind.

VII

ON THE PSYCHOGENESIS OF
AGORAPHOBIA IN CHILDHOOD
(1913)

NEUROTICS who are afraid of walking in the street without being accompanied by a particular person usually suffer from a second phobia also: the fear of being alone indoors. The unconscious of such patients does not permit them to be away from those on whom their libido is fixated. Any attempt by the sufferer to defy the prohibitions set up by his unconscious is visited by an anxiety state.

A five-year-old boy afflicted with both these phobias recently produced quite spontaneously, that is to say without being questioned by the doctor, a confirmation of this psychoanalytical observation. What he said is so amazingly appropriate and succinct that I should like to quote it here and to add a few words of comment.

So severe was his anxiety that the boy could not be induced to leave his parents' home to go by himself to visit relatives living next door, although he had not even to cross the road to do so. He also became frightened if his mother went out, even when his nurse stayed with him. Recently he reached the point where he actually refused to go out with his nurse.

Once when his mother asked him to go for a walk with the nurse he protested, declaring in firm tones:

'Ich will kein Spazierkind sein, ich will ein Mutterkind sein.' (I do not want to be a walking-child, I want to be a mother's child.) [1]

This remark is noteworthy in several ways. The boy expresses his wish for the closest possible tie with his mother: to be a 'Mutterkind'. He refuses to allow a person whom he does not love to take him by the hand: to be a 'Spazierkind'. Most striking, however, is the fact that the boy does not speak of his fear but of his desire. His fixation to his mother cannot be disregarded. The question arises as to how the phobia de-

[1] Editor's note: The epigrammatic flavour of this remark can hardly be conveyed in English; the notion expressed by it is that he did not want ever to leave his mother's side.

veloped in view of the fact that his desire to be a mother's child was so near his consciousness.

The objection implicit in this question can easily be met. According to Freud's theory of the neurosis, it is not the boy's wish to be with his mother which undergoes repression, but his incestuous wish for sexual possession of her. A second remark made later the same day provides confirmation of this view. It shows the little boy to be involved in the struggle with the Oedipus complex and proves him to be dominated by the desire to be his mother's sole possessor.

The little boy's father had gone away for a few days. During this time he was allowed to sleep beside his mother in his father's bed. When, one morning, his mother told him that his father was returning that day, the boy declared: 'How much nicer it would be if daddy never came back at all!' In these words he gave unequivocal expression to his death wish against his father, at the same time staking his claim to sleep at his mother's side.

Both these remarks showed the boy's ingenuous confession of his infantile wishes. At the same time they clearly show the hallmark of repression, and it can be demonstrated that underlying the openly expressed wishes is a deeper layer of wishes which remain unexpressed. This deeper layer corresponds to the Oedipus complex.

Such observations taken from the early stages in the development of the neuroses provide particularly valuable confirmation of the theories based upon material gained with the aid of psycho-analysis only with great difficulties in cases of fully-developed neuroses.

VIII

SOME REMARKS ON THE ROLE OF GRAND-PARENTS IN THE PSYCHOLOGY OF NEUROSES

(1913)

IN my work as a psycho-analyst I have always been struck by the fact that some neurotic and psychotic patients would always return to speaking of their grandfather or grandmother. Yet in no single case of this kind had the grandparents exercised a decisive influence upon the course of the patient's life. However much these cases differed from one another, their analysis invariably led to one uniform conclusion: the special emphasis given to the grandfather or grandmother was always rooted in a violent rejection of the father or mother.

The deeper causes of this singular manifestation, like many other characteristics of the neurotic, become comprehensible to us if compared with the behaviour of children. Two examples from the life of a normal or only slightly abnormal boy may serve to illustrate this.

This boy indulges in the typical day-dream of being the prince of an imaginary kingdom. He ascribes to the king of this realm just those qualities which he most respects in his own father. Later he endows this king with a father, thereby himself acquiring a grandfather, to whom he attributes the power of creating things by his command, that is to say, divine omnipotence. The result is clear: the father who in the eyes of the small child had been omnipotent, is in turn subjected to a higher power which he, too, must respect. In this way the omnipotence previously ascribed to his father is challenged. It should be noted that the boy knew neither of his grandfathers and therefore he had created the grandfather-figure in his phantasy-kingdom mainly from his own imagination.

The same boy was on one occasion punished by his mother. In tears he explained: 'now I'll marry granny'. He thus indicates to his mother in an indirect way that he had really meant to marry her. Feeling her treatment of him to be unfair, he rejects her, albeit only temporarily, and shows her that there is someone placed above her, kinder and more powerful than she, in whose eyes he finds greater favour.

The boy plays off his grandparents against his parents, thereby giving expression to his phantasy that there are persons who surpass the parents in power and kindness. It is perhaps worth pointing out that language encourages this assumption by the child. 'Grandfather', 'Grossvater', 'grandpère', and similar designations lead us to suspect that the child in his evaluation of his grandparents merely repeats what mankind has done from time immemorial. Here, as elsewhere, the child takes the word at its full original value.

We are reminded of this boy's behaviour, if we consider the following passages from a case history from the psycho-analytical point of view. It concerns a young man who developed dementia praecox at a very early age. In his hallucinations and delusions his maternal grandmother played a role which was at first incomprehensible. The patient often spoke of this ever-recurring vision as that of his 'great-grandmother'.

As a small boy, the patient had been attached to his mother to a quite unusual degree. He had guarded her with the greatest jealousy and had begrudged his father and his siblings even a moment of her attention. Later when his psychosis gradually became manifest, he shut himself off from his mother with extreme hostility. Just as the patient's whole being had earlier been entirely dependent upon his mother so in his psychosis he felt himself dominated by his grandmother. In his visions she appeared before him, imposing commands and prohibitions upon him. He heaped the vilest abuse upon her apparition just as he rejected his mother in the harshest way whenever she came to visit him.

The patient's attitude towards his mother was one of constant hostility. He did unceasingly what the normal boy of the first example did in a momentary emotional outburst: he substituted the grandmother for the mother. Here the over-determination of psychic reactions becomes apparent. The patient can direct his vituperation against his grandmother or great-grandmother far more freely than against his mother. They are not as real to him as is his own mother, to whom he is in truth just as fixated as before. Moreover, the substitution of the grandmother for the mother permits him to retain an infantile attitude towards the hallucinatory person, an attitude which he obviously cannot give up. Another patient, an obsessional neurotic, showed his extremely violent rejection of his father in many ways. He measured his father against his maternal grandfather. The patient had been brought up puritanically by his father, whose means were modest. One day he went with his mother to visit his grandfather in his home town. The old man, who was well-to-do and delighted with his grandson's visit, heaped presents upon him and spent sums of money which to the boy seemed enormous. From that time onwards his resistance against his father took a definite shape. More than ever before his father appeared to him as a mere tyrant whilst the generous grandfather was elevated to the position of a father-ideal. During the course of psycho-analytical treatment the patient once dreamed that he was travelling with his mother to the home town of his grandfather, who incidentally had been dead for years.

In the thought-sequences of another neurotic patient the image of his father was accompanied with the constancy of a shadow by the image of his maternal grandfather. Psychoanalysis could prove that the son's hostile and rebellious attitude towards his father was expressed in this greatly mitigated form. Among other relevant material the patient recalled that in his early childhood his grandfather, who already lived in retirement, had always seemed to him like a dethroned god, such as Kronos. By putting the dethroned grandfather side by side with the still ruling and youthful father, the boy secretly comforted himself with the thought that his father, too, would not rule for ever but would one day be deposed just like his grandfather.

Sometimes, too, a neurotic turns away from his father with a strong feeling of hatred. As a substitute, however, he establishes in his phantasy a relationship between himself and his remotest forbears (his 'forefathers'). I have at present the opportunity of observing such a case but practical considerations prevent my communicating it in detail.[1] I have illustrated similar phenomena in my study of Amenhotep IV.[2]

Psycho-analysis teaches us the numerous pathways taken by neurotic phantasies in order to neutralise the power of the father- or mother-complex. Such phantasies of neurotics may be divided into three groups. The most far-reaching of these consists of phantasies of elimination. It is well known that neurosis can express death-wishes against either the father or the mother in many ways.

A second group of phantasies serves the denial of the parents, particularly of the father. These are the phantasies of different parentage.

[1] The patient's most intense anger was connected with an event, which had originally caused him the most intense excitement, that is to say, witnessing the primal scene between his parents.

[2] *Imago* (1912), **1**, No. 4. See this vol., Part III, p. 262.

Lastly the neurotic may defend himself against this complex concerning his parents by debasing the power of the father or mother. Such debasement may take the form of putting a more powerful figure above that of the father.

In connection with this last group it should be remembered that some neurotics tend, consciously or unconsciously, to play off one authority against another. Resistance against the analyst often takes this form in the course of psycho-analytical treatment.

The religious faith of some neurotics, too, may be largely fed from these sources. Faith in divine omnipotence or in pre-destination comforts the neurotic. It gives him the feeling that even the father on whom, by reason of his unconscious fixation, he feels wholly dependent, is not omnipotent but is himself in turn subject to a higher power.

Finally I would draw attention to an analogous phenomenon to be observed in folk-psychology. A displacement of authority from the father on to remoter forbears may well be the basis of ancestral cults. Here, however, it is no longer the individual idolising one of his forefathers. A larger community of men endows one common ancestor with the power which has its prototype in paternal authority.

IX

ON NEUROTIC EXOGAMY: A CONTRIBUTION TO THE SIMILARITIES IN THE PSYCHIC LIFE OF NEUROTICS AND OF PRIMITIVE MAN

(1913)

UNTIL recent times the only special significance attached to marriages between close relatives was that they were regarded as genetically unsound. In an earlier paper [1] I have pointed out that marriages between relatives must be considered to be essentially psychopathological phenomena. Starting from the sexual deviations of neurotic patients made known to us by psycho-analytical investigation I reached the conclusion that many such neurotics failed to transfer their libido on to persons outside their family. They failed because even after puberty their libido remains incestuously fixated. For the neurotic, who must avoid not only the object of his original incestuous wishes, but also women outside his family, marriage to a kinswoman constitutes a compromise.

In the paper mentioned above I have shown that in order to appreciate correctly the psychological significance of the tendency towards inbreeding, this phenomenon must be ranged with certain other manifestations. At one end of the scale we find true incest. This is far less rare in psychopathic families than has been hitherto supposed. At the other extreme is complete and permanent avoidance of all heterosexual relationships.

Closely akin to the first extreme is the inclination towards cousins and other cognate members of the family. Closely akin to the other extreme is the manifestation which I should like to call 'neurotic exogamy'. This occurs where a man [2] experiences an insuperable aversion to any close relationship with a woman of his own people or nation. Or, to put it more correctly, of his

[1] 'The Significance of Intermarriage between Close Relatives in the Psychology of the Neuroses.' *Jahrbuch für Psychoanalyt. Forschungen*, (1909), 1. See this volume, Part I, p. 21.

[2] As in the paper quoted above I am here again mainly considering the manifestations met with in men. The reasons for this have been given in that paper.

mother's people. This is an indication of special measures taken to avoid the possibility of incest. The neurotic takes flight from women who typify his mother and turns to women who in appearance and character are as different as possible from his mother or sister. This flight is a result of his exaggerated phobia of incest.

An example will illustrate the course of events here described.

A neurotic patient of fair, north German type, showed the strongest aversion to women of the same type. Nothing in a woman was permitted to remind him of his original love-object, his mother. He could not even bear women who spoke his native dialect. Only foreign, brunette women attracted him. In the course of years he had been interested in several women, all of them foreigners. At the same time he showed a tendency to which Freud applied the term 'Reihenbildung'— having a series of women. The patient was quite incapable of a lasting and successful attachment to one particular woman. His fixation on to his earliest love-object was too overpowering.

I have had the opportunity of analysing a number of similar cases, and I have come to the conclusion that this aversion on the part of certain men to women possessing their own or their mother's personal or racial characteristics is specifically determined. Weiss [1] published an interesting observation of the same kind. His communication concerns a man who was unable to marry any girl who came from the same neighbourhood as himself, or his father or mother. He also felt shy with girls whose hair or eyes resembled those of his sisters.

With some neurotics the underlying reason for this sexual diffidence remains completely unconscious, whilst with others it is fully conscious.

One patient told me that being himself a Jew, he could never marry a Jewess, for he could not help seeing his sister in every Jewish girl. In fact this patient had an unusually strong incestuous fixation to his mother and sister, as was borne out by the form of his neurosis, which was agoraphobia. During puberty there had been some degree of sexual intimacy between him and his sister.

A second patient, also of Jewish parentage, made very similar statements concerning his taste in women. He repeatedly fell in love with girls whose appearance was in complete contrast to that of Jewish girls, one being, for instance, a blonde Danish girl.

In a third exactly similar case, the patient was unaware of the basis of his racial sympathy and antipathy.

[1] *Internat. Zeitschr. für ärztl. Psychoanalyse*, 2, 161.

In all the cases I investigated closely a pronounced hatred against the patient's nearest relatives existed side by side with an exaggerated love for these same relatives. This hatred may be directed mainly against the mother, in which case the explanation for it is to be found in disappointed incestuous love. Alternatively, it may be directed against the father, in which case it clearly derives from the son's Oedipal attitude.

Such hatred leads a son to turn his back first upon his kinsfolk and then upon all who belong to the same people.

This approach sheds new light upon two common occurrences.

First, there are the so-called mixed marriages. In Christian countries such marriages take place mainly between Gentiles and Jews, being brought about sometimes by the fear of incest and sometimes as a result of a hostile rejection of the family. I could cite many cases which bear out this contention.

In the second place we should bear in mind those men who, spurred on by a desire for independence felt in adolescence, emigrate early in life and marry a foreign woman in a strange land. I have in mind a number of most instructive observations of this kind.

Freud's most recent investigations have drawn our attention to certain similarities in the psychic life of neurotics and of primitive peoples. In this connection the most important thing to remember is the exaggerated phobia of incest to be found both in neurotics and in primitive peoples. This incest phobia is most strongly expressed in the laws of those peoples who give first place to its prevention. The most effective and far-reaching measure of this kind is an institution existing in many primitive tribes, called exogamy. It prohibits sexual relations not merely between close relatives but even between members of the same tribe.

We have seen that some neurotics, driven by an inner necessity, direct their affections exclusively towards persons belonging to another nation. This inner drive has the same result for neurotics as is produced in primitive tribes by the external prohibition of their laws. We are therefore fully justified in applying the term exogamy to the phenomenon here described. We apply the same term to both the neurotic and the ethnological aspects of this phenomenon since both have the same origin and fulfil the same purpose.

X

A CONTRIBUTION TOWARDS THE UNDERSTANDING OF THE SUGGESTIVE EFFECT OF MEDICINE IN THE NEUROSES[1]

(1914)

ONE of my patients tells me that people meeting him for the first time often communicate their most intimate secrets to him. With emotion he said: 'A man once told me that he was not going to marry, because he was disappointed by every girl after he had once had intercourse with her.'

It struck me as significant that he should mention just this example. The next associations were as follows: 'My anxiety sometimes lessens if I see a pretty girl in the tram who attracts me sexually, even though she is a complete stranger to me. . . . Is it possible, doctor, for sexual feelings to drive out anxiety?' After I had commented on this, he continued: 'If I am frightened, I always get most help from medicine which I have only carried in my pocket and have never taken. Once I have taken a medicine, I am always disappointed.'

We now understand why the patient had chosen this particular example. In it he identified himself with that marriage-shy acquaintance. He himself had never 'taken' a girl. He is completely fixated to his mother through his anxiety; only near this woman, untouchable to him, is he free from anxiety.

[1] Editor's note: This was published in a section on 'Experiences and Examples from Psycho-analytical Practice,' in the *Int. Zeitschrift für Psycho-analyse*, 2, Part IV.

XI

SOME ILLUSTRATIONS ON THE EMOTIONAL RELATIONSHIP OF LITTLE GIRLS TOWARDS THEIR PARENTS

(1917)

A MOTHER, in telling me about her four-year-old daughter, whom we will call Elsie, said that she showed particular love and tenderness for her father. Recently she had particularly liked to play at being father's wife. When the mother asked her why she wanted to be her father's wife she replied that she would 'like to know what it was like', and added that she could then at last find out 'what coffee tastes like'. 'I asked her', the mother continued, 'what is to happen to me, and she had her answer ready: "You will just be our child".'

'On one occasion', the mother continued, 'Elsie related to her elder sister a story she had herself made up. It began: "Once upon a time there was a dwarf who had seven little dwarfs. Their mother had died a long time ago". When I asked why the mother had died the child explained: "Oh, she was already over a hundred and very poorly". Some months ago at the zoo, Elsie stopped in front of a cage in which there was a wild sow with a large litter. Elsie exclaimed with the greatest delight: "Look, there is a father pig with his children!" I explained that it was the mother, but she insisted, "No, the father". When I assured her once more that it was the mother she asked: "But where is the father?" Only when I said that he had probably just gone a little walk did her face brighten again.

'Once Elsie spoke of the day when she would be a bride. I asked: "Who would be the bridegroom?" Her answer came out pat: "Well, my darling daddy, of course". Some weeks later she said goodbye to her father with the words: "Bye bye, dear husband".'

This is just a selection from a large number of similar statements made by the same child. They all clearly show how the four-year-old child gives her love mainly to her father and how she takes him away from her mother, as it were, and calls him her husband. Conversely, she readily gets rid of her mother or makes her into the child, thus changing places with her. In these examples the mother's elimination is an indirect one; it is not the child herself, but the dwarfs or the little pigs who have no mother but only a father.

The example of another little girl shows the same tendencies, but in her case the death-wish against the mother and the erotic feelings towards her father were even less disguised.

Helen, aged four, once gave vent to her feelings whilst having dinner with her father in her mother's absence in these words: 'Isn't it nice that mummy is not at home today?' When her father asked her why she was so pleased about it, the little girl replied: 'Because she cannot butt in when we talk'. Some weeks later these death-wishes became even clearer when Helen asked her mother: 'Mummy, when are you going to die?' She was apparently not satisfied with the answer she received, for a few days later she enquired: 'Mummy, ten years from now will you still be alive?' In the following month or so these questions were repeated many times. They always concerned the mother and never the father. When her mother said on one occasion: 'If I die, you won't have a mummy!' she promptly replied: 'But I'll still have my daddy'.

About this time the same little girl said on one occasion during dinner: 'Daddy, perhaps I could see you naked some time'. This was only said once in so direct a form. It apparently was easier for her to give up the fulfilment of this wish than to abandon her hostile attitude towards her mother.

From the behaviour of older children and of adults Freud has drawn the conclusion that these primitive impulses have been repressed and sublimated. He has also pointed out how frequently the original impulse is changed into its opposite, a process called reaction-formation. It was therefore interesting to see this process at work in a young child as could be done with little Helen.

For a time her death-wishes against the mother had been expressed without inhibition. There followed a period of some weeks during which she spoke neither with special hostility nor tenderness towards her mother. Then one day when out with her mother little Helen began to ask her mother to look at all sorts of things in shop windows. Then she would ask of the various things they saw: 'Which hat do you like best?' 'which dress would you like?', just as adults usually do with children. If her mother pointed out what she liked best, the little girl would assure her each time: 'When I'm grown up, I will buy you that hat' (or whatever it might be). To a child presents are especially important as tokens of love. Helen had already overcome her death-wishes and now showered her mother with proofs of love. Obviously she could only give her promises for the future. Herein, however, lies a remarkable compromise formation. Helen no longer demanded that her mother should be dead when she was grown up. She was content to change places with her, as already described in connection with little Elsie. Her behaviour expressed the thought: 'When I am grown up I shall have money because I shall be my father's wife. Then you will be our child and will have to let me buy you things.'

XII

SOME REMARKS ON FERENCZI'S PAPER ON 'SUNDAY NEUROSES'

(1919)

TEMPORARY exacerbations of nervous disorders in connection with Sundays, feast-days and holidays have often come to my attention. The remarks which follow on the aetiology of such fluctuations are intended not to contradict Ferenczi's thesis, but to supplement it in one particular direction.

A large number of people are only able to ward off the outbreak of severe neurotic symptoms by working at high pressure. There is in these people, as a result of too severe a repression of instincts, a constant danger of the conversion of accumulated excitation into neurotic symptoms. By their strenuous efforts in their profession, in study, or in some other round of activity, they divert their attention from their libidinal demands. They develop the habit of working to an extent which is far beyond the requirements of any real necessity. Work in ever-increasing dosage becomes as indispensible to them as the habitual drug to the morphine addict. If at some time such neuropaths develop a neurotic illness, doctors and laymen alike are quick to produce an apparently plausible aetiology. 'Overwork', they say. In some of these cases, however, work does not succeed in keeping the pressure of libidinal forces always at bay. Eventually these forces break through by way of conversion. In other cases, with which we are particularly concerned here, neurotic symptoms of greater or less acuteness and severity break out when, for external reasons, work is interrupted. The psychic equilibrium so strenuously maintained by constant work will be overthrown in the course of a Sunday or a holiday or a longer period of inactivity. Such patients feel better again as soon as they resume work.

There is another noteworthy factor. The great majority of people use their Sundays to enjoy themselves, to go dancing, and generally to spend their time in the company of the opposite sex. For this reason Sundays are a painful reminder to our patients of their own libidinal restrictions and particularly of their inability to make contacts with the opposite sex. One of my patients stayed indoors on Sundays so as to avoid seeing couples in the streets. Unhappy and restless, he remained at home. Such painful feelings of inferiority disappear when Sunday is over. On Monday morning these patients may even feel superior to their fellow beings because they excel them in their work.

During the war I saw several soldiers who performed their military duties with exaggerated punctiliousness. In this way they contrived to keep relatively free from symptoms. Periods of leave, however, had a bad effect upon them and produced an increase of neurotic manifestations. One officer, for instance, suffered from severe neurotic symptoms during the enforced inactivity of trench warfare. He always asked his superiors to send him to any particularly active part of the front-line, in order to rid himself of his symptoms.

Physical illness or accident, forcing inactivity on its victims, may often precipitate an outbreak or exacerbation of neurosis. One tends to link such a neurosis aetiologically with the pre-ceding infection or accident. It can often be established, however, that the patient felt overwhelmed by his suppressed libido during his enforced idleness.

In connection with the regular reappearance of the 'Sunday neuroses' I should like to mention another periodical variation in the severity of neurosis which is well known but which has not so far been considered in psycho-analytical literature. I refer to the fluctuations occurring in the states of neurotics in the course of the day. Particularly familiar to the physician is the type of neurotic who is depressed in the morning and euphoric in the evening. It would be rewarding to make this pecu-liarity, which is to be seen in many neuroses, the subject of a separate study. From one single observation I also know of an annual exacerbation of a neurosis: a case of anxiety hysteria, occurring each winter at the time of the solstice and invariably disappearing with the advent of the longer days.

XIII

TWO MISTAKES OF A HEBEPHRENIC PATIENT
(1921)

A YOUNG girl suffered from an insidious type of hebe-phrenia. She was suspicious and negativistic, showing various signs of the onset of delusion-formation, but so far she had not developed any delusional system. Her suspicions were directed in particular towards the possibility that others might defraud her or steal from her.

One day the patient told me, in great excitement, that a 50 mark note was missing from a suitcase in her room. She would not hear of any explanation other than that somebody living in the same boarding-house had stolen it from her. During a care-ful search, in which she was helped by another person, she found her money. She herself had put away the note in such a way that it could easily be overlooked. She had put it inside a folded sheet of writing paper which she had then put with the other sheets.

A short time later there was a new upheaval. The patient had lost 150 marks. She said that she had searched high and low for them, but without success. The next day it was discovered that the missing money was in fact no longer in her possession be-cause she had spent it.

The cause underlying the two errors was noteworthy. The patient admitted to possessing a so-called 'dreambook', which she consulted as to the portents of her dreams. One morning she awakened from a dream in which she had been wearing a watch on a gold chain round her neck. The dreambook gave the following meaning to this dream: 'You will be robbed'. We can appreciate how completely this prophecy fulfilled the patient's unconscious wishes. On the following day she missed the 50 mark note. By the manner in which she had put the money away, she had unconsciously arranged to make it appear as if the note had been stolen.

When she told me about the loss of the money, she explained to me in detail that it was impossible for her to have spent it, and enumerated with painstaking exactness all the various items of her recent expenditure. After thus demonstrating how particularly reliable her memory was, the second error, also arranged by the patient's unconscious, could the more readily appear to be due to theft. It was based upon the purposive failure of that very function whose dependability the patient had so much vaunted. Any suspicion of her having forgotten was thus made to appear remote.

These two mistakes are of special interest, because they demonstrate how a person with paranoid tendencies is able to fulfil the unconscious desire to be injured.

After I had written this short note the patient committed a further mistake which served the same tendency. She lost the key to her room so that she could no longer lock the door. When the first two mistakes, which were designed to simulate thefts, had been cleared up too rapidly, the unconscious changed its tactics. Instead of arousing the suspicion of a theft, the patient now arranged for the possibility of being robbed. The persistence with which she committed these mistakes resembles the tenacity with which she and other patients like her cling to the idea of being persecuted.

XIV

PSYCHO-ANALYSIS AND THE WAR NEUROSES[1]
(1921)

DURING the war academic neurology has come more and more to regard the aetiology of the traumatic neuroses from the psychological point of view. Despite the rapprochement referred to by Ferenczi, however, there are two respects in which it continues to differ from our way of thinking. It takes account almost exclusively of the reaction of the ego-drives to the trauma, and it confines itself to the obvious manifestations of the neurosis. The object of this paper is to emphasise the importance of the unconscious and of sexuality in addition to the recognised factors.

When, before the war, psycho-analysis proclaimed the sexual aetiology of the neuroses, the case of traumatic neuroses was said to disprove this theory. Some people still maintain that the origin of the war neuroses refutes our theories. Shock, the fear of repeated exposure to situations of danger, the wish for a pension, and a predisposition the nature of which was far from clear, were held to be adequate causes of this illness. The great number of neuroses which broke out during the war were thought to demonstrate the unimportance of the sexual aetiology.

My peace-time experience with traumatic neuroses had long ago led me to believe that the sexual factor in such cases had as great a significance as in other neuroses; but before the war they were not numerous enough or the evidence conclusive enough for publication. I should like to mention the case of a young girl who had a slight tram accident at a time when she was passing through a serious erotic conflict. Analysis showed that this accident provided, as it were, the pretext for the outbreak of the neurosis. The symptoms were connected with the erotic conflict; the trauma was unimportant in comparison with it. I would further mention that in several cases within my experience in which the patients made constant complaints about an accident they had suffered all were found, on detailed examination, to be impotent. This latter disturbance

[1] Originally read at a Symposium held at the Fifth International Psycho-analytical Congress, Budapest, September 1918.

was precipitated by the accident, but appeared to have its true causation in old unconscious sexual inhibitions.

The investigation of war neuroses has fully confirmed the inferences I drew from such observations. Moreover, I was struck by the reappearance in war neuroses of certain symptoms which were familiar to me from peace-time, both in traumatic and also in two non-traumatic types of neurosis. I refer to the symptom-complex which we were so often able to observe in cases of anxiety-tremors: trembling, restlessness, irritability, over-sensitiveness, insomnia, headache, anxiety, depressive moods and feelings of insufficiency. The two non-traumatic types of neurosis in which these symptoms were displayed, although in a less obvious form than in war-neuroses, were those of the impotent man and the frigid woman. So far-reaching a similarity of external manifestations leads one to suspect a similarity in the inner processes.

All my experiences are in full accord with those Ferenczi has already described. The effect of trauma on the sexuality of many persons is to give rise to a regressive change in the direction of narcissism. I should like to say that we have both come to the same view, expressed here today, without having discussed it beforehand with each other. It is only a proportion of those involved in the war, however, who are affected by trauma in this way. We therefore cannot exclude entirely the assumption of an individual predisposition, but we are better able now to define it more exactly than is done in current academic neurology. A few examples will assist us to state the problem more clearly.

A soldier, called up at the outbreak of war, was wounded on the 12th of August 1914. Before he was completely cured, he secretly left the military hospital, returned to the front, and soon afterwards received a second, and some months later, a third wound. When he returned once more to the front, he was buried by an exploding shell and was unconscious for two days. After this fourth trauma he showed emotional but no neurotic disturbance and certainly no signs of anxiety, depression or agitation. Another man went to the front, fell into a pot-hole during night fighting, was unhurt, but immediately afterwards developed the most severe type of neurotic tremors and presented the picture of a nervous breakdown. How are such differences to be explained?

The histories of such people, and even more a deeper analysis, reveal to us why one man remains essentially well all through the most severe physical and mental trials of the war, whilst another reacts to a relatively small incident with a severe neurosis. It is found with great regularity that war neurotics were even before the trauma—to call it for the time being by the common name—emotionally unstable, especially with regard to their sexuality. Some of them were unable to fulfil their duties in everyday life; others were able to do so, although they showed little initiative or driving power. In all cases sexual activity was restricted, and libido inhibited by fixations. Many of them had already before the war shown poor or limited potency. Their relationship to the female sex was disturbed by partial fixation of the libido in the developmental phase of narcissism to a greater or lesser extent. Their social and sexual functioning was dependent on certain concessions to their narcissism.

In wartime these men are placed under entirely different conditions and are faced with extraordinary demands. They must at all times be prepared to sacrifice themselves unconditionally for the general good. This involves the renunciation of all narcissistic privileges. Healthy individuals are able to suppress their narcissism entirely. Just as they are able to transfer their love, so they are able to sacrifice their ego for the community. In this respect those predisposed to neurosis fall behind those who are healthy.

At the front they are obliged not only to endure perilous situations—a purely passive performance—but also to undertake something which is given far less attention. This is the aggressive action for which the soldier must be ready at all times; besides the readiness to die, a readiness to kill is demanded of him. A further factor influencing the unstable sexuality of those predisposed to neurosis is that they are living in an almost exclusively male environment. The sexuality of normal people is not harmed thereby: but this is not the case with men whose narcissistic traits are stronger. Our knowledge of the connection between narcissism and homosexuality makes this comprehensible to us.

The attitude towards women, which had previously been unstable, will be seriously upset under such conditions. If the instability of the relationship to the other sex is very great, it does not need a war trauma to bring about the outbreak of a neurosis.

I had occasion, for instance, to observe a man who on return from his home leave suffered a convulsive fit and was brought into the hospital, where he showed signs of severe anxiety and depression. This man had always attracted attention because of his soft and unmanly personality. In his marriage his potency had been weak, and he had always been inclined to jealousy. When he came home on leave, he was completely impotent with his wife. His fears that his wife would be unfaithful to him reached a climax, and soon after his departure from his home town he suffered a convulsive fit.

Men with unstable heterosexual drives need support for their sexuality. They often gain this support from their wives, upon whom their libido becomes entirely dependent, or they have to ward off again and again feelings of sexual insecurity by going to prostitutes for confirmation of their potency. So, too, they need in wartime a support for their wavering capacity for action. Their military usefulness is likewise dependent on specific conditions. They are often useful in the ranks where their capacity for action is reinforced by their comrades. A changed situation, an incident which, in cases of strong predisposition, may be only very slight, upsets their balance and makes the man who was formerly weakly active, entirely passive. This passivity is apparent not only in the sphere of the ego drives, but equally in the sphere of the sexual drives. Narcissism breaks through. The capacity for transferring the libido is lost, like the capacity for making sacrifices for the community. On the contrary, we are now faced with a patient who himself needs nursing and consideration from others, and who in a typically narcissistic manner is in constant fear for his life and health. The obtrusiveness of the symptoms, such as tremors, fits and so forth, can also be regarded as narcissistic. Many patients show the traits of complete feminine passivity in the way they abandon themselves to their suffering. In their symptoms they relive over and over again the situation which caused the outbreak of their neurosis, and try to gain the sympathy of others.

Here I should like to refer once more to the fact that in our patients the fear of killing has a significance similar to that of the fear of dying. It is only when seen in this light that some of their symptoms become comprehensible. Particularly instructive is the case of a man who relapsed at the front into the neurosis from which he had suffered six years earlier. At that time he had developed a severe tremor of the arm after dreaming that he had killed somebody; hand-to-hand fighting in the front line reactivated the old symptom. Hysterical convulsions are not only brought on by danger situations or shock; not infrequently a suppressed aggressive act is expressed in them. Such attacks often follow a disagreement with a superior officer. The suppressed impulse to violence finds in the attack its motor abreaction.

The complete instability of many war neurotics, their deep depression, and their tendency to harbour thoughts of death, find further explanation in a special effect of the trauma. Many neurotically disposed persons manage, until they are unsettled by a trauma, to keep themselves going with the help of an illusion deriving from their narcissism, namely a belief in their immortality and invulnerability. An explosion, a wound, or some such disaster, suddenly destroys this faith. Narcissistic security gives way to a feeling of powerlessness, and the neurosis sets in.

The extent to which regression may develop is shown in those cases described in medical literature, in which patients behave like very small children. One of my patients, who had previously been neurotic, was reduced to such a condition by the shock effect of an exploding mine. For a long time he behaved like a frightened little child. For weeks he could make no answer to questions about his illness except the two words: 'Mine bangs'. He had thus reverted to the manner of expression of children in the second year of life.

The following example is apparently a notable exception to this rule. A young man, previously healthy and professionally and sexually fully capable, was overtaken by a severe neurosis at the front. He suffered from a serious astasia and abasia, and from a strong emotional over-excitability. An explosion had hurled the lower part of the patient's back against the wall of a trench; he had therefore suffered a trauma, and had already been treated by various neurologists for 'traumatic hysteria'. Detailed physical examination revealed distinct signs of a disease of the conus medullaris, obviously a haematomyelia. It was found that after the trauma the patient had been unable to retain his urine and faeces. Despite this he remained at his post as he considered these symptoms to be the result of shock. His condition improved in the succeeding weeks, but at the same time he became aware of the cessation of all sexual feelings. At first he attempted to make light of this disquieting manifestation, ignorant of the fact that he had acquired an organic impotency. During home leave he became convinced that there was no possibility of overcoming his lack of sexual feeling. His neurosis then broke out, not as a psychological consequence of the explosion, but as a reaction to his traumatic organic impotency. Incidentally, this neurosis differed from the usual traumatic neuroses in that it was accompanied by moods of euphoric, and at times actually manic, elation.

This difference deserves special attention. Surprisingly

enough an elated mood is often found in patients who have suffered severe organic injury. I have, for instance, always observed that on amputation wards there is a remarkably cheerful atmosphere. At the outbreak of war my attention was drawn to this euphoria of the severely injured by a particular incident. On a ward in a general military hospital I had to treat four soldiers who had all suffered a severe injury to the right eye by splinters from the same grenade. All four had already undergone enucleation of the eye in another hospital. They were in no way depressed, but were in a carefree and cheerful mood. On the day they each received an artificial eye, a strange scene took place. The men exuberantly skipped about, danced, and laughed, just like children working themselves up into a frenzy of joy. There is no doubt that this, too, was a regression to narcissism, albeit of a restricted type. These patients repressed their awareness that by their injuries they had suffered some degree of impairment, particularly in the eyes of the female sex. What they had to forego in love from outside, they replaced by self-love. The injured part of the body gained a significance as an erotogenic zone, which it had not previously possessed.[1]

All the experiences recounted here demonstrate that the war neuroses are incomprehensible without due consideration being given to sexuality. This conception receives valuable confirmation from observation of psychoses of war-time which, like all psychoses, reveal their latent phantasy content much more openly than the neuroses. As other observers have already stated, only a few of the psychoses developed at the front are connected with delusion-formations. If a delusion is present, however, it has a clearly manifest sexual content. In some of the cases I have observed, I found delusions of jealousy, in others the delusion of homosexual persecution by comrades. I would like to mention the paranoic illness of a soldier which broke out when, after long service at the front, he went home on leave and proved to be impotent with his wife. A clearly transparent symbolism, as well as other indications, pointed with certainty to the significance of the homosexual component in the development of the delusion. Another man had the delusion that he had been infected with syphilis by his comrades whilst he slept in the hospital ward. The origin of this delusion, too, lay in the incomplete repression of homosexuality.

[1] The hallucinations experienced by those who have undergone amputations of still possessing the part of the body which they have lost (phantom limb), may find their explanation in this source.

In this connection another notable observation may be mentioned. In 1915, whilst I was working in a surgical ward, a man was treated for a bullet wound in the penis. The operation, carried out by a well-known surgeon, was very successful. Two years later the same patient came to my psychiatric ward. Having previously been psychologically normal, he now showed a paranoid mental illness. Questioning revealed that as a consequence of his injury he had developed complete genital insensibility. Here, too, the psychosis seemed to be closely connected with the loss of masculine potency.

The reasons usually given to explain the avidity with which some war casualties seek a pension are just as unsatisfactory as those usually given to explain the symptoms of the neuroses. Like neurotic symptoms, such avidity is connected with changes in the libido. On the surface it appears as if the patient is fighting merely for compensation for stiffness of the wrist, for a lost finger, or for neurotic symptoms. The fact that the neurotic feels within him the change which his libido has undergone is usually entirely overlooked. He is overcome by the feeling of an immense loss, and in this he is justified, in that he has actually lost his ability to transfer his libido, and thereby an important foundation for his self-confidence. Before the war an injured man told me that he had agreed with his insurance company on a certain sum by way of compensation. Hardly had this agreement been reached, when the thought occurred to him that this sum did not nearly cover his real loss. From then on the sum which, in his opinion, he should have demanded mounted rapidly until it became astronomical. The pension compensates merely for the reduction in earning capacity which can be objectively assessed, and not for that which is far more important in the eyes of the patient, his impoverishment in object love, for which he cannot be adequately compensated. Here, too, the patient's behaviour is due to narcissism. Where a capacity for devotion, in every sense of the word, had formerly existed, narcissistic greed is now dominant. The genital zone has lost its primacy; anal eroticism is increased. It is obvious that the pension encourages the development of these character traits; but this is only possible in cases where the injured person had previously shown an inclination to react narcissistically to an external blow to his integrity.

We now come to the question of therapy, and especially to that of psycho-analytical therapy.

At the outbreak of war little attention was paid to neurotics. They were sometimes sent to convalescent homes, but without

c

being given adequate treatment. The large number of neurotic illnesses made other measures necessary. The old method of curing by 'shock' was resuscitated; then followed a period of active therapeutic methods, of which Kaufmann's was the best known. These methods were at first misleading because of the rapid improvement they brought about in a great number of patients. In respect of the duration of such improvement, however, they have not fulfilled expectations; moreover they brought certain undesirable manifestations in their wake. The military medical authorities therefore show keen interest in putting alongside the too 'active' methods, other effective, though less drastic, ones.

Is psycho-analysis able to bridge the gap? Theoretically we may say that it is, because of all therapeutic methods psycho-analysis is the only causal one. We also have practical experience on our side. I refer to a publication by Simmel, and to his paper which is to follow mine. In view of this paper, I will be brief in recounting my own therapeutic experiences. For us psycho-analysts the greatest reserve in treating war neuroses was essential, since before the war papers read at medical conferences and medical literature had shown only too plainly the rejection of our ideas and aims on the part of the profession. When in 1916 I opened a ward for neuroses and psychoses, I dispensed with all active interference, as well as hypnosis and other means of suggestion. I let the patients abreact in a waking state, and attempted by means of a simplified psycho-analysis to make them understand the origin and nature of their illness. I succeeded in giving them the feeling of being understood and of considerable relaxation and improvement. Later on my hospital took on the character of an observation ward, particularly for psychotics. I could therefore collect but few therapeutic experiences.

The objection that psycho-analysis is too slow is not borne out by our experience.

More recently it has been found that the patients treated by Kaufmann's method often relapse when they are removed from the influence of the physician, or when they are exposed once more to the dangers of front-line service. Whether psycho-analysis will have more durable effects, experience alone will show. I will conclude by mentioning the instructive result of the private treatment of a neurosis, carried out recently. I succeeded in a few weeks in curing a twelve-year-old boy of a severe phobia of air attacks. This cure proved to be lasting after the patient had returned home. There he was once more exposed to the danger of daily air attack, and stood up to this situation just like any other person. This success may justify the expectation that psycho-analysis may fill the existing gap by providing a cure which is enduring in its effects. Psycho-analysis more than any other method of observation enables us to look deeply into the structure of the war neuroses; it may also gain therapeutic supremacy in this sphere.[1]

[1] The institution of wards for psycho-analytical treatment which was under consideration by the medical department of the Prussian War Ministry did not materialise because of the deterioration of the political situation soon after the congress.

XV

THE RESCUE AND MURDER OF THE FATHER IN NEUROTIC PHANTASY-FORMATIONS

(1922)

WE are familiar with and well understand the wishful ideas of neurotics which take the form of rescue phantasies, since Freud in 1910 interpreted their unconscious meaning and showed that they derive from the parent complex.[1] In these phantasies the neurotic saves sometimes his father, sometimes his mother, from mortal peril. The phantasies of mother-rescue arise for the most part from the tender feelings of the son, but according to Freud's analysis, alongside the desire to rescue they contain the wish to give the mother a child. Later these phantasies were specially studied by Rank.[2] Rank[3] and also Harnik[4] have helped us to understand why phantasies of mother-rescue appear in poetical works.

With regard to phantasies of rescuing the father, Freud has pointed out that here the son's impulses of defiance find their chief expression. He has further indicated the general form usually taken by such phantasies. The son generally saves from mortal danger a substitute of the father, such as a king or some other exalted personage. Elsewhere[5] Freud cites an example of a typical phantasy of father-rescue, but without giving a detailed analysis. I have often encountered the same phantasy in my patients, and I assume that it is also familiar to other analysts. I should here like to make a detailed examination of its unconscious content, and particularly of its symbolism, and to show that it is not enough merely to discover for oneself in such a neurotic product a manifestation of infantile defiance

[1] *Jahrb. f. psychoanalyt. Forsch.*, **2**; also in *Kl. Schr. z. Neurosenlehre*, **4**, p. 210. 'Über einer besonderen Typus der Objektwahl beim Manne' (A Special Type of Choice of Object made by Men: Standard edn., Vol. 11).

[2] 'Belege zur Rettungsphantasie', *Zentralblatt f. Psa.* 1910.

[3] *Das Inzestmotiv in Dichtung und Sage*, 1912, and **2**, *Int. Journal*, (1914), 43 *et seq.*

[4] *Imago*, Jahrg. I, 5.

[5] In the *Traumdeutung* in the discussion of day-dreams, and also in the discussion of an example in the *Psychopathology of Everyday Life*.

already recognised by Freud. A deeper analysis seems to me to be necessary. It also provides, as I shall show in this paper, valuable clues to the understanding of the patient's unconscious. Finally it gives us insight into the deeper layers of related phantasy-formations which we shall draw upon for comparison.

In the phantasy which I have in mind the patient imagines himself walking in a street. Suddenly he sees a carriage with the king, or some other highly placed person in it approaching with alarming rapidity. Boldly he seizes the horses' reins and brings the carriage to a standstill, thus saving the king from mortal danger.

If we look first of all only at the manifest content of the rescue-phantasy, we find that it is in easily recognisable contrast to the Oedipus myth. The neurotic saves the king's life instead of taking it like Oedipus. The danger in which the king is placed is, still considering only the manifest content, in no way connected with the son; indeed the son risks his life for the sake of his father.

On the other hand the similarity between the two phantasy-formations in their manifest content is remarkable. In both the encounter with the king is represented as a chance occurrence. It is particularly striking, moreover, that in both the king rides in a carriage.[1]

If we now use our established knowledge that to the unconscious king stands for father and rescue for killing, then the close concurrence of the rescue-phantasy with the Oedipus legend becomes clearly apparent. In the latter the killing of the king is certainly unconcealed: but this difference is readily explained by the fact that the myth, at its most superficial level, describes an evil deed which took place in the distant past, from which every member of the people which created the myth feels himself far removed in consciousness. The neurotic, on the contrary, is himself the central figure in the manifest content of the rescue-phantasy. The transformation of attack into rescue is thus explained by the stricter functioning of the censorship.

The rescue-phantasy contains quite a number of elements whose determination is in no way clear, even when we have recognised in the king the father, and in the rescue its ambivalent significance, since it also stands for destruction. Among these details, which are mainly of a symbolical nature, we may enumerate the following: the driving, the carriage, the horses, the running away, the road, the accidental encounter, the

[1] Dr. Karl Müller-Braunschweig drew my attention to this parallel in a discussion at the Berlin Psychoanalytical Association.

stopping of the horses. If we begin by trying to understand the first of these details, namely the driving, we are reminded of a sexual symbolism whose meaning is familiar to us. We then arrive at a layer of latent phantasies whose meaning is as follows: the son unexpectedly becomes the onlooker whilst his father performs the sexual act.

The symbolical meaning of the horses, too, now becomes clear. Here the over-determination of every element is shown in a particularly instructive manner. In the cases of the rescue-phantasy which I have analysed the carriage was always imagined to be drawn by a pair of horses. The two animals in motion become comprehensible to us as symbols of both parents. Now the meaning of the running away, too, becomes clear to us. In many dreams and in frightening phantasies of neurotics, coitus or masturbation is represented by movement of ever-increasing rapidity which one is powerless to check or to stop.[1] We may recall, for example, the fear of some neurotics of going down hill or descending a staircase. Their anxiety refers to the danger that they might become involved in a movement which they could not stop and which is out of their control. The same patients also show a fear of travelling in any vehicle which they cannot stop at will, for instance a train. These patients ward off the danger to which they feel they would be exposed if they let go even for a moment their grip on their libido. They displace their anxiety, however, on to the fore-mentioned situations, which are well suited as symbolical substitutes for the repressed content.

If the running away of the animals stands for the sexual act, then the arrival of the son, who stops the horses, can only stand for the tendency to prevent the parents from coming together. The intention to separate the parents belongs to those instinctual manifestations which derive with particular frequency from the Oedipus complex. The censorship conceals this design and replaces it by chance, which brings the son on the road at the very moment when the violent movement starts.

Whilst the positive element in the rescue-phantasy finds expression in the manifest content, in the deeper layer the element of defiance is more dominant. This defiance, as Freud has already recognised, is the essential motive of the father-rescue. At the same time a contrast to the phantasy of mother-rescue becomes clear; just as in this wishful-phantasy the son begets a child by his mother, so in the phantasy we are here considering

[1] We cannot here go into the relationship of such phobias to urethral eroticism.

he prevents his father from doing the same. The close connection of the two phantasies now becomes fully apparent. In addition, there is the further wish, recognised by Freud, to become 'quits' with the father by rescuing him. Now he owes his life to the son, just as the son owes his to his father.

The foregoing analysis, however, has not yet done justice to the manifold determination of the horse as a sexual symbol. The associations lead, just as in the analysis of dreams of a similar content, to the further meaning of the horse as a symbol of masculine potency and of the male sexual organ. We know that the following dream symbols have the same meaning: engine, motor-car, and steamship. They share in common the quality of pushing forward with overwhelming force. If the son successfully stops the runaway horses, he proves by doing so that his masculine potency is superior to that of his father, whom the child in his admiration had idealised into a king, that is, into the most powerful man. By preventing the father, however, in the deeper layer of the phantasy, from performing the act symbolically represented, he also robs him of the masculinity which he previously admired. The rescue-phantasy is now seen to contain, besides the desire to murder the father and separate the parents, the further wish to castrate the father. Our daily psycho-analytical experience teaches us that phantasies of killing and of castration are always intimately connected. We must return later to the symbolism of castration, and especially to the representation of the son's genital superiority. First, however, we will consider the further determination of the horse and the significance of the carriage in the rescue-phantasy.

The king, who originally embodied all the ideals of masculinity, proudly drives in his carriage as befits his rank. The carriage is a vehicle and the horse is a beast of burden. Both are symbols of the woman, that is, of the mother. If, then, the horses run away, we can see in this the expression of a further wish: the mother is in alliance with the son; she runs away from the father. She even puts him into mortal danger, and delivers him up to the son.[1] If, however, the mother endangers the father's life whilst the son is trying to save it, the son's neurotic guilt feelings are effectively allayed. I shall later in this paper recount a dream which supports this assumption.

[1] In this connection we may recall the saying: 'Einem die Frau ausspannen'. Here, too, we can see the substitution of the horse for the woman. Editor's note: There is no corresponding phrase in English. Ausspannen means to unharness, as with horses. Einem die Frau ausspannen thus means to take a man's wife away from him.

There remains one symbol to be considered: the road in which the incident takes place.

In the Oedipus myth, the murder of the father does not occur in the royal palace, but in the road. This detail, no less than any of the others, cannot be without significance. We know the road as a common symbol of the female genitalia. If therefore we use our knowledge of symbols we can find in the rescue-phantasy, as well as in the Oedipus legend, elements which have hitherto passed unnoticed.

The road over which father and son quarrel now hardly needs further commentary. The idea of a struggle for the mother's genitalia covers, however, two very different unconscious phantasies.

The first one is easily recognised. The duel between father and son is a recurrent theme in myths and dreams. In the Oedipus legend, however, the struggle is represented by its particular symbolism as a struggle for genital supremacy.

King Laius is not the only traveller in the carriage. He is accompanied by a driver, a herald, and two servants. The king and the driver attempt to push away the approaching Oedipus. He resists, and strikes the driver. Then the king strikes Oedipus a blow across the head with his knobbed stick. This causes Oedipus to attack the king with his staff. He kills him, the king falling backwards from the carriage. Then follows a tussle between Oedipus and the king's servants, in which he is victorious.

The symbolical language is here transparent.[1] The blow on the head is a typical castration symbol. Oedipus uses no real weapon, but his staff, again a common sexual symbol, against his father's dangerous weapon, and so lays open the way to the mother. The slaying of several men serves to underline the hero's supremacy. They are all merely derivatives of the father-figure. It is significant that the father first uses force against the son, whereupon the son replies with a blow, which, however, he does not direct against the father himself, but against the driver, that is to say, a substitute for the father. Then the father attacks the son, and it is only at the end, and as an act of self-defence, that the son kills him. Here the same sequence occurs as in the beginning of the myth. The father threatens the life of the newly-born son, so that the later deed of Oedipus bears the character of retaliation and is thus to some extent mitigated.

We are familiar with a typical neurotic phantasy which

[1] It is not my intention in this paper to give an exhaustive analysis of the myth; I am limiting myself to a few remarks on the content of the symbolism.

places the encounter between son and father not in the son's youth but in his remotest past, that is during the foetal stage. Every psycho-analyst is familiar with the strange phantasies in which the son, during his life in the womb, becomes the witness of parental coitus. Among these phantasies are to be found dreams in which the dreamer tries to pass through the birth canal, but finds it blocked by the father, that is to say, by his penis.

One of my patients dreamt that he was travelling in a ship which passed from the sea into a canal. The ship ran into a kind of morass, and there the dreamer came across a coachman driving in his carriage in the opposite direction.

Ship and carriage are easily comprehensible in this connection as male genital symbols. The muddy canal represents the mother's bowels, the bowels of the earth. According to infantile theory conception and birth take place there.

The fact that the dreamer comes in his ship from the sea reminds us of the representation of the birth of the hero in many myths.[1] Water is one of the commonest of birth symbols. I shall not discuss here the significance of the dream for the particular dreamer, but shall turn immediately to the birth symbolism concealed in the Oedipus myth.

At the time of the fateful encounter with Laius Oedipus is on his way to his parents, who are still unknown to him. In a narrow pass he meets his father, who comes along in his carriage just like the driver in my patient's dream. There is no doubt that a birth phantasy is also present in this part of the myth. The son must somehow get rid of the father so that he can be born. We are again reminded of the starting-point of the legend, which is the oracle prophesying to Laius that his son would kill him and would take his own mother for his wife. After hearing this Laius orders that his newborn son shall have his feet pierced—a symbolical castration—and be exposed in the mountains. Here, then, the father, by exposing his son in the mountains, bars his way to life, and by castrating him bars his way to the mother. Oedipus' later journey to Thebes is a second representation of his birth. Again the father bars his way, but this time the son kills his father, whom he does not know, as a newborn child does not yet know his parents.

In the rescue-phantasy these wishes have been made more unrecognisable than in the myth with which it has been compared; this has been brought about by means of repression and distortion, involving the turning of these wishes into their

[1] Cf. Rank: *The Myth of the Birth of the Hero.*

opposite. Just as the analysis of the rescue-phantasy gave us clues to the symbolical content of the Oedipus myth, so the analysis of the Oedipus myth sheds new light upon those deeper layers of the rescue-phantasy which undergo more far-reaching distortion.

Our understanding of the rescue-phantasy and of the Oedipus complex can be increased from yet another side. Neurotics who produce phantasies of father-rescue occasionally produce dreams which supplement them in a peculiar way. Here is an example. The dream is as follows:

'I am sitting on the left side of my mother in a small two-wheeled carriage, a dogcart, which is drawn by one horse. To the right of the carriage, close to the wheel, stands my father. His attitude signifies that he is speaking, or has just spoken, to my mother, but no word is to be heard, and certainly my mother does not react in any way. He looks noticeably tired and pale. Now he turns silently away from the carriage and walks off in the opposite direction to that in which the carriage is facing. Whilst I watch him disappear I have the expectation that he will soon come back again and I turn to my mother with the words: "We could meanwhile drive up and down." Mother now makes a slight movement with the reins which she holds in her hands, whereupon the horse slowly begins to move. After a few moments I take the reins from her hands, whip up the horse, and we quickly drive away.'

The fact that this dream derives from the Oedipus complex is easily recognisable to the initiated. In the carriage, which only has room for two persons, the son takes the place at the mother's left side which belongs to her husband. The father is got rid of. He looks tired and pale, is silent, and disappears. The anticipation of his return may be considered as a product of dream-distortion necessary to circumvent the censorship.

Whilst the disposal of the father is represented in a relatively simple way, the second essential part of the Oedipal phantasy, namely that of the union of the son with the mother, is concealed behind a complicated symbolism which deserves our particular interest.

The incest is represented by mother and son driving together. It begins, characteristically, at the moment when the father disappears. Our dream therefore starts where the rescue-phantasy ended: the father's death. Up to this moment the mother had kept a rein upon the libido of herself and of her son, the libido being represented by the horse. Now when the son suggests that they drive up and down, a symbolical representation of the act of coitus, she herself gives the signal to start and the horse begins to move—a symbol of erection. Then follows the movement with increasing rapidity, which we understand in the sense previously discussed.

We therefore find in this dream as in the rescue-phantasy the horse again representing masculine activity and at the same time feminine libido; it is also a symbol of the penis. It is interesting to note that in the one case as in the other the son takes hold of the reins; by this means in both cases he takes over the role of the father. A particularly striking concurrence of the forces at work in both phantasy-formations is to be found in the running-away. In the dream the mother runs away with the son with the increasing rapidity of the horse, just as in the phantasy of the runaway horses.

The foregoing analysis leaves no room for doubt that even what appear to be the simplest of day-dreams owe their creation to the interaction of the most variegated instinctual impulses. That is why they need a careful analysis with an investigation of every detail. In the case under discussion this analysis enables us to draw instructive comparisons with other phantasy-formations employing a strikingly similar symbolism. The symbolism of the carriage, the horses, the driving, and of the increasing speed is suitable for the expression in a condensed form of a number of repressed sexual tendencies. In this way we gain insight into the changing phases of the conflict between instinct and repression, not only in the individual but also in the communities which have created the myth.

XVI

MISTAKES WITH AN OVER-COMPENSATING TENDENCY

(1922)

It may be said of all the manifold phenomena described by Freud in his *Psychopathology of Everyday Life* that they are contrary to the conscious intentions of the person concerned. The tendency running counter to conscious intention, however, takes a different course in various forms of mistakes. It may fall a victim to repression; this happens, for instance, when we forget words, proper names, and so forth. In the example concerning 'aliquis' given by Freud, forgetting the word prevented certain painful associations from becoming conscious. Mistakes in speaking or writing produce a different effect; here the tendency that is unacceptable to consciousness asserts itself so as to interfere with the carrying out of the intended action. Mistakes might be divided into two categories according to their effects; namely, those in which the tendency that is rejected by the conscious is stifled, and those in which it achieves partial expression.

For some time past I have in my psycho-analytical work occasionally come across mistakes which seem to belong to a third category, one not mentioned in the *Psychopathology of Everyday Life*. I recently met with a frequently recurring example of this kind in a patient, and this provides the subject for the present note.

The patient, a teacher, whose articulation is usually quite normal, tends to duplicate the first syllable of proper names by a slight stutter. This condition troubles her very much and keeps her in a state of anxiety whilst teaching in class. She is afraid of having to read aloud for fear of coming across a proper name which would cause her to stutter.

One day she told me of a name she had distorted on such an occasion. The mistake certainly consisted in the distortion of a word, but not of the duplicating kind just mentioned. She had altered the Greek name Protagoras into Protragoras.

Her associations very soon led to another type of mistake which actually involved a duplication of the first syllable, and which had occurred a few moments before the mistake 'Protragoras'. She had said 'A-alexander' instead of 'Alexander'. She easily connected this mistake with an infantile habit she had indulged in to an unusual degree, namely, that of playing with names or words by distorting them so that they came to sound like 'naughty' nursery-words. It is hardly necessary to remind readers that baby talk nearly always consists of words of two similar syllables. These words are used for persons, animals, and objects familiar to the child, and particularly for the names of various parts of the body and bodily functions. These latter words often remain in use long after the child has adopted the language of adults and no longer says 'bow-wow' but 'dog'. For a long time my patient was inclined wherever possible to make words sound like the forbidden words, and this applied especially to words in which the syllables 'a' or 'po' occurred.

Freud has already discerned the significance of such tendencies. He finds that this playing with words is also occasionally carried out involuntarily.[1]

The first syllable of the name Protagoras had been changed into the word 'popo' (buttocks) which was unconsciously in the patient's mind, by the simple device of leaving out the 'r' and duplicating by a stutter the first syllable of the word. The patient had actually done this kind of thing many times. The variation in the present instance is explained by the feeling of anxiety carried over from the immediately preceding mistake. The tendency to express further forbidden words undergoes repression. Instead of the indelicate and therefore objectionable omission of the 'r' in the first syllable of 'Protagoras', an 'r' is wrongly inserted in the second syllable. This mistake has the effect of preventing an infantile sexual tendency from entering the conscious stream of thought. The mechanism used, however, is the exact converse of that which had given rise to the forbidden tendency. The mistake bears the character of over-compensation.

During treatment a few days later the patient in speaking of a death omitted the first 'n' in the word 'Kondolenzbrief' (letter of condolence), saying 'Kodolenzbrief'. This mistake also proved to be one of over-compensation, in the service of an avoidance.

The disturbing influence in this instance did not proceed from a word used by children, but from the foreign word 'Kondom' (condom), usually pronounced by Germans in the French manner, as though the second syllable ended with a nasal 'n'. After overcoming some resistances the patient brought to light a peculiar association between the words condom and con-

[1] *Psychopathology of Everyday Life.*

dolence. Some time previously a death had occurred in the patient's family, and the relatives had assembled in a room belonging to her brother. The young man had neglected to put away a couple of condoms which were lying on the table packed up in a letter envelope. This created a painful impression on the condoling relatives. If I mention that the patient had since childhood envied her brother's masculinity and more recently his sexual freedom, it is not difficult to recognise that an element of infantile sexuality, the castration complex, is also concealed in this example. Considerations of discretion prevent me from giving further details.

The effect of the mistake is obvious. The disturbing idea associated with the 'Kondom' could easily have caused her to substitute an 'n' for the 'l' in 'Kondolenzbrief', especially as the first syllable also contained the letters 'on'. In fact, however, the opposite happened: the 'n' was eliminated from the first syllable. The mistake has, therefore, the same effect of over-compensation as we saw in the first example, but the mechanism is converse. In the first example a consonant belonging to the first syllable is inserted in the second syllable as well, whereas in the second example a consonant is removed from the first syllable to produce the effect of assonance (Ko-do).

A few days later the patient told me a dream in which she was discovered by her mother in a compromising situation with a man. She added that the scene took place in the 'partrerre' of a house.[1]

The mechanism of this mistake is the same as that of 'Pro-tragoras'. I should imagine that the superfluous 'r' in the second syllable counteracts the tendency to omit the same letter from the first syllable. 'Paterre' sounds like the Latin 'pater'.[2] The latter word had occurred not long before in another mistake and had clearly referred to her father. The man in the dream with whom the patient was surprised by her mother very soon turned out to be a representative of her father. It is to be noted that a duplicating pronunciation of the commencing letters of 'parterre' would produce the revealing word 'papa', and this had been avoided in a manner exactly similar to that of the for-bidden word 'popo' in the first example.

On the basis of these examples I consider it justifiable to speak of over-compensating mistakes. I can express no opinion as to their relative frequency in comparison with the frequency

[1] Editor's note: Parterre is often used in German for ground floor.

[2] Editor's note: This refers to the German pronunciation of the Latin word.

of the recognised types of mistakes. In order to show that these examples observed in the same person are not unique, I will mention a mistake of a similar character made by a man. I can only repeat it as he recounted it to me, for I was not able to analyse it with him. I feel, however, that my interpretation contains a large measure of probability.

My friend said: 'Whenever tonsillitis is mentioned I am always embarrassed because of the clinical name for the disease. I am always about to say "Angora" instead of "angina".' I expect that the word 'vagina', which has a similar sound, was seeking expression instead of the word 'angina'. The error then concerned the first syllable of the word. Such a slip, if made in the presence of other people, would be exceedingly embarrassing; therefore the mistake was displaced on to the last two syllables. To refer to tonsillitis as 'angora' was merely an amusing slip, lacking the painful element of the mistake thus avoided. In fact, however, the mistake had never actually occurred. There was only a constant anticipation of its occurrence. It is also clear that here the defensive mechanism keeps the upper hand.

Mistakes of this kind ought not to be thought of as being essentially different in character from other mistakes. It is noteworthy, however, that an instinctual impulse is converted into a defensive, over-compensating phenomenon. Our psychological experience teaches us that such processes may take various forms. After an anxiety-dream has been analysed it is not the anxiety, defence or flight which seems to be the essential element in the dream, but rather the impulse of the dreamer which the dream seeks to fulfil; this is true whether the wish-fulfilment is achieved or inhibited.

Even more apt is the comparison of the phenomena here described with some of the symptoms of obsessional neurosis; for instance, the repeated confirmatory testing of gas taps. An escape of gas might kill the relatives of the neurotic. His hand would like to obey the unconscious injunction to leave the gas tap turned on. The typical outcome of the conflict in obsessional neurotics is a victory for the dictates of caution. Although this is the outcome, psycho-analysis rightly lays the emphasis on the repressed impulses and their unconscious significance. The same is true of the cases here described, which express a superficial victory of the censorship similar to that in anxiety-dreams and in many obsessional symptoms.

XVII

AN OCTOGENARIAN'S MISTAKE
(1922)

In the Berliner Tageblatt of the 25th March, 1922, there appeared an amusing article by the actor, Ludwig Barnay, who had recently celebrated his eightieth birthday, on the honours he had received both in former and in recent times. He jokingly mentioned that all the tokens of esteem usually bestowed only on the dead had been conferred on him in his lifetime. In one town a monument had been erected to him; in another a commemorative tablet had been placed on the house in which he had lived; in a third a street had been named after him. He then posed the question what honours remained to be conferred on him after his death, and gave the following reply:

'In any event a funeral, the usual memorial service and an obituary notice in the public press. But the funeral obsequies will have to do without this threefold celebration, since I have directed in my will that my demise shall not take place until after my cremation.'

The mistake which appears in the last sentence shows very clearly the writer's wish not to die at all, and gives us a good insight into the deep unconscious conviction of his own indestructibility held by every human being.

It is worth noting that the words 'take place' are not the words which should have been used. Some such phrase as 'My demise shall not be announced . . .' should have been used. The mistake, however, was apparently facilitated by the words 'take place' occurring in the same sentence.

No less interesting psycho-analytically is the fact that neither the editor nor the proof-reader had noticed the writer's mistake. I might add that readers of the paper had also passed over the passage without noticing the mistake, thus indicating that they unconsciously sympathised with the writer's feelings.

XVIII

TWO CONTRIBUTIONS TO THE STUDY OF SYMBOLS [1]

(1923)

1. *Observations on the Symbolic Meaning of the Triad*

THE frequent occurrence of the triad in the various products of human phantasy has long been familiar. We know that its symbolical meanings vary. There is the well-known use of the number three as a representation of the male genitalia, and as an allusion to the triad of father, mother, and child. In the dreams of my patients I have several times met with the triad where it has another, less familiar meaning. It is not my intention to consider here any of the numerous possible meanings for the individual of the symbolical significance of numbers; but rather to formulate a generalised interpretation based on common cultural concepts.

There are three orifices of the human body which principally attract the child's attention. Their attraction is due not only to the fact that they serve for the intake of food and for evacuation, but also because they possess an erotogenic significance of the highest importance. They are the oral, anal and uro-genital orifices. It is apparent that these orifices are represented in dreams by the number three, particularly when the establishment of genital primacy has failed and when the three erotogenic zones are competing for primacy. A neurotic patient of mine, whose dreams very clearly revealed to me the significance of the number three, harboured in her unconscious an abundance of wish-phantasies, partly of an oral-cannibalistic and partly of an anal character.

It seems worth pointing out a similar significance attaching to the number three in fairy tales and in myths. Psycho-analysis has revealed how closely they correspond with individual phantasies. A very impressive counterpart to the meaning of the triad above referred to is contained in Grimm's fairy-tale of 'The Wishing Table, the Gold Ass, and Cudgel in the Sack'.

[1] 'Zwei Beiträge zur Symbolforschung: (*a*) Zur symbolischen Bedeutung der Dreizahl; (*b*) 'Dreiweg' in der Oedipus-Sage. *Imago* (1922), 9, 122.

A father sends his three sons to a distant country. Each of them learns a craft and at the end of his apprenticeship receives a gift from his master. The eldest is given a little table which, when the appropriate words are spoken, becomes laden with everything one could wish to eat. The second gets an ass which on the order, 'Bricklebrit, spew forth gold', at once produces pieces of gold from his bowels. The third son gets a sack containing a cudgel, which at his master's bidding comes out of the bag, thrashes any adversary of his master, and returns to the bag at the latter's command.

The first gift denotes a wish-fulfilment connected with the oral zone. Every child probably has the wish to obtain by means of the omnipotence of thought any desired food at any time.

The second gift has a similar meaning. The attaching of value to faeces and the identifying of faeces with gold are familiar to child psychology. The second gift means the fulfilment of the wish to provide oneself with unlimited wealth by way of anal production.

The meaning of the third gift is not quite so obvious, but it becomes easily comprehensible if we remember the typical symbolical significance of the cudgel. The meaning of the sack containing the stick is unmistakable. The orders given to the cudgel by its owner: 'Out of the sack, cudgel', and 'Into the sack, cudgel', clearly refer to erection followed by its opposite. The third son is thus endowed with the gift of unlimited potency which he can evoke at will.

The fairy-tale thus contains three wish-fulfilments corresponding to the three erotogenic zones. It is noteworthy that their sequence coincides with the three phases of libido development discovered by Freud. In the first phase the erotogenic significance of the mouth is paramount, in the second that of the anus, and in the third and final phase, that of the genitalia.

Furthermore, it is interesting to note that at the beginning of the story the two elder brothers laugh at the youngest. The eldest brother, however, soon loses his magic table to a fraudulent inn-keeper at whose inn he stays the night on his journey home, and who replaces it by an ordinary table. On his arrival home, the father derides him when he vainly tries to obtain delectable dishes by means of the table. The second brother fares no better with his ass. He, too, is cheated by the inn-keeper and derided by his father. On the basis of the psycho-analytical interpretation of fairy-tales it may be presumed that both inn-keeper and father symbolise the jealous father. The youngest son alone defeats the inn-keeper through his virility, the symbol of which is the cudgel. Only he obtains his father's recognition on his return.

The fairy-tale thus confirms the experience of reality that it is not by infantile phantasies of an oral or anal character that a boy attains maturity, but only through the successful establishment of genital primacy. What is particularly instructive, however, is the symbolism of the triad.

2. 'The Trifurcation of the Road' in the Oedipus Myth

In a short paper on the symbolism of a neurotic rescue-phantasy [1] I have sought to prove that the phantasy of rescuing one's father shows a remarkable correspondence to the Oedipus myth, and that this is true not only with regard to the latent content of the myth. I have tried to show that both phantasy structures make use of a similar symbolism in their representation of a similar content. This similarity of symbols has not hitherto been given sufficient attention. In the latent content of both phantasy structures, the son witnesses the act of sexual intercourse between his parents; he seeks to prevent this by killing his father, and in that way rescuing his mother.

In the Oedipus myth, the son's encounter with his father's fast moving carriage, symbolising coitus, occurs at a particular place. In the various versions of the myth a 'narrow pass' and 'crossroads' are mentioned. If the narrow pass is a symbol of the female genitalia, it falls into place with the rest of the symbolism employed. With the second symbol the interpretation is more difficult. ὁδὸς σχιστή literally means not 'cross-roads', but 'divided-road'—which might be translated by some such phrase as 'parting of the ways'. We find the expression 'trifurcation' (Dreiweg) in a German translation of the Sophoclean version of the tragedy. The symbol of the 'narrow pass' easily fits into our theory; the 'trifurcation', however, appears at first sight not fully comprehensible.

Professor Freud drew my attention to the difficulty this point raises when I showed him the above-mentioned paper for his opinion. One possible interpretation readily suggested itself. The parting of the ways might, as in the case of Hercules, symbolise a doubt on the part of the traveller; for Oedipus, at the moment of his encounter with King Laius, is seriously troubled about his parentage. Such an explanation, however, would be much too rationalistic; it fails to take sufficient account of the latent content of this part of the myth and in

[1] 'Rescue and Murder of the Father in Neurotic Phantasy-Formations, this vol. Part I, p. 68.

particular to meet one specific point. The narrow place is described as being wide enough for either Oedipus or the carriage of Laius. If it were a 'divided road', it would be particularly easy for either one to make room for the other. Hence only an interpretation of ὁδὸς σχιστή which explains this peculiar feature of the story can be regarded as satisfactory.

Having regard to these difficulties, I entirely omitted the consideration of this particular question from my previous paper. Shortly afterwards, a dream brought by a patient of mine provided an explanation of the trifurcation which in my opinion is completely satisfactory. The dream was as follows:

'My mother has died, and I am attending the funeral. The scene then becomes indistinct. I go away and then return to the grave. I have the impression that I am in Russia, and that Bolsheviks have violated the grave. A hole has been dug in the ground. I see something white at the bottom of it; it may be the shroud. Then the scene changes again. Now my mother's grave is at a place where two roads meet, converging into a wide highway. The grave protrudes only slightly above the surrounding ground; vehicles pass over it and disappear. Now I myself am driving backwards and forwards over it.'

Analysis reveals the incestuous character of the dream. The patient's unconscious contains pronounced necrophilic phantasies. Not until his mother was dead could he possess her. The violation of his mother signified by the digging of the hole in the ground is attributed to the Bolsheviks; this is due to the working of the 'censorship'. Frequently in the dreams of our patients the Bolsheviks represent those wishful impulses which outrage conventional morality. According to the free associations of the dreamer, the shroud which is visible down below signifies the fact that the body is naked. 'White' produces from the patient the association 'dark' symbolising pubic hair. In the dream, therefore, in place of the dreamer's own unconscious urge to violate his mother, we find the act of violation already perpetrated by other persons. It should be noted that we speak of violating a grave as well as of violating a woman.

The indeterminate number of violators in the shape of Bolsheviks recur in the dream in the form of the many vehicles passing over the grave. If in the first part of the dream the grave symbolised the mother who has been dishonoured by many men, the identification of the mother with a prostitute becomes only too apparent. A place where several roads meet suggests the idea of particularly heavy traffic. We remember that busy places like railway stations and department stores are frequently used as symbols of prostitution. At the same time we remember that the road symbolises the female genital organs, the vehicles those of the male. The true meaning of the driving backwards and forwards over this particular spot can no longer remain in doubt.

Another feature of the manifest content of the dream is of importance, namely the fact that the grave protrudes a little above the ground. The explanation for this is that in the repressed phantasies of my patient a protuberance representing a penis is attributed to the female body. In many of his dreams his mother appears in a masculine role, he himself in a feminine role. In the dream in question he plays the active part, but in the special circumstances that his mother is no longer alive.

His mother's grave represents her body, and especially her genitalia. Both dream-scenes contain allusions to the genitalia. In the first part of the dream the hole in the ground, and in the second the slight protuberance referred to this. The site of this well-worn grave provides an unmistakable clue. The two roads which merge to form a wide highway are the two thighs which join at the trunk. The junction is the site of the genitalia.

The dreamer approaches the scene just as a number of men are engaged with his mother. They vanish and he takes possession of her. This is exactly what happens in the Oedipus myth. Oedipus encounters Laius, who is accompanied by other men, at the trifurcation. Oedipus kills Laius and the others. He then sets out to find his mother. If we interpret the symbolism of the ancient legend in this way, Oedipus' struggle with Laius is a struggle for the mother's genitalia. This makes it clear why neither father nor son can give way.

We therefore come to the unexpected conclusion that the trifurcation has the same meaning as the narrow pass. The former symbolises the site of the female genitalia; the latter their shape. Nevertheless the phantasies underlying the two versions are not the same. The version of the trifurcation, the place of heavy traffic, clearly represents the mother as a prostitute; the encounter in the narrow pass gives expression to another phantasy, that of encountering the father inside the mother's body before birth; the phantasy of observing coitus from within the womb. Further discussion of this problem is to be found in the paper referred to above.

XIX

PSYCHO-ANALYTICAL VIEWS ON SOME CHARACTERISTICS OF EARLY INFANTILE THINKING [1]

(1923)

PSYCHO-ANALYTICAL interest is focussed on the question of the origin of psychic phenomena. In terms of psycho-analysis the problem is this: by what instinctive forces, conscious and unconscious, are these phenomena determined? The analysis of psychological products regularly reveals in them the combined workings of the 'ego-instincts' and the 'sexual instincts'. Psycho-analysis attributes to the latter a far wider significance than that ascribed to them by other schools of thought. It is not necessary for the purpose of this paper to enter upon a discussion as to whether psycho-analysis is right in this respect; the task before us is a more general one.

Psycho-analysis took as its starting-point the investigation of neurotic symptom-formation. But the more thoroughly the psycho-genesis of a symptom was explored the more definitely did the associations of the patients lead back into the past, and ultimately to early childhood. In this way certain necessary hypotheses suggested themselves with reference to the instinctive life, and especially the sexual life, of the child, which were in opposition to the traditional views. These hypotheses were confirmed by direct observation of children, and thus we attained new points of view about the psychology of childhood. Amongst other results we came to know that thinking in early childhood is in a special degree under the influence of the instinctive life. My intention now is to show how certain phenomena of infantile thinking are determined by peculiarities, with which we are familiar, of the instinctive life of the child. As the title of this paper indicates, I do not pretend to give an exhaustive account of the subject; I am conscious of the fragmentary character of my essay.

Thinking is the intellectual side of our relation to the outside world; it is based upon sense-perceptions, the experience of the

[1] This paper was delivered by the author at the International Congress of Psychology at Oxford, on July 31st, 1923.

individual. At the earliest period of our lives the contact with the outside world which is of the greatest practical significance is made by means of the mouth. The twofold importance of the mouth as an organ of nourishment and an erotogenic zone is a matter which, as I have said, I do not propose to discuss here. Without passing any judgment, therefore, as to the correctness or otherwise of that psycho-analytical conception I will merely lay stress upon the fact that at this earliest period of life the instinct of sucking is the most powerful one that there is. At a rather later stage the instinct of biting acquires a similar importance. It is only gradually that the child apprehends the outside world by means of eye and ear. The tendency to put every object into his mouth and chew it with his teeth, with a view to completely incorporating it, becomes strikingly evident from the moment that his hands have the power of grasping. To the child at this stage the outside world consists of all those objects which delight him and which he would like to incorporate in himself but has not yet so incorporated. The ego and its interests are more important than the object-world. At the stage of the primitive pleasure in biting there is as yet no inhibition to check the destruction of objects: the child is still wholly without adaptation to the outside world. In the realm of the ego-instincts egoism is wholly dominant, as is narcissism in that of childish sexuality. Thus we see that the child's primitive attitude towards objects is a simple matter of pleasure or pain. The outside world is regarded purely subjectively according to its effect, pleasurable or painful, upon the ego. This is true to a considerable extent with regard to the thinking of adults as well, but there is nevertheless a great quantitative difference in the two cases. In adults the function of consciousness has a moderating and regulating influence upon the instinctive life; consciousness has the power of confronting the impulses with criticism and applies to our desires the standard of reality.

Thus the psychic attitude of the young child towards objects is determined simply and solely by the pleasurable or painful effect produced upon him by those objects. Side by side with this important fact of the infantile mental life let us hasten to set another phenomenon which is closely related to it. I refer to the discovery that, when two objects arouse in the child similar feelings of pleasure or of pain, he proceeds unhesitatingly to identify them. The critical mode of thinking by which we compare and differentiate is wholly absent at this early stage. A few examples may serve to illustrate this mode of thinking by identification which belongs to early childhood.

A little girl of eighteen months was somewhat afraid of dogs. If she saw one she would cry out in alarm: 'Bow-wow bite!' ('Wau-wau bei't'). When winter came and the house was heated she once went too near the stove and burned her hand slightly. She began to cry, saying 'Bow-wow bite!' The fact that a dog that bites and a hot stove both hurt was enough to make the child identify the two. Because the hot stove hurt her it was a bow-wow.

Another baby, about two years old, spent much time by the cage of a canary which she kept on calling by its name 'Hans'. One day she called a feather dropped by the bird 'Hans' and after that she gave the same name to all feathers and before long to one of her mother's hats which was trimmed with feathers, to her mother's hair and to her own, to a soft cushion and so on. Everything which felt soft was in her language 'Hans'. To the adult, whose thinking differentiates, a canary and a woman's hair are two very different things. Thought which differentiates will ascribe to both the same quality 'soft', but in so doing it will not neglect the more important differences between the two objects.

We find analogous thought-processes amongst primitive peoples. The primitive form of thinking persists moreover in the symbolic mode of expression as we meet with it in myths and fairy-tales of different races and in the dreams and other phantasy-creations of individuals. As the child grows older he finds great scope in play for thinking by the method of identification, though of course he has by this time become conscious of the imaginary character of his play. One example will suffice to illustrate my meaning. A boy of seven years old, when out for a walk, removed some scattered pieces of paper from the pavement with a stick, saying as he did so: 'I am the old general!' A retired general did as a matter of fact live near the boy's home and made it his business to keep the street tidy. In his play the child identified himself with the general simply on the strength of the imitation of this habit of his. To adult thought a vague analogy of this sort is trivial and could never be made the basis of an identification of two persons.

Owing to this peculiarity of infantile thinking it is possible for any person who acts in the same way as another has done previously quite easily to take the latter's place in the child's mental life. A little boy had lost his father in the war. An uncle took charge of him and gave him much affection, and it seemed as if the child was on his side much attached to his uncle. In about a year's time the latter died, whereupon another relation appeared on the scene with the intention of taking charge of the little orphan. It happened that the child was asked if he were sad because his uncle had died. The boy, who was four years old at the time, answered: 'Oh no; you see we have the other uncle now and he gave me a piece of bread and marmalade twice'.

It is only gradually that differentiation in thinking establishes its claims. An important motive in this process is the child's tendency to emphasise points in which he is superior and thus to contrast himself with the outside world. A two-year-old boy was asked if he liked his new baby-sister. The child, who was not yet able to frame connected sentences, answered quickly: 'No teeth . . . red . . . smelly!' It is easy to see that the leading motive in this typical way of comparing himself with little brothers and sisters is the child's narcissism.

Another and particularly interesting instance of identification should be mentioned here, and that is the substitution of animals for people in the animal-phobias of children. Psychoanalysis succeeded in proving that in these cases there is regularly an identification of the father or mother with an animal. Here the psychological process is clearly exactly analogous to the phenomena of the animal-totemism of primitive peoples. Originally the prevailing tendency in the child's relation to objects was the desire to incorporate them in itself. Gradually this aim is replaced by another, namely the craving to possess and master the object. 'I want, I want!' ('Haben, haben!') is the phrase with which the child reacts to the sight of any object. This attitude towards the object includes a tendency to preserve and protect it and this is the first step in the direction of adaptation to the outside world; it is on this basis only that the adaptation of thought to reality is possible. We cannot follow out this process of adaptation in detail here.

Even at this stage of intellectual development the child is still far removed from adult modes of thinking. The influence of narcissism on his thinking is still paramount and is seen particularly in his ideas of his own power. He ascribes to his desires and thoughts an unlimited omnipotence which can so operate on the outside world as to effect changes in it. Only gradually does his critical faculty teach him the bounds which are set to his influence upon that world. To follow out this process further would be a tempting task and, if we did so, we should be able to convince ourselves that in its later stages it is intimately connected with the child's attitude towards those with whom he has the closest relations. Here we enter the sphere of the 'Oedipus complex' which embraces the most important phenomena of infantile sexuality.

In this paper it is not possible to do more than indicate briefly the subsequent fate of the child's ideas of omnipotence. They become displaced on to some being who is endowed with peculiar authority (father, God).

To return once more to the manner in which thinking in early childhood is dominated by the pleasure-principle, I want further to call attention to the fact that free thinking, unadapted to reality—that is to say, phantasy—is in itself an important source of pleasure. Children play with thoughts as with toys and just on that account logical thinking, in accordance with reality, replaces only gradually this pleasure-giving play.

Thus we see that, in childhood, thinking is far more influenced by the instinctive life than in riper years. The regulative factors which are derived from the repression of the instincts have not as yet been brought to bear upon it.

Psychology has busied itself much with the development of the intellect in children, but it has generally treated the subject from points of view very different from that of psycho-analysis. Either the interest has been focussed on purely quantitative processes, as, for example, the number of words that a child learns within a given period, or else only formal phenomena have been taken into consideration—for instance, the child's capacity for expressing his thoughts in the form of sentences. These problems are deserving of the greatest interest, but the development of infantile thinking includes a number of questions which are not generally regarded but must take the chief place in our discussion.

Psycho-analysis urgently calls attention to the importance of infantile instincts in the evolution of thought. Our justification for laying so much stress on them must be that in the evolution of both the individual and the race the instincts are earlier than thought. Psycho-analysis therefore takes the position that it is impossible to give a correct account of any mental phenomenon without thoroughly analysing its instinctual determination.

XX

PSYCHO-ANALYSIS AND GYNAECOLOGY[1]

(1925)

GENTLEMEN, the previous speaker has given you a general idea of what the gynaecologist needs to know about psychotherapy for the purposes of his own subject, and how he can put such knowledge to practical use. Where he has touched on psycho-analysis I agree in all essential points with what he has said, so that further discussion is unnecessary. It therefore only remains for me to speak about the special importance to gynaecology of the psycho-analytical method. I cannot confine myself to a mere discussion of the therapeutic aspect of psycho-analysis for reasons which I shall mention. Psycho-analysis started some decades ago from the treatment of hysterical conditions. At first with the aid of hypnosis and later without it, it investigated the psychic life of patients more thoroughly than had ever been done before. Freud, the founder of psycho-analysis, obtained in this way some surprising psychological results. In his search for the psychic origin of nervous symptoms he was led further and further back and ultimately into the earliest years of childhood. 'Repressed' impulses, wishes and memories which had disappeared from consciousness proved to be the driving force in such illness. This discovery made a general investigation of instinctual forces imperative. In particular, the importance of sexuality in the aetiology of the neuroses, hitherto only suspected, had to be closely investigated and assessed.

Psycho-analysis undertook the investigation of ego drives serving self-preservation as well as of sexual drives. It created a completely new psychology by demonstrating the influence upon psychic processes of repressed and therefore unconscious elements of the instinctual life. Thus, apart from its therapeutic importance, psycho-analysis became a method of psychological research and a science. I must therefore discuss two questions: first, how far is gynaecology interested in the theoretical findings of psycho-analysis, and secondly, how far is it interested in its therapeutic results. This twofold task is so great that within the limits of a short paper I can only give a

[1] Editor's note: This paper was read at a meeting of the Berlin Gynaecological Association in March 1925.

condensed survey, referring briefly to the most essential points rather than embarking upon a detailed exposition.

The pathology and treatment of the neuroses in the female sex are based upon a knowledge of female psycho-sexuality. A carefully worked out and radical treatment therefore pre-supposes a psychological understanding of the causal relation-ships involved. On that same basis rests also the medical and personal understanding of the patients which are the essential pre-requisites of therapeutic action.

Before embarking upon a survey of the psycho-analytical findings which concern us here, one fact I must mention is that such findings have been obtained entirely by empirical means. The discovery that nervous disorders in adults can be traced back to their early infantile sexuality was fully confirmed by direct study of instinctual processes in the child.

In the psycho-pathology of female neuroses one factor has turned out to be of particular importance. This concerns the patient's attitude towards the fact of her own femininity. In many cases this attitude may readily be seen to be equivocal, or even one of patent aversion. Such an attitude can always be traced back to the time when the child first discovered the difference between the sexes. A girl's normal reaction to this discovery is first of all to show an easily understandable envy of something a boy has and she has not. The little girl cannot immediately comprehend a permanent shortcoming in her own body. She expects that she will eventually be compensated, and aided by her phantasy, she visualises various ways in which her desire will ultimately be fulfilled. Not until she has matured somewhat does she abandon such hopes. Another phantasy invariably met with among little girls is that they once had a penis, of which they were subsequently deprived by means of an operation or in some other way. The female configuration then appears to be the result of a sort of castration and the female genitalia as a wound. In the course of normal development masculine wishes are superseded by adaptation to reality. This is facilitated by the girl's love-relationship to her father and by her identification with her mother. Phantasy is now imbued with the wish to take her mother's place and, like her, to have children by the father. This is where maternal impulses have their origin. Such transformation of the original wishes, how-ever, is not always accomplished. The wish for masculinity then persists, later to be reinforced by logical reasons. Where de-velopment is normal every incident in the process of maturation serves to increase the expectations for the future. The acquisition of feminine attractions reconciles the girl to her 'loss'. If development departs from the normal, as invariably happens with neurotics, all incidents of sexual maturation and of sexual life produce a traumatic effect on the feminine psyche. The development of the female figure finally shatters the hope for masculinity. The onset and recurrence of menstruation, to be followed later by defloration, confinement, maternity and meno-pause all serve to reactivate the old castration-phantasy which lives on in the woman's unconscious. The incidents just enu-merated are bound up with two repetitive manifestations, namely pain and loss of blood. This serves to keep alive the idea of a wound. Moreover, adolescence makes further psychic demands upon girls which boys do not have to meet in the same way. Firstly, a greater measure of instinctual repression is de-manded from the female sex. Furthermore, after puberty a pro-cess occurs in women which has no counterpart in male develop-ment. In order to understand this process we have to use Freud's concept of 'erotogenic zones'. In infantile sexuality the ob-taining of pleasure is connected with certain parts of the body which are particularly susceptible to excitation. These are called erotogenic zones. Among these are included in particular all the orifices of the body. Only with maturation does one eroto-genic zone gain primary significance in both sexes, that is the genital zone. From then on this zone gives the principal satis-faction, whilst the other erotogenic zones merely produce 'forepleasure', thereby promoting the impulse towards full satisfaction. Up to this time the genital zone is only one among several serving to produce auto-erotic pleasure. In the female sex a complication here arises. In early infancy auto-erotic genital stimulation is exclusively centred in one part of the external genitalia, namely the clitoris. Later, however, in sexual activity with men the main centre of excitation should be the vagina. Normally this change-over takes place successfully, but in neurotics it generally fails to occur. The consequences of such failure will be considered presently. For the moment it is only necessary to emphasise how beset with dangers is the psycho-sexual development of women. Where such development fails to take place the results are to be met with on all sides in the pathology of the neuroses. According to the type of disturbance and to certain pre-disposing factors we find either the formation of nervous symptoms or of perversions. There is a close con-nection between neurosis and the perversions. In both, normal impulses are repressed from consciousness. In the pervert they are replaced by abnormal sexual impulses, in the neurotic by actual symptoms. Hysterical manifestations prove to be the result of unconscious fixation of the libido on to persons or situations important to the patient in his childhood. The symptoms of hysteria are localised in those parts of the body which serve as erotogenic zones. The mouth, for example, is an erotogenic zone. In the realm of the perversions we find sexual impulses translated into the exploitation of this part of the body for sexual purposes; in hysteria the mouth may be the site of nervous manifestations which partly serve to express resistance against such sexual impulses. Hysterical vomiting is an illustration of this.

Certain disturbances of psycho-sexual development may thus give rise to a variety of neurotic manifestations. Not all of these are expressed in the form of physical symptoms. Some, particularly the multifarious forms of anxiety, are mainly psychological, though they are usually accompanied by physical symptoms. In neurotic women erotic desires and hopes are frequently interwoven with anxiety. Likewise, unsatisfying and disappointing incidents in their love-life may produce anxiety.

If we assemble all the various examples of the ways in which women may reject their femininity under the heading of 'castration complex' it enables us to see clearly how many of the disorders constantly met with in the practice of gynaecology originate from this source. Confining ourselves to one single group of symptoms, namely disturbances of sexual sensitivity in marital relations, both nerve specialist and gynaecologist will readily agree on the frequency and importance of such symptoms. As to their causation they are all due to divergences from normal development as just described. Their consequences have recently been given special gynaecological attention. I am referring to Kehrer, who traces certain changes in the reproductive organs to frigidity. I merely mention in passing his opinion that even a tendency to the formation of fibroids may be caused by frigidity, though I am unable to test the correctness of this opinion from my own experience.

Some manifestations in neurotic women prove, even without a detailed psychological analysis, to be signs of resistance to certain functions. Among them is the occurrence of the menstrual period outside the normal cycle as a sign of resistance to sexual union. Vomiting in pregnancy is partly determined by an unconscious resistance to carrying the baby to full term. Sudden interruption of lactation may often arise from the mother's unconscious hostility to her child.

The many and various symptoms arising from an **uncon-**

scious rejection of feminine tasks amply demonstrates the importance of this point of view. It was psycho-analysis which first gave this point of view the consideration it deserves, just as it was first to give due consideration to the factors of psycho-sexual development and their significance for the formation of neurotic symptoms. All the symptoms here mentioned may either be found in conjunction with organic symptoms or as plausible-looking substitutes for them. It is clear that in either case true understanding of such pathological processes is only possible on the basis of psycho-analytical observation. These examples may suffice to show the importance to the gynaecologist of psycho-analytical insight for his speciality.

With regard to psycho-therapeutical treatment, the scope of my paper, unlike that of the previous speaker, is limited to those disorders which cannot be treated by the gynaecologist himself but which need radical treatment by a psychological specialist. First I would like to say that the gynaecologist cannot be expected to learn the psycho-analytical technique. Both psychological theory and psycho-analytical technique require a separate course of study. The ability of a physician to use this method largely depends upon the extent of his interest in psychological processes. A keen interest in organic disease, in gynaecological technique and particularly in surgical procedures is but rarely to be found in combination with an inclination for the thorough investigation of the patient's psychic life. There are different types of medical temperaments: the surgeon's rapid intervention appeals to some, the tentative and patient attitude of the psychologist to others. Even where both types of inclination and ability are found combined in one physician, however, it would be impracticable for him to do justice to two such contrasting tasks. In psycho-analytical practice each patient is treated over a period of time in daily sessions lasting an hour. Such a routine of work, involving a regular time-table filling up the whole day, is incompatible, for instance, with surgical practice. Finally there are additional reasons against combining these two therapeutical methods in the hands of one person. A woman undergoing detailed physical examination and treatment will form too strong a personal attachment to her physician if he also subjects her to psycho-therapeutical treatment which reveals to him all her conscious and unconscious psychic life. If anyone were disposed to believe, however, that because of its special technique psycho-analysis can easily and with certainty succeed where other forms of treatment fail, I should have to disillusion him. Psycho-analytical treatment is in

every case both for the doctor and the patient a long and difficult undertaking, somewhat comparable to the orthopaedic
adjustment of malformations dating from early childhood. In
the severe and chronic cases, with which psycho-analysis is
mainly concerned, we should not overestimate its therapeutic
possibilities. No one has a better opportunity than the psycho-
analyst himself of observing in his daily work the psychic forces
in the patient which obstruct his cure. Nonetheless our experience certainly justifies us in not underrating our therapeutic potentialities. This is not the place to consider therapeutic technique. A few practical examples may suffice to
illustrate which of the cases most often seen by the gynaecologist
can most successfully be improved, or even completely cured, by
psycho-analysis.

First there are the various forms of dyspareunia. By psycho-
analytical means such symptoms as frigidity and vaginismus
can be permanently removed. This has results which go far
beyond the effect upon the sexual life of such women. Experience has repeatedly shown that the neuroses of unsatisfied
women cause suffering not only to their husbands but also
to their children. In this way the seeds of nervous disorder
are sown in the children. These women are also inclined
to particularly severe disturbances during the menopause.
These examples will make clear to gynaecologists the value of a
method of psychotherapy which tries to get to the root of the
neurosis.

I would like to mention in this connection how frequently
it happens that both partners in a marriage have a mutually
harmful effect on each other, so that they both become increasingly neurotic. Among the symptoms regularly met with in
such cases are, in the husband the gradual decline of potency,
and in the wife a rejection of sexuality amounting to disgust.
Here the treatment of both partners leads to a far-reaching
improvement in the marriage.

Among the various nervous disorders producing physical
manifestations I will mention only one. Gynaecologists frequently encounter in their patients signs of nervous skin irritation. Local treatment is usually unsuccessful. Psycho-analysis
reveals the connection of this symptom with repressed sexual
wish-phantasies and can often demonstrate that such irritation
may migrate from its original site in the genital area to other
points on the body surface, and ultimately to distant parts of the
body such as the scalp or the knees. These forms of pruritus are
certainly amenable to psycho-analytical treatment.

Finally I would mention the disturbance, characterised especially by nervous anxiety, frequently met with in young girls about to be married. Prompt intervention in such cases may prevent serious consequences.

Owing to the limited time at my disposal I must restrict myself to these few examples. They should suffice, however, to indicate to the initiated the many points of contact between psycho-analysis and gynaecology. Psycho-analysis can show the gynaecologist how to approach the problem of investigating the psychological make-up of his patients. Psycho-analysis itself must be left to deal, however, with cases involving a neurotic disturbance demanding more from the physician than mere human and psychological understanding.

For a long time medical science was dominated by the concepts of structural pathology. Under their influence medicine made great strides. At the same time such a structural approach distracted medical attention from the importance of psychological factors. The result was that every branch of medicine lost touch with psychology. We must aim to restore the psychological aspect to its rightful place beside the structural point of view. Both can easily be blended and probably all branches of clinical medicine would derive new stimulus and valuable points of contact if greater emphasis were laid on the psychological factor.

Gentlemen, this evening is an important one in the medical life of Berlin. This society, which has honoured me by inviting me to read this paper, is the first clinical association to recognise that the achievements of psycho-analysis deserve attention. It is probably no mere coincidence that it was a gynaecological society which was the first in Berlin to take such a step. Rather is it due to the close connection between our respective sciences. Let me end on a personal note. Exactly 25 years have passed since I listened in this very hall to Olshausen's clinical lectures. It gives me great satisfaction to stand in the same place and to add my small contribution to the general body of medical science.

D

XXI

CONCURRENT PHANTASIES IN MOTHER AND SON

(1925)

A YOUNG man who was in psycho-analytical treatment with me had noticed since early childhood that his mother had an intimate extra-marital relationship with a man. In connection with this fact he had typical phantasies on the pattern of the Hamlet story: that the mother together with her lover would kill his father. These daydreams, recurring over many years, were analysed and were dispelled when the patient became conscious of his own previously repressed wish to get rid of his father with his mother's assistance. One day, after extensive analysis of the patient's phantasies of hostility against his father, he told me of a strange incident. Whilst the whole family were at dinner the mother related a peculiar dream she had had the previous night. A strange man had mocked at her and had derided her abilities and character. She had then turned him out with the assistance of Mr. X (her lover).

The story of his mother's dream had aroused my patient's attention and he had understood at once that the stranger could have been none other than his father, who the mother, together with her lover, threw out: that is to say, did away with him. He rightly concluded that his mother's phantasy was concerned with the same crime as his own earlier phantasies. The correspondence between the two phantasies went even further. He, too, had often in phantasy reproached his father for his failure to appreciate his wife's excellent qualities. She now justified the killing of her husband by the same argument.

This example shows the extent to which one person's daydreams can coincide with the phantasy-formations of another.

Part Two

REVIEW OF C. G. JUNG'S *VERSUCH EINER DARSTELLUNG DER PSYCHOANALYTISCHEN THEORIE (ATTEMPT AT A REPRESENTATION OF PSYCHO-ANALYTICAL THEORY)*[1]

(1914)

T HE title of Jung's recent work and the introduction to it which appeared in book form, lead the reader to expect a presentation of the theories of Freud and his school. The author tells us that he will expound his views, taking as a basis his own experiences in relation to those of Freud. By 'a modest and moderate criticism' he seeks to further the psycho-analytical movement and to put his own formulations alongside those of Freud where they appear to him more accurately to express the facts observed.

If the paper had indeed carried out this project it would have been a welcome addition to our literature. A clear and concise introduction to the field of psycho-analysis would be desirable; we would also be grateful for any objective criticism. There is no need to conceal the fact that opinions are divided within the psycho-analytical movement. We have, after all, put the 'Proceedings of the Vienna Psycho-analytical Association', which reveal the differences of opinion within our ranks, before the forum of public opinion.

The position, however, is quite otherwise. The present reviewer cannot content himself with recounting the author's views and criticising them. He has, in addition, the unusual and unpleasant task of showing that Jung has given a totally incorrect exposition of Freud's teachings.

Before embarking upon the details of these two points, I must emphasise some of the general characteristics of this latest work of Jung which are in striking contrast to the merits of his earlier writings. Like the 'Study of the Transformations and Symbolisms of the Libido', this new work contains a number of

---

[1] Nine lectures given in New York in September, 1912. *Jahrb. f. psychoanalyt. Forsch.*, **5**. Published in book form in Vienna, F. Deuticke, 1913.

contradictions, so that we have entirely opposing views on the same subject matter in two different places. Sometimes the exposition is so confused that one is scarcely able to follow the writer's train of thought. Certain of Freud's doctrines are baldly set forth, without the underlying reasons being given. It is also striking that Jung repeatedly gives his views on scientific research and criticism, only to violate them in the most flagrant way in the same paper. These general shortcomings must cause the critical reader to view the author's treatment of particular topics with great scepticism.

I shall turn first to Jung's treatment of the theory of sex and of infantile sexuality.

Jung defends the extension of the concept of sexuality which Freud deemed necessary, but does so in a most challengeable manner. Thus he says that the psycho-analytical school means by sexuality the instinct of the preservation of the species (p. 16).[1] It may be said in passing that the instinct of the preservation of the species is nothing more than a teleological fiction. The instincts of the individual, and by no means only the sexual instinct, indirectly serve also the preservation of the species. There is no justification for saying any more about them in this respect. Furthermore, it is obvious that certain manifestations of the sexual instinct, such as homosexuality, do not serve any such purpose. In fact, however, Freud has extended the concept of sexuality in the opposite direction: infantile sexuality, in the sense in which he uses that term, strives merely for the gaining of pleasure. According to Freud, sublimated sexual impulses and neurotic symptoms are alike derivatives of the sexual instinct; both are concerned with the preservation of the species only indirectly if at all.

Jung expressly concedes to Freud the right to designate as sexual those phenomena of childhood which are 'merely indicative and preparatory', but with 'certain conclusions' he is not prepared to agree (p. 16). 'Freud is inclined to see in the act of sucking at the mother's breast a kind of sexual act. This opinion has brought heavy reproaches upon Freud. It is, however, we must admit, quite ingenious, if we assume with him that the instinct of the preservation of the species, that is to say, of sexuality, is in a way distinct from the instinct of self-preservation, thus serving the function of nourishing and therefore undergoing a special development from the time of conception. This line of thought seems to me biologically unsound' (pp. 16–17).

[1] The page numbers of the quotations refer to the book edition.

The passage just quoted would not cause us any surprise if we found it in the criticism of an opponent, who was insufficiently informed about Freud's writings. It contains a misrepresentation in two respects. One would not have expected this from Jung. In the first place Freud obviously recognises the act of sucking as serving the purpose of nourishment. At the same time, however, he sees it as an act which gives rise to a pleasurable stimulation of the mouth as an erotogenic zone. What Jung quotes is in conformity with Freud's views on the significance of infantile thumb-sucking. Secondly, Freud himself assumes that the two instincts are primarily united, and only secondarily differentiated.[1]

After delivering his first blow against infantile sexuality by means of very doubtful arguments, Jung prepares for yet a second blow. On page seventeen the following assertion appears in italics: 'This period, that is, earliest infancy, is characterised by the absence of sexual functions.' There is it, baldly stated, only a few lines after the admission that nothing can be said

[1] The following is a quotation from *Three Essays on Sexuality:* Standard edn., 7, 181.

'Furthermore, it is clear that the behaviour of a child who indulges in thumb-sucking is determined by a search for some pleasure which has already been experienced and is now remembered. In the simplest case he proceeds to find this satisfaction by sucking rhythmically at some part of the skin or mucous membrane. It is also easy to guess the occasions on which the child had his first experiences of the pleasure which he is now striving to renew. It was the child's first and most vital activity, his sucking at his mother's breast ... that must have familiarised him with this pleasure. The child's lips, in our view, behave like an erotogenic zone, and no doubt stimulation by the warm flow of milk is the cause of the pleasurable sensation. The satisfaction of the erotogenic zone is associated, in the first instance, with the satisfaction of the need for nourishment. To begin with, sexual activity attaches itself to functions serving the purpose of self-preservation and does not become independent of them until later. No one who has seen a baby sinking back satiated from the breast and falling asleep with flushed cheeks and a blissful smile can escape the reflection that this picture persists as a prototype of the expression of sexual satisfaction in later life. The need for repeating the sexual satisfaction now becomes detached from the need for taking nourishment.'

Jung incidentally states further that Freud traces the sexual quality of the act of suckling from the similarity between the excitation and gratification ·in suckling and the analogous manifestations in the sexual act. I leave it to the reader to investigate the correctness of this representation with the help of the above passage.

against Freud's sexual terminology, 'as it rightly designates all the precursors of sexuality as sexual.' Jung is content to reinforce his opinion with some biological arguments, but he omits to provide any convincing proof.

With further astonishment one reads on page 18 that a sexual quality can be attributed to the thumb-sucking of the infant 'far more readily' than to the act of sucking. After all this is precisely what Freud had asserted. The vagueness of Jung's mode of expression goes hand in hand with the feebleness of his arguments. We shall encounter it time and time again. He seeks to escape from the difficult position in which he finds himself by weakly contending ('proving' is hardly the word) that thumb-sucking is not a sexual pleasure, but a 'nourishment pleasure'.

There is even more to come. Jung suddenly recognises, starting from masturbation and tracing it back to the development of early infantile 'bad habits' such as nail-biting, and ultimately to thumb-sucking, that all such manifestations are but early phases of masturbation and are thus sexual (p. 17). It is only with regard to thumb-sucking that he shows some reservation in a later passage.

What is this but making complete havoc of Freud's clear and careful arguments? No reader can possibly discern the author's real opinion from his contradictory statements. Jung, who on page 8 declares it to be unjust to attribute to 'a mind like Freud's the clumsy mistakes of a beginner', being completely blind to the shortcomings of his own arguments on page 18 reproaches his 'revered master' with the crude illogicality of 'petitio principii'. Or he puts forward propositions like this: 'The obtaining of pleasure is in no way to be equated with sexuality'. Hitherto we have heard such objections only from our opponents, who thereby thought to refute something which Freud was supposed to have asserted.

I will omit some of Jung's further arbitrary statements about the earliest sexual manifestations, and turn to his criticism of the 'polymorphous perverse' disposition of the child.

The relevant views of Freud about erotogenic zones and partial instincts, are so incompletely described that no one can obtain a true understanding from what he says. Jung then gives the following résumé:

'According to this way of thinking, therefore, the later normal and monomorphous sexuality consists of various components. First of all, it falls into a homo- and a hetero-sexual component, to which is added an auto-erotic component as well as different erotogenic zones.'

As many mistakes as there are words. Jung, in his presentation, completely overlooks the fact that these are phases of development. Freud has called the earliest manifestations of the libido 'auto-erotic', that is to say, without an object, and has shown that the libido progressively frees itself from the erotogenic zones to which it is at first attached, but this process is never completely carried through. Freud has further described how the originally autonomous erotogenic zones become subject to the primacy of the genital zone, and how in this way the normal sexuality of the adult is achieved. Freud has given particular attention to the process of finding an object. By omitting all the essentials, Jung gives the misleading idea that according to Freud sexuality first of all falls into a homo- and a hetero-sexual component. Freud nowhere speaks of an auto-erotic 'component', still less does he say that this is added to the earlier forms of sexuality. Jung is here actually turning Freud's theories upside down.

Jung gives his readers an entirely incorrect picture when he states that Freud artificially splits up sexuality. The exact opposite is true. Freud has brought together under the concept of sexuality a great number of manifestations which previously had remained wholly incomprehensible. Through the investigation of infantile sexuality he has established the fact that there is a continuity between the instinctual life of the child and that of the adult. He has demonstrated that many instinctual drives, which had seemed to be utterly conflicting, in fact complement each other and form a unity. In short, he has introduced the great unifying concepts into the theory of sexuality and of the neuroses.

Furthermore, no one has appreciated as much as Freud the capacity of the libido to transform itself. One needs only to remember, for instance, his theory of the origin of neurotic symptoms, his teachings on sublimation and reaction-formation, his terminology, such as object-cathexis and withdrawal of the libido from the object. Nevertheless he is reproached by Jung for having split up the libido into fixed, watertight components. In this case Jung's pretentions so far exceed what is justifiable that a firm protest is necessary. Not only does he arrogate to himself the credit for introducing unifying concepts into psychology; he even regards his work as comparable in importance to the introduction into physics of the concept of energy, as though the dynamic concept had been previously unknown to psycho-analysis. In reality the only novelty is the serious mistake of confusing psychological, biological and physical concepts.[1] Jung however, lays down this proposition: Just as physics, optics, mechanics, etc. have lost their autonomy, so the 'established' components of sexuality must inevitably lose theirs. Freud's partial component instincts are put side by side with the 'psychic power' of the older philosophers.

What does Jung put in the place of what he has discarded? His completely vague concept of libido and the 'applicability' of the libido.

There is no need to embark on a criticism of Jung's concept of the libido. I will merely refer to Ferenczi's trenchant exposition in Part 4 of the first volume of this journal, to which I shall make only just a few additions.

With regard to the 'possibilities of application' of the libido, which has for a long time been the common property of psycho-analysis, its establishment does not absolve us from the task of explaining what these 'possibilities' are. Freud has here taken as his starting point certain biological facts from which I will mention bisexuality as an example. Repression then explains the ascendancy of one set of impulses in consciousness, whilst impulses of the opposite kind are repressed into the unconscious. Jung, however, contents himself with words which can have no meaning for us. I here quote from a brief report of one of his case histories: 'The disappointment drove the patient's libido from the heterosexual mode of application back into the homosexual form.' Here again Jung's method of expression is extremely obscure. What are we to understand by 'homosexual form'? The author should, before making use of such loose expressions, explain where the libido gets its ability to choose other 'forms'. It must be emphasised that in his *Three Contributions*,[2] Freud begins by laying a biological foundation upon which to base his theory of sexuality. Jung, on the other hand, introduces his libido-concept, that is to say, a philosophical construction, and then interprets the facts in the light of this theory.

The vagueness of Jung's concept of the libido and its 'possibilities of application' is illustrated in a later section of his work (p. 79). Jung there says by way of illustration: 'A mountaineer, who is unable to attain the summit of a peak he longed to climb, would henceforth "turn his libido into useful self-criticism".'

[1] The caution with which Freud, in contrast to Jung, proceeds along this line is shown by his recent article: 'The Claims of Psycho-analysis to Scientific Interest', 1913. Standard edn., **13**.

[2] Editor's note: Now known under the title: *Three Essays on the Theory of Sexuality*.

Unfortunately Jung does not add how the mountaineer would do this. If he really knows, one can only wish that he himself would in future make extensive use of this 'possibility of application' of the libido.

Jung cannot deny the 'polymorphous perverse' disposition of the child. He deals with this topic in a vague and roundabout way (p. 25 ff.). At one point he says that the child's manifestations are very striking, and even more obvious than in adults; later on he refers to them as 'mere indications'. Of these 'indications' Jung says, however, that they 'still bear the character of infantile, innocent, and harmless simplicity'.

Jung stresses over and over again this 'innocence' of the child. Later he even adds that the child is not capable of planned intentions (p. 63).

Jung thereby not only disregards his previously expressed opinions, which after all everybody is free to do, but he also ignores facts which he himself had previously published. What does he wish to imply by his constant stressing of childish 'innocence'?

It is one of Freud's great merits that he freed psychology from ethical evaluation of a child's instinctual impulses. For the psychologist these impulses are natural manifestations which he observes and tries to understand. They should not be called either innocent or wicked. For this reason Freud has asserted that the unconscious is amoral. The fundamental content of the unconscious is formed, according to our view, by repressed infantile, primitive, impulses. Jung takes what from the scientific point of view is a seriously retrogressive step by assuring his readers over and over again of the innocence of infantile impulses. Worse still, he later ascribes moral tendencies to the unconscious.

The three stages of libido-development claimed by Jung have already been criticised by Ferenczi. Making use of Ferenczi's exposition, I will proceed to discuss further statements by Jung which were not contained as such in the 'Wandlungen', and which well exemplify Jung's method of attacking Freud's teachings.

Jung is quite wrong in stating that Freud explains the difference between infantile and mature sexuality as stemming from 'a diminutive of the infantile'.

Furthermore, Jung attempts to explain (p. 38–39) the original polymorphism of sexuality by saying that nourishment libido moves from the mouth in other directions. According to him an essential part of hunger libido is transformed into sexual libido.

The attempt to make the mouth the only starting-point of this entirely hypothetical movement of the libido shows the complete onesidedness of Jung's ideas. He entirely neglects all erotogenic zones except the mouth, and this certainly is from the scientific point of view one of the most reactionary steps. Are we concerned exclusively, however, with physical manifestations of the libido? How, for instance, does Jung explain the child's sexual curiosity and exhibitionistic tendencies?

The part of Jung's work which is most open to attack is that which deals with the Oedipus complex. This exposition suffers from a notable lack of clarity (p. 62 et seq.). One tries in vain to gain from these vague expressions a clear idea of what he is driving at. The reason for this lack of clarity is easy enough to discern. It is due to leaving out of account repression and the unconscious. The word 'repression' does, it is true, occur here and there in Jung's writings, but is always used vaguely; it has even lost its meaning. In this exposition of psycho-analysis the unconscious appears only sporadically. Nowhere do we find him taking up a clear attitude towards the fundamental problem of the unconscious. Without any introduction Jung makes such peremptory statements as: 'in the child's unconscious, phantasies are considerably simplified', or 'in the unconscious these wishes and intentions gain a more concrete and drastic form'. He does not, however, give any elucidation of the unconscious and of unconscious phenomena.

That Jung sees in the Oedipal relationship a mere symbol, and denies all real meaning to incestuous impulses, is already known from the second part of his work on *Wandlungen und Symbole der Libido*: here again I refer to Ferenczi's critical review. Nowhere is it so clear as in this part of the book that Jung is in retreat from psycho-analysis towards superficial psychology. Just one example of this. On page 63 we find the statement that in early childhood the mother has for the child 'naturally no appreciable sexual significance'. Not long before—and I here refer to the first part of the *Wandlungen*—Jung had found quite natural the exact opposite of what he is here saying. In support of his present doctrine the psycho-analyst Jung falls back on the findings of an American doctor, who discovered through questioning children that they liked to define their mother as the person who feeds them. After he has practised psycho-analysis for ten years, as he tells us in the introduction to his book, he is suddenly content with the sayings of children which can consist only of what is conscious and conventional. Why then bother with laborious psycho-analyses? Jung does not even notice that by doing this he comes very close to psychological mass-investigators such as William Stern.

Jung uses this opportunity to stress once more the importance of feeding pleasure. Here he goes to the length of saying: 'The great orgies which took place during the decline of the Roman empire may, so far as I am concerned, be due to anything but to repressed sexuality; for this could not be laid at the door of the Romans of that time. That these excesses were a substitute cannot be doubted; not, however, a substitute for sexuality but for neglected moral functions. . . .'

The uninitiated reader must gain the impression that Freud —to whom of course one could not attribute the elementary errors in logic that a beginner might make—at some stage expounded this palpable nonsense. Those who have read any passages in Freud's works where questions of cultural history are discussed, will remember how different is the spirit which pervades them. Jung's remark just quoted therefore recoils with all its banality upon his head.

For the incest barrier among civilised peoples, Jung gives the wholly inadequate explanation that everyday occurrences lose their attraction for human beings. All the facts of cultural history, no less than those of individual psychology, give the lie to this view.

According to Jung, the 'Oedipus phantasy' develops 'with increasing maturation', and in the 'post-puberty period, with the now completed separation from the parents enters into a new phase', of which the 'sacrifice' discussed in detail in the *Wandlungen* is the symbol. In Jung's view, during this time the unconscious phantasy of 'sacrifice', that is to say, the resolution to 'give up infantile wishes', appears.

We seek in vain for an explanation of this phenomenon. The unconscious has been endowed with moral tendencies: it makes sacrifices. All our foregoing experiences, none of which is refuted by Jung, demonstrate the amorality of the unconscious, the ruthless egotistical driving force of the instincts which have been forced into the unconscious. In addition to the concept of repression Freud also postulated the valuable concept of sublimation. With the help of this latter process the repressed and previously asocial drives are enabled to return in a transformed, that is to say, socially acceptable, form into consciousness. Jung's 'exposition' does not pay any heed to this process. In his description mentioned above the unconscious is something wholly vague; but this is not all. By suddenly producing a phantasy at a certain time of life, which Jung calls a 'sacrifice', thereby giving it a distinctly religious connotation, the unconscious becomes a kind of well-spring of mysticism. At this point Jung in fact ceases to be a psycho-analyst and becomes a theologian.

A further step backwards into surface-psychology may be seen in Jung's attempt to draw a sharp borderline between the psychic conflicts of the child and those of the adult (pp. 67–68). He says: 'Those cases which have suffered since childhood from chronic neurosis, no longer suffer from the same conflicts as in childhood. The neurosis may have broken out when the child had to go to school. At that time it was the conflict between pampering and stern necessity, that is to say between the child's love of the parents and the obligation to go to school. In adult life it is a conflict between the pleasures of a comfortable middle-class existence and the rigorous necessity to work. It only appears to be the selfsame earlier conflict.' Unfortunately Jung forgets to state the actual difference. That the adult neurotic, who is past school age, does not use his neurosis to escape from school, is an obvious platitude. The conflict has, therefore, merely changed its outer aspect. It is precisely Freud's merit to have recognised the same conflict continuing in its varying metamorphoses. Jung's view in this case is just as reactionary as that of the 'hostile critics', to whom he felt himself so superior in his preface to his work.

Jung's objections to the importance of incestuous wishes as the central complex of the neurosis had already been partly refuted before Jung himself raised them. For the rest, Ferenczi has sufficiently dealt with this question. I will therefore not now go into Jung's views regarding the purely regressive significance of this phenomenon, but will take up only one of his objections. According to Jung, the Oedipus phantasy cannot be pathogenic because it is common to all mankind. To become pathogenic it would need 'a special activation'. The actual attitude of psycho-analysis to this question is too well known for it to be necessary to set it out here. I am not referring to Jung's objection here merely in order to refute it, but because it is so well suited to demonstrate the inner instability of Jung's method of argument. On page 116 Jung states that the incest complex is 'reactivated' by man's indolence, which makes him recoil from the effort of adaptation. In the same place, however, he describes this 'indolence' as common to all humanity. In this way Jung reveals the absurdity of his own arguments. After promising to give a specific instead of a general cause for incestuous propensities, he hits on 'inertia', which is well-known to be the most universal quality of all matter.

Jung is particularly critical of the concept of the 'latency-period'; whereas in reality his attacks are nowhere less justified than here. On page 35 of his *Three Contributions*, Freud expressly admits that our understanding of the processes of the latency-period in children is as yet hypothetical in nature and lacking in clarity. Jung, who on page 19 declares theories to be no more than tentative suggestions, completely loses sight of this qualification when dealing with Freud's theory. In agreement with Fliess, Freud felt it necessary to assume a period of latency to which he ascribed the important function—left unquoted by Jung—of building up inhibitions against primitive instinctual impulses. Freud has also emphasised that even during the latency-period manifestations of libido are not absent, and he speaks of them as 'breaking through'. Therefore Jung's comparison with a flower, which develops backwards into a bud, is refuted. Such inner contradictions are particularly striking in this part of Jung's work.

Jung raises an objection to Freud's views on infantile and neurotic amnesia; the latter, according to Freud, follows the pattern of infantile amnesia. Jung finds in this a contradiction, and declares that the expression 'amnesia' is entirely inapplicable to early childhood. The differentiation of the two phenomena given by Jung on page 73 in no way corresponds to what is to be observed in children and in neurotics. Once again he makes an unauthentic statement. To refute Jung's contention, I need only mention those neuroses in which the amnesia of childhood is not, as is usually the case, manifest up to the fifth or sixth year only, but extends right up to the eleventh year or even further. In such cases infantile amnesia is directly succeeded by neurotic amnesia, and it is therefore not legitimate to regard them as in contrast to each other.

I have now reached the question of the theory of the neuroses, and can deal with this more briefly, as the same process is found to be repeated once more. Freud's theory of hysteria is presented in an utterly inadequate manner. Jung deals at great length with the old 'trauma theory' (which by the way he wrongly designates a 'theory of disposition'). He then describes how Freud came to attach greater importance to neurotic phantasies. Of the theory of the special psycho-sexual disposition of the neurotic, of the repressed wishes as the driving force of the neurosis, of the ambivalence of emotional impulses in neurotics and others, the reader hears not a single word. In his presentation of a case of hysteria (p. 41 et seq.) Jung explains how it would have been interpreted under the 'old theory'. Both here, and several times again later on (pp. 46, 76, 77), he makes it appear as though Freud adhered to his 'trauma theory' and was searching for the causes of the neurosis exclusively in the events of the distant past. This is objectionable the more so as he himself expressly condemned the methods of attack used by the opposition. The neurotic's insufficient adaptation to reality, which Jung so rightly stresses, has been fully dealt with by Freud, in particular in his paper 'Formulations on the Two Principles of Mental Functioning'. To be more specific, Freud has particularly emphasised (in his 'Fragment of an Analysis of a Case of Hysteria') that the neurotic shrinks from the demands made by reality upon his sexuality. In his paper on Obsessional Neurosis (1909) he dealt in particular with the avoidance by the patient of any decision. Above all in the article on 'Types of Onset of Neurosis' (1912), Freud showed his full awareness of the actual conflict in the neurotic. He recognised, however, that this was merely a new version of earlier conflicts, and for that reason stressed the significance of the latter. If Jung now designates the actual conflict as the only one essential for the understanding of the neurosis, this is by no means an original idea on his part; he is simply straying on to the misleading path, the path taken by non-analytical neurology, which Freud has taught us to avoid.

After discarding Freud's method as a purely historical one, Jung cannot help admitting that Freud 'recognises the final orientation of the neurosis to a certain extent' (p. 77). This is perhaps the most glaring example of 'misrepresentation' of psycho-analysis which Jung commits. Is it really necessary to repeat what Freud has taught us about the tendencies of the neuroses, and about symptoms as means of representation of unconscious wishes? It is true that Freud has not gone so far as to confuse these tendencies of the neuroses with finality in the metaphysical sense. I am loth to waste further words on this matter. All that has in fact been achieved here has been achieved by Freud alone, whilst Jung has added nothing but the superfluous words 'final orientation'.[1]

According to Jung, the neurotic shrinks from the 'duties' which he has to fulfil in life. This view in no way does justice to the facts. Instead of bringing many counter-arguments, I will mention only one. Among neurotics we find a great

[1] I shall deal elsewhere with the use of neurotic phantasies as 'productive and rehearsing material'.

number of people who show the most marked devotion to duty, who devote themselves entirely to their work or to other activities. If we study such neurotics in detail, we always find that certain inhibitions of the libido (I refer here of course to the sexual meaning of this word) prevent them from obtaining gratification, and that work serves them as a substitute gratification. Jung's view is by no means original, but merely a repetition of Freud's view on the avoidance of the sexual demands of reality. Jung has simply 'desexualised' it, to use a word coined by himself.

Jung reduces the significance of the unconscious in the neurosis almost to nil. We read for instance the following statement: 'They (that is, the neurotic phantasies) are often only present in the form of feelings of expectation, hope and prejudice. In such a case one calls these phantasies unconscious.' It hardly needs pointing out that we are here faced with a drastic whittling down of the concept of the unconscious. Jung gives no reason for thus changing the psycho-analytical views on the unconscious.

Jung seems consistently to avoid the term 'repression'. Instead we find such vague expressions as: 'The libido was not acknowledged' (p. 72 and elsewhere).

He writes at length about 'transference' without adding anything essential to what is already known. On the other hand the phenomenon of 'resistance' is almost entirely overlooked.

One of Freud's important tenets which Jung completely sacrifices to 'regression' is the neurotic's fixation to the infantile.

Towards the end of the book Jung gives an account of an analysis which was undertaken on an eleven-year-old girl. Here, too, the neglect of the unconscious greatly adds to the confusion. It is noteworthy, incidentally, that this child refutes Jung's views in some important respects. For example, she developed in the fifth year of her life a strong sexual curiosity, and at the same age fidgeted in a certain manner which, according to Jung, 'must be regarded as indicating a sexual undercurrent'. The latter expression, again, is as vague as it could possibly be.

Jung sees the last basis of the neuroses in the 'inherent sensitivity' (p. 92). As he himself looks upon this as 'a mere phrase', discussion is superfluous. In my opinion Freud has, here too, given us something more tangible.

I will deal very briefly with Jung's exposition on the question of dementia praecox. Here again I am in accord with Ferenczi's opinion. On the question of 'loss of reality' Jung takes as a starting-point the same passage from Freud's *Paranoia-Analysis* as he took in his earlier paper. Of the two possibilities which Freud suggested for the elucidation of the concept of the 'end of the world', Jung omitted to consider the one which Freud himself was inclined to adopt. He now tries to come to grips with the second explanation for such loss of reality. He does not, however, in my opinion succeed in refuting Freud's theory in any way.

Jung's remarks on the dream must arouse our opposition in several respects. Once again Jung gives an inadequate account of Freud's theory by saying that the technique of interpretation consists in 'trying to remember where the pieces of the dream originate from' (p. 55).

Jung is further mistaken when he calls Freud's interpretation of dreams 'an exclusively historical method'. Freud in fact looks for the wishes which are concealed in the dream under many disguises. Such disguises are, however, only to be understood from a historical point of view. The tendency of the dream is projected into the future; the dreamer, however, forms his conception of the future in his unconscious phantasies after the pattern of his remote past.

Jung demands a more detailed consideration of the 'teleological' function of dreams in contrast to the view of Freud who regards dreams as being determined exclusively by historical factors. This 'prospective' element in the dream has long been known to us. Every analyst meets it daily in his dream analyses. In his *Interpretation of Dreams* (1900) Freud has already pointed out that such elements of a dream as intentions merely form its superficial layer. It is the task of psycho-analysis to lay bare its deeper layer. In a later paper entitled 'Fragments of an Analysis of a Case of Hysteria' Freud has explained his views on this point in greater detail. The 'prospective' tendency is not therefore an original discovery of Jung or Maeder, but simply a new name for a false trail, which Freud had avoided from the beginning. The same holds good for the analogous function which Jung ascribes to the neuroses.

I have omitted considering in this article a number of other untenable positions taken up by Jung, especially those which Ferenczi had already discussed. I would add that for this reason I have not dealt with Jung's psycho-therapeutic technique.

I believe, however, that I have proved that Jung has not substantiated his claim to give us a logical development of Freud's ideas (p. 135). To use his own expression (p. 135), he merely uses 'as different as possible a nomenclature for as contrary as possible a point of view'. When Jung proclaims in his Introduction that he is 'far from seeing in his modest and moderate criticism a defection or a schism' I am very ready to believe that he himself is a victim of self-deception. I myself, however, see no reason to avoid these expressions. I will go further, and state that Jung has no longer the right to apply the term 'psycho-analysis' to the views he propounds.

The reason which has led me to say this is that Jung has once more put aside all the essential concepts of Freud's teaching.

Infantile sexuality, the unconscious, repression, the concept of psycho-sexuality, the wish-fulfilment theory of the dream and of the neuroses—all these indispensable concepts of psycho-analysis have partly disappeared, and partly shrunk into insignificance. Of the important details of Freud's teachings which have met with a like fate I will mention only auto-eroticism and narcissism, ambivalence of feelings, sublimation and reaction-formation. Nor can I forbear to comment that important parts of psycho-analytical theory have found absolutely no mention in Jung's work, for instance the theory of obsessional neurosis, of anxiety, and of depressive states.

In these circumstances no one will see in my radical rejection of Jung's ideas a rigid adherence to a narrow partisanship. Rather do I believe that I have proved Jung's 'presentation' to be a complete distortion of psycho-analytical theory. I see in Jung's writing mainly destructive and reactionary tendencies at work: I can see no sign of any positive or constructive achievement.

I will conclude by pointing out that Jung has offended against his own most fundamental principle (p. 13) to take truth, and not moralistic sentiments as his guiding principle, by approaching infantile sexuality and the unconscious from the point of view of ethical and theological evaluation. It is against such evaluation that I take my stand, for psycho-analysis must be shielded from influences which seek to make it what philosophy was in former times: the handmaiden of theology.

II

THE CULTURAL SIGNIFICANCE OF PSYCHO-ANALYSIS [1]

(1920)

PSYCHO-ANALYSIS, whose origin and development we owe in the first place to the Viennese physician and psychologist, Sigmund Freud, has grown, in the course of time, from a therapeutic method into a science of psychology. It has brought new and surprising revelations, not only as to the psychic life of the individual, but also as to social groups such as the family, the community and the state. Since its method of approach has proved fruitful in various other branches of knowledge, it has gradually attracted ever-widening interest. In recent times psycho-analysis, both as a medical method and as a psychological theory, has sometimes been called a fashion, and a short life has accordingly been prophesied for it. Only those who have no knowledge of its history can share this view. It is forty years since the basic discoveries were made on which psycho-analysis is founded. During this period a growing number of collaborators have helped in building, stone by stone, until a great and organically integrated structure has been erected. This structure is by no means complete; the workmen are still busily engaged in expanding it and in rectifying faults in its construction. Thus psycho-analysis is revealed as a constantly growing and developing science, whose possibilities can not yet be assessed, and to which the future appears to belong. It is therefore anything but the transitory product of a passing fashion.

This strange course of development of a science, this reaching out of its newly-gained knowledge into ever-wider spheres of intellectual life may well claim our interest. Let us then turn to the beginnings of the new theory. In following its progress up to the present time, we may hope to gain an insight into the significance and implications of the psycho-analytical way of thinking.

In 1880 a Viennese physician, Dr. Joseph Breuer, succeeded by means of hypnosis in reawakening in a girl suffering from severe hysteria, memories of the events which led to the ap-

[1] First published in *Die Neue Rundschau*, October 1920.

pearance of her nervous symptoms. These memories had apparently been completely lost. During the hypnotic sessions he made his patient re-live those scenes which had become completely estranged from her consciousness, and which had led to the outbreak of her various disturbances. After she had given expression to these memories, accompanied by a vivid show of emotion, he roused her from the hypnotic sleep. Each time he found her relieved, as if eased from an inner tension. By persevering with this treatment he gradually brought about an improvement of the grave illness. Breuer later communicated his experience to his younger colleague, Dr. Freud, who, at first in association with Breuer, but subsequently alone and independently, pursued this line of research and not only created the particular method of treatment known as psycho-analysis, but also opened up new pathways in psychology.

Breuer's discovery had drawn attention to a strange fact on which all further research was based. A memory could disappear from human consciousness, to be replaced in consciousness by a pathological symptom or by a strange phantasy, without the individual being aware of the connection between them. If the memories 'repressed' into the unconscious could be successfully brought back to consciousness, the substitute-formation became unnecessary and disappeared. According to the first findings only such psychic material was banished from consciousness as was incompatible with the individual's feeling of self-respect because of the painful emotion associated with it. Freud postulated a psychological process of 'defence', by whose help one might get rid of unwanted ideas and emotions, and this process he called repression. At the same time, however, he recognised that the very same psychic forces which had brought about the repression, would oppose, in the form of 'resistance', the coming back into consciousness of the repressed material. When hypnosis had proved to be unreliable and frequently unable to overcome this resistance, Freud found another way of exploring the unconscious: the method of 'free association'.

The principles underlying this procedure are easily comprehensible. We have all experienced, for instance, the forgetting of a name. The more we try by strenuous thinking to trace the elusive name, the more it escapes us, or wrong names come to mind, as if to mock us. The correct one persistently evades our memory. A few hours later, however, when we have turned our attention in other directions, the word which we have vainly sought before suddenly enters our mind. We then say that a thought has just occurred to us. It is clear that the forgotten name had not really disappeared, but had only been temporarily repressed, that a psychic resistance had prevented its return into consciousness, and that this resistance had increased with the increase of our concentration. When attention was diverted, the repressed content could find its way back into consciousness. Freud then encouraged his patients to bring the thoughts occurring to them whilst their attention was relaxed; that is to say, he made them associate freely, excluding all conscious aim, and by this method he gained a deeper and far more complete insight into the unconscious. The new method, which dispensed with hypnosis, was given the name psycho-analysis.

There is one obvious objection to all this. One might suppose that the thoughts thus produced would be arbitrary and due purely to chance, and that instead of the image that actually emerges, there might equally well have been another. The patient undergoing analysis also raises such objections. His free associations often appear to himself at first meaningless, and without any psychological connection. We ask him to express these thoughts before he begins to criticise them. If he follows our advice, and goes on to bring a chain of thoughts whose sense and inner connection remain completely obscure, there comes at some point an association which leads straight to the repressed material. The links of the chain which hitherto appeared meaningless then become comprehensible, revealing to us psychic processes which had previously been withdrawn from our understanding. In this way the strict causality of even the most trivial psychic process becomes apparent.

Psycho-analysis thus proves that in the psychic realm, which was previously regarded as the arena for chance and arbitrary forces, the rule of causality holds undisputed sway. It demonstrates in every psychic process the working of opposing instinctual forces, each of which strives for primacy in consciousness.

The growing volume of experience led to the establishment of a technique of interpretation which permitted the understanding of the hidden meaning of nervous manifestations and other psychic products. Two conclusions of particular significance were revealed with the help of this technique. The repressed material is endowed with a driving force of its own; the discovery of this fact necessitated a modification of Freud's original views. It is not merely memories that have to be repressed because of their emotional significance, but also inner drives of a distinctly wishful character, which are undoubtedly connected with memories strongly charged with emotion. The repressed wishes, however, originate in the realm of sexual drives.

Psycho-analysis was compelled to extend considerably the concept of sexuality, to which at first it had given no particular attention. The working of unconscious sexual impulses was discerned in many psychic processes. The new theory devoted especial attention to the early stages of sexuality to be observed in children; it was able to trace many pathological manifestations in the psychic life of adult neurotics back to childhood. Psycho-analysis does not neglect the ego-drives, such as those which derive from the need for food and for self-preservation, which exist side by side with the sexual drives; it attaches the greatest significance to the interplay of ego-drives and sexual drives in both normal and abnormal psychic life.

Man is born with a diverse, unorganised mixture of varying and opposing instinctual impulses. We call the earliest impulses of his sexuality auto-erotic, because they do not yet demand an external object; they are concerned rather with the pleasurable stimulation of certain parts of the body, to which we apply the term erotogenic zones. At this stage the genital zone is by no means the focal point of the growing sexuality. We can see that in earliest infancy the most pleasurable auto-erotic sensations are attached to the mouth as an erotogenic zone. In suckling the child obtains both nourishment and pleasure. It also derives pleasure from sucking the thumb, or other objects, an activity which some children continue for a long time. No part of psycho-analytical theory has aroused so much opposition as the evaluation of sucking as a sexual activity. The facts, however, have compelled us to draw such a conclusion, for these manifestations of infantile instinctual life merge imperceptibly into definite sexual manifestations, particularly infantile masturbation. Pathology has made us familiar with cases of abnormal development, in which pleasurable sucking retains the primacy in sexual life, and inhibits the development of the other component instincts. We cannot go more fully into the evidence supporting the propositions here put forward. It should be emphasised, however, that these and other psycho-analytical theories, which at first sounded so strange, spring not from preconceived notions, but solely from unprejudiced observation and practical experience.

The auto-erotic phase is followed by a second, in which the libido is directed on to an object. This object, however, is the child itself, which during this phase of its instinctual development knows only its own interest, loves only itself, and accordingly over-estimates its power in a most ingenuous way; it demands all sorts of proofs of love, which it regards as its due. This is the stage of development we call narcissism. The word is taken from the Greek legend about the youth who fell in love with his own reflection. The self-love of the child at this period goes hand in hand with an entirely ruthless selfishness in the sphere of the ego-drives. The child's cry 'I want it, I want it', is the clearest expression of this state.

Gradually, however, the libido is turned to other objects. The juxtaposition of opposing drives is characteristic, so that friendly and hostile impulses, love and hatred, may be directed towards the same person. Other drives, later classified as sexual, show their active and their passive aspects simultaneously. We may mention here scopophilia and its opposite, the wish to exhibit; the wish to attack and conquer, as well as its passive counterpart. During this time, that is, around the fifth year, the child's sexual curiosity is very strong. We can here only mention in passing that it is at this time that the child clearly shows his need for love from his environment, and that the mutual attraction of the sexes becomes apparent; we shall have to deal later with this process.

The small child lacks all those inhibitions in the instinctual life which we take for granted at a later age. The gradual adjustment to its immediate and more distant environment to be observed in the growing child, is based upon the process of repression, by which a considerable part of the primitive instinctual impulses are subdued. It is just these parts of infantile sexuality which form the basis of the unconscious. The unconscious then becomes more and more the repository in which is collected all that is unbearable to consciousness because of its painful content. This repressed instinctual material is to a large extent integrated and in that way diverted into socially acceptable or desirable aims, and so it becomes again admissible to consciousness. Part of this instinctual energy goes, for instance, to construct those important barriers to sexuality known to us as shame, disgust and pity. This process is called sublimation.

Sexuality attains its final form at the age of maturation. The procreative function takes the foremost place, and the genital zone becomes the centre of sexual life. Under its primacy the component instincts blend to form a unity. In the normal course of development, it is only at this stage that an integrated direction of sexual impulses is achieved. The opposite sex becomes the sole sexual object, and coitus the sexual aim. Disturbances of this course of development, however, bring about those deviations from normality which we call perversions.

The unconscious, in the sense described above, is that part of man's psychic life which is barred from his conscious insight. This does not mean those ideas which are put aside because of the mental limitations to consciousness, but which remain accessible to our memory. We call this latter psychic sphere the pre-conscious, so as to distinguish it from the conscious and the unconscious. We regard the resistance whose function it is to prevent the return of repressed ideas from the unconscious, as a barrier between the unconscious and the pre-conscious. Freud has appropriately called this resistance 'the censorship'. This term is easy to understand. Under governments exercising strict censorship over the press, any literary product which is not acceptable to those in power is suppressed. Those who wish to give expression to their dissentient opinions must conceal them behind oblique references, or distort them in some other way. When Montesquieu wanted to criticise the French monarchy before the Revolution, he wrote the *Lettres Persanes*. Under the guise of describing conditions in Persia, he actually portrayed those of his own country. Our unconscious constantly makes use of such indirect modes of representation, when it wants to enable the products of its phantasy to enter consciousness.

We are fully justified in speaking of unconscious phantasies, since our unconscious contains a large number of wishes which are unfulfilled and which, we may add, are very largely incapable of fulfilment. That aspect of human thought-processes in which our innermost longings are represented as fulfilled or at least capable of fulfilment is called phantasy. Here we can once more find proof for the close connection between the unconscious and the primitive instinctual life of infancy. In early infancy the thoughts of the child are governed by his own pleasurable instincts. Just as his activity consists of play, so his thoughts consist of phantasy. His thoughts are gradually adjusted to reality, but the element of phantasy never completely disappears. At a later stage we may distinguish two forms of conscious thought, the phantastic and the realistic. The unconscious, however, which represents a primitive, infantile stage of our psychic development, consists entirely of unrealistic thoughts derived from repressed wishes.

If we glance back at the course which the development of psycho-analysis has taken, we see the importance of Breuer's original discovery. A device used by the physician for the understanding and treatment of a nervous disorder has become a powerful instrument of psychological and biological discovery. Psycho-analysis opened up the way to the understanding of the human unconscious, and created a new theory of the instinctual forces active in mankind, especially that of sexuality. It recognised that the pathological psychic processes found in nervous patients differed only quantitatively from the psychic processes found in normal persons. Psycho-analysis can therefore justly claim to be a psychology of both normal and abnormal psychic processes.

On the basis of these new discoveries psycho-analysis was able to explain a psychic phenomenon which had aroused man's interest from the earliest times, namely the dream. Here it was no longer dealing with pathological manifestations of purely medical interest, but with a product of normal psychic life, albeit one which was difficult to understand. Psycho-analytical dream interpretation became our most important means of understanding the unconscious. This is easily comprehensible, for during sleep the function of consciousness is to a large extent suspended. Psychic products created in sleep must therefore be of the greatest assistance in understanding unconscious psychic processes.

Earlier attempts at dream-interpretation had assumed that the dream represents psychic impulses in pictorial form, but they had failed to do justice to the manifold problems of dream-psychology, or to recognise the unconscious and the laws governing unconscious mental processes. Moreover they were unable to discover the wishful impulses which created the dream, or to explain the function of the dream in the psychic life of the individual.

Freud differentiated between the external appearance of the dream, the manifest content, from the repressed wishes and other ideas indirectly represented in the dream. He contrasted the hidden, latent dream-content with the manifest content. The manifest content of a dream, as we remember it on awakening, usually appears to our consciousness strange and incomprehensible, even confused; it therefore needs to be interpreted. The method of interpretation is the same as that which Freud used for the understanding of nervous symptoms. Starting from each single detail of the manifest dream-content, we elicit the associative material by asking the dreamer to exclude all conscious direction or criticism of his thoughts whilst putting them into words. The direction which his associations take inevitably leads us to the latent dream thoughts. Interpretation thus proceeds in the opposite direction from that of the psychic process which had distorted the latent dream thoughts into the manifest content, and which we call the dream work.

Children's dreams are naturally the simplest. They represent wishes which have not been fulfilled in waking life, such as the wish for sweets which the child has been denied. In childhood every wish can become the stimulus to a dream. Here the egocentricity of the dream is fully apparent and undisguised. In the dreams of adults the dream-stimulus is a repressed wish, or at any rate a wish which is strengthened from unconscious sources. The wish-fulfilment is nearly always made unrecognisable by dream-distortion. Here we meet once more with that resistance which we have already come to know by the name of censorship.

The dream blends together material from many different sources. First of all there are actual wishes, whose fulfilment has been denied in the dreamer's waking life. These prove, however, as has already been pointed out, to be mere repetitions or, one might say, new editions of infantile wishful impulses. This is particularly evident in the case of certain dreams which with very little variation are common to all men. Dreams about being naked are an example of this. Everyone has probably dreamt at some time or other of being insufficiently clad in company, in a restaurant, or in the street. Such a situation certainly does not gratify any conscious wish, as can be inferred from the painful feelings of anxiety with which such dreams are usually accompanied. At some period in his past, however, there was a time when nakedness was not shameful, but a source of pure pleasure. This was during the period of early infancy. Those who carefully observe children cannot fail to notice with how much elation they behave whenever they are free from the constraint of clothes. They derive particular pleasure from showing themselves naked to those they love most. The Paradisean state of nakedness without shame is one of the happy liberties of the child, for which man unconsciously longs in later years.

In the same connection we may mention the frequent occurrence of dreams of the death of a near relative. It is not unusual to dream of the death of a beloved person, whose life we consciously value above all others. In the dream we live through this happening with all the signs of anxiety, terror and distress. This might be thought to indicate that such dreams are the expression of a fear and certainly not that of a repressed wish. It is only to be expected that psycho-analysis, which ascribes a wishful character even to these dreams, should meet with the most violent opposition. Let us investigate the matter impartially. If these dreams spring only from loving tenderness, how are we to explain the fact that the dreamer so often awakens from them with painful feelings of guilt? It is just this feeling of guilt which serves as a pointer. There was a time in our life when we put to death in phantasy any person who thwarted or hurt us in any way. Again this was during the period of early infancy. A child between two and five years of age, who has hitherto been an only child, reacts to the advent of a rival in the shape of a second child with unconcealed hostility. A four-year-old girl, watching her newly-born brother being bathed, said to the nurse: 'Do let him drown.' A three-year-old boy feels himself unjustly treated by his father, gets into a fury and utters the words: 'Daddy is to have his head off!' This primitive form of human reaction lives on in the unconscious, whilst in consciousness the more civilised upper layer of the psyche completely denies its existence. Repression frequently is so extensive that we feel justified in asserting that we have never had such impulses. Adults like to emphasise over and over again the innocence of the child. If, however, we observe the child's instinctual life as impartially as psycho-analysis demands, we shall no more praise the child as innocent than condemn him as wicked. Rather shall we stress the fact that in the earliest phase of his life the child is dominated by his instinctual impulses, so that his wishes and actions cannot be judged by moral standards. We can trace death dreams back to this amoral period of childhood.

It is striking that men dream mainly of their father's death, women mainly of the death of their mother. Once more the explanation of this peculiar phenomenon is to be found in the early stages of psychological development. In the first half of the fifth year the little boy turns with particular tenderness to his mother, whilst displaying definite signs of jealousy and hostility towards his father, and asks when his father will die. He is far more loving towards his mother, wants to be alone with her and tries in an amusingly childish way to act like a man. He shows himself naked to her with undisguised intention. There is no doubt that we are here faced with the signs of infantile sexuality. A girl of corresponding age tries to attract the father's tenderness, and at the same time plies the mother with questions, such as: 'When are you going to die? Will you still be alive in ten years time? Will you still be alive when I am big?' When one little girl was asked by her mother what she would do without her, the answer came back promptly: 'Then I shall marry Daddy.' One day she said: 'Daddy, I might see you naked some time.' 'I might' is no doubt a mitigated form of 'I want'. We shall understand this better when we hear that only recently this little girl had had a baby brother, and that she had noticed the anatomical differences between him and herself with keen interest.

The boy's infantile erotic attitude towards his mother and his jealous hostility towards his father are to be seen in close juxtaposition in the Greek legend of Oedipus, where the hero kills his father when he bars his way, and afterwards marries his own mother. This motif, which is also to be found in other legends, springs from that psychic conflict which is of deep and far-reaching importance in the infancy of every human being. If the child is able to transform his primitive eroticism into a de-sexualised tenderness towards his mother, and to restrict his hostility towards his father, the accomplishment of this task is the best guarantee of success in making those adjustments which life so often demands. If the child fails to overcome the Oedipus situation, he is liable to severe disturbances in the further development of his emotional life, and hence to nervous illness.

In the dreams of adults repressed tendencies of this type seek expression in many ways. I will give as an example a dream of an adult man: 'I am sitting to the left of my mother in a two-wheeled carriage, like a dogcart. On the right-hand side of the carriage stands my father, silently, and with a serious expression. Then he turns and walks away in the opposite direction to that in which the carriage is moving, and soon disappears from our sight. I have already suggested to my mother that we should drive up and down, as if waiting for someone. She gives a slight pull on the horse's reins, which she is holding, so that the horse begins to move. At that moment I take the reins from her, whip up the horse, and quickly drive away with her.'

This dream is not taken from any incident in real life, as neither the dreamer nor his parents had ever possessed a carriage of any kind. No similar incident had ever taken place in the dreamer's waking life and there was no apparent reason why this kind of scene should appear in the dream. We should remember, however, that the manifest dream content does not show the true purpose of the dream, and we should try to follow the dreamer's thoughts. In this particular case they led to phantasies of getting rid of the father. These phantasies, though originating in infancy, had been reactivated by the dreamer's actual conflicts with his father. The father is silent and turns away; we discern in this the allusive and tentative manner in which the dream refers to the phantasy of the father's death, which must not be permitted open expression. It now becomes easy to understand why, immediately after the father's 'disappearance' the son takes his place next to his mother and why he takes the reins, a symbol of control. We may later be able to gain deeper insight into the latent meaning of the dream. We can already recognise its wishful character and its close relationship to the Oedipus situation.

In comparison with these dream stimuli, namely the wishful impulses of the present day and of infancy, other factors in dream formation are of very much less consequence. In popular dream interpretation as endorsed by some psychologists, physical stimuli such as a full stomach or bladder are considered of great importance. There is no doubt that such physical sensations play a part in dream formation, but are in themselves insufficient to account for the dream. It is also true that the same physical factor produces in different persons, or in the same person at different times, entirely different dreams. From this we may conclude that the physical sensations may have a precipitating influence on the dream, but that the true latent content derives from other sources.

The process which we have already come to know as dream work serves to circumvent the censorship. This latter prevents unconscious impulses from breaking through into consciousness during waking life. During sleep it admits them only conditionally. In many cases the censorship demands that the emotions accompanying the dream-thoughts be suppressed or changed into their opposite and that a far-reaching distortion of the dream-thoughts themselves should take place. The dream-work takes many different forms, which cannot all be discussed here. It may, for instance, merge several similar ideas into a single one, which thereby becomes over-determined. It must also cast the dream-material into a form which is suitable for representation, like a scene in a play. Thus abstract concepts have to be translated into pictorial representations of those concepts. Furthermore, dream-work makes abundant use of symbolical representation.

Since we have already become aware of the indissoluble connection between our unconscious and sexuality, it will hardly surprise us that the various symbols used in dreams mainly refer to sexual matters. The organs and functions of the sexual instinct are represented by numerous symbols. Many of these symbols are also familiar to us in waking life; they occur in witticisms, in folk-lore, and in the representational arts. By using this knowledge we can penetrate more deeply into the meaning of the dream previously discussed. All activities like walking and driving, which in the dream are performed with a person of the opposite sex, are allusions to sexual intercourse. Thus we can now recognise in such dreams the complete fulfilment of Oedipal wishes.

The following short dream may serve to illustrate simple symbolism. A girl in a nursing-home makes the acquaintance of a young doctor whom she praises highly. During the night she dreams that this doctor approaches her bed and pushes a dagger into her abdomen. The accompanying anxiety leads us to conclude that the dream contains a wishful impulse, which is unacceptable to consciousness. The dreamer's unconscious demands from the man the satisfaction of her instinctual wishes. If in the dreams of women assault is among the most frequent occurrences, the reason for this, as we see in the dream under discussion, cannot be in doubt. The dreamer appears as the innocent victim of male aggression; she does not need to reproach herself for her dream, even though it contains a wish-fulfilment, for this is concealed by anxiety.

These are but a few of the problems connected with the dream, which we have merely touched upon rather than discussed in detail. Other important problems of dream psychology have likewise been solved satisfactorily by psycho-analysis, but these need not concern us here. It was, after all, not our intention to deal fully with the problem of dreams but only to illustrate from one example of dream-interpretation the attitude which psycho-analysis adopts towards the phenomena of normal psychic life. We shall now be much better able to understand the relationship of certain psychological phenomena of waking life to the unconscious.

The effects of repression in healthy persons are by no means to be discerned only in dreams, but also in waking life. We have already mentioned that certain memories, for example, of names, may at times escape us. Psycho-analysis can show that in every case of this kind the forgetting is purposeful. It has the function of keeping out of consciousness ideas which are unpleasant, and for that reason unacceptable, to our conscious mind. If we forget a familiar name, address or telephone number there is always a motive for this repression. We are reminded here of the memory disturbances of nervous patients which, according to Breuer's discovery, are connected with the cause of the formation of their symptoms. The forgetting of dreams on awakening follows the same rules. We are often aware that at the moment of waking the memory of a dream somehow eludes us.

Motivated forgetting can be grouped along with other manifestations under the term 'slips and faultily performed actions'. When we make slips in speaking, reading, or writing, when we mislay anything or when, intending to take up one thing we take hold of something else instead, or make any other kind of mistake, such actions only appear to be accidental. In fact even these trifling happenings obey strict laws. Unconscious motives of an opposite kind interfere with the carrying out of the conscious intention. The slip appears to be due to mere clumsiness. If, however, we analyse examples of these slips, we are surprised at the practical ingenuity and logical consistency with which unconscious impulses contrive to find expression.

A woman is unhappily married. Consideration for her children and her parents prevents her from seeking a divorce. Her repressed wish betrays itself when she signs her letters with her maiden name, thereby denying the name she had taken on marriage.

Another young wife receives a letter from her parents-in-law, complaining that she does not write to them often enough. Her reply contains this slip: 'You must forgive me for writing so infrequently in the future'. It should have been: 'in the past.' Her disinclination to write to people she did not care for forced itself into the open. The writer announced that she would continue to write infrequently.

I will now give some examples of slips of the tongue.

A newly-appointed professor says in his first lecture: 'I am not inclined (geneigt) to assess the merits of my predecessor.' The word should have been 'qualified' (geeignet).

During a debate in the Reichstag in November 1908, a right-wing member solemnly declared, with reference to certain remarks of the Kaiser: 'We must express our opinion to the Kaiser spinelessly (rückgratlos).' A storm of laughter interrupted the speaker, who corrected himself by saying 'unreservedly' (rückhaltlos). It was too late, however, for his secret intention to give way to the Kaiser had already betrayed itself in his speech.

Getting on the wrong tram or a tram going in the wrong direction, so as to be taken back to the starting-point; losing and breaking things; self-inflicted injuries; many accidents, and many other events of everyday life, great and small, fall within this category. This can be demonstrated by observing the basic rule of psycho-analysis, that is to say, taking the event as the starting-point, freely associating to it, and not allowing ourselves to be side-tracked by the emergence of resistances.

The same holds good for the so-called chance actions which occur in everyday life and which appear to be so trivial. A married man, whilst describing his complaints in a doctor's consulting room, takes off his wedding-ring and drops it, so that it rolls across the floor. It soon becomes clear that his nervous symptoms are connected with the intimate side of his marriage, and that he cannot bring himself to decide on a divorce.

It would be possible to bring an infinite number of such examples, but we are limiting ourselves to these few. It is worth mentioning, however, that cases like this last one of the dropping of the wedding-ring are often regarded by the people as omens. The explanation which psycho-analysis gives to them is far better, for it is founded on their unconscious psychic function. Psycho-analysis seeks to trace many superstitions to their unconscious sources.

To the uninitiated it must seem strange that, after Freud had succeeded in throwing light on the significance of errors and on the problem of dreams, he chose to turn to the psychology of wit. It is impossible to expound here the entire psycho-analytical theory of wit. I will indicate briefly some of the ways in which it can be shown that wit and dreams stand in a similar relationship to the unconscious. It was this relationship which aroused Freud's attention.

If when we indulge in wit we put aside strictly logical thinking, we are only reverting to the freedom we enjoyed in early childhood. The process of repression, which sets in during the fourth year of life or thereabout is, in wit, temporarily suspended. The psychic energy which would otherwise have been used for repression is released with pleasurable effect; this takes us back for a short time to a state of childhood liberty and freedom from convention. The psychogenetic study of wit leads back to the child's playing with words; that is to say to a stage of mental development in which reality was not yet heeded. The older child has need at times to set reason aside. The pleasure he takes in nonsense produces jokes, which constitute the second preliminary step in the formation of wit. The third step consists in the harmless witticism, which serves to give expression to a significant thought free from the restraint of criticism. Finally, intentional wit, which gives expression to aggressive or sexual impulses, among others, ranges itself on the side of strong impulses fighting against repression.

E

In common with the dream, wit uses specific technical means of representation, such as the condensation of different psychic elements into a unity, and representation through opposites. Furthermore, the material of wit, just like that of dreams, springs from the unconscious. Wit is instantaneous and not a product of conscious psychic activity. Wit, too, is opposed by the restricting force known to us as censorship. In contrast to the dream, however, wit is a social process. The person producing the witticism needs to communicate it to an appreciative hearer. In this other person repressions are suddenly suspended, and the repressed is abreacted by laughter. Whilst the dream serves to prevent unpleasure, wit strives for a positive gain of pleasure.

Let us now look back for a moment at the path which psycho-analysis has taken. It has demonstrated the conflict between repressing forces and repressed instinctual impulses not only in pathological states, but also in important manifestations of normal psychic life. It has revealed not only the wealth of material, which is individually coloured according to the inborn constitution and the personal experiences of each human being, but all that is characteristic of, and common to, the unconscious of all mankind. Such psychological findings must necessarily be no less significant for other spheres of human knowledge. The following survey is intended to give, in broad outline, without claim to comprehensiveness, the disciplines which have a scientific or practical interest in the discoveries of psycho-analysis.

Adult individuals have as a rule no understanding of the instinctual life of the child because they have, through their own instinctual repression, become too far removed from childhood behaviour. Psycho-analysis has given us a fundamental insight into the wishes and the phantasy-life of the child, and especially its sexuality. Erroneous views are still widely held, particularly in respect of infantile sexuality. It is obvious that education can derive great benefit from the results of our science. In particular, it can show the teacher how many expressions of infantile instinctual life are only apparently eradicated by suppressive measures. The forcible suppression of instinctual forces paves the way for nervous illnesses in the child. An upbringing which proceeds according to psycho-analytical findings will avoid such mistakes. It will attempt, in an appropriate way, to get rid of pathological inhibitions, which stand in the way of a sublimation of the instinctual life, and will in particular pay careful attention to the child's sexual phantasies. An upbringing of this kind might in the future become of great importance in preventing the development of nervous disorders.

Not every individual, in growing up, easily finds the way from the wish-fulfilling dreams of infancy to realistic thinking. Between the normal person, who has successfully travelled this road and the neurotic, who has more or less foundered on it, a third type is to be found. This is the artist, in whose creations wish-fulfilment plays a role similar to that which it plays in the dreams of the rest of mankind. Without having solved all the problems of the artist or of art, psycho-analysis has thrown an entirely new light upon the unconscious drives governing the artist's work, and upon the effects of works of art upon those who enjoy them. The artist obtains from his work a self-liberation similar to a cathartic abreaction, in which he allows others, in whose psychic life the same repressed wishes are at work, to participate. Of particular interest are certain findings of psycho-analysis concerning the relationship between the artist's childhood impressions and the events of his life on the one hand and his work on the other. We merely mention this in passing. Those who wish to go further into these questions should read the essays on the psychology of art, of which a number have been published by Freud and his followers. These essays deal with poets as well as with painters, sculptors, and their work.

Psycho-analysis has not confined itself to the investigation of the phantasy activity of individuals, whether children or adults, normal or pathological, but has also made successful advances into the realm of mass-phantasy. In discussing typical dreams we recognised striking parallels to certain myths. This analogy between dream and myth is very far-reaching, and extends to content as well as to form. The myth, too, has a latent as well as a manifest content, the former being concealed behind many varied symbols and strange condensations. Much of the material used in myths is also to be found in dreams. The themes of incest and of nakedness are common to both. We may regard the myth almost as a dream of the people. Just as the content of the individual's dream takes the dreamer back to a forgotten time of his infancy, so the content of the myth goes back to the prehistoric epoch of mankind. Psycho-analytical investigations of myths and fairy-tales have yielded a wealth of understanding of the phantasy creations of the unconscious of the people. What psycho-analysis has to teach us about the causes of myth-formation deserves particular attention. The true psychological cause of this phenomenon cannot lie in the need to explain mysterious natural processes, as has sometimes been suggested. The same instinctual strivings as we have discerned in the dream are operative here.

These investigations revealed surprising analogies between the childhood of the individual and the pre-history of mankind, and the insight thus gained became of great importance for the comprehension of other products of the human mind, such as religion, ethics, law, philosophy, customs and conventions. All such systems are founded on the need for a transformation of those instinctual drives to which direct satisfaction must be denied. They are thus equivalent to the products of individual sublimation.

Here, too, a comparison between the ideas of the primitive human mind and those of the child is very fruitful. Psycho-analysis has shown how the child originally harbours the phantasy of the unlimited power of his own wishes; many of the animistic and magical ideas of primitive peoples are similar to this concept of the child's. The most primitive social systems known to us rest entirely on the incest barrier of primitive man. The significance of incestuous wishes as the cause of one of the earliest childhood conflicts has become known to us through psycho-analysis. One of Freud's greatest achievements is his discovery of certain parallels between the most primitive forms of religion and the psychic life of the child.

Among a great number of primitive peoples we find a social system in which religious and secular functions are not yet differentiated and which is known to ethnology by the name of totemism. The totem is usually some kind of animal; less frequently it is a plant or an inanimate object. We will confine ourselves here to a discussion of the more usual form. Every animal of the species worshipped as a totem by the tribe is given special treatment. It must not be caught, killed or hunted. On one special, solemn occasion called the totem-meal, however, the totem-animal is killed and eaten by the whole community whose totem it is, this meal being accompanied by strange rituals. All the members of the tribe stand in a special relationship to the totem. They regard themselves as descendants of the totem, and in return for treating it favourably, they in their turn expect it to show them a friendly spirit and to refrain from hostile actions.

This system, which we regard as a primitive forerunner of the historic religions, is bound up with other institutions which are equally remote from the conceptions of civilised peoples. A man who belongs to the kangaroo totem is not allowed to take a wife who belongs to the same totem. In other words, he is not only forbidden to marry a blood-relation, but, as if to reinforce the incest barrier by further measures, the prohibition is extended to all the members of the tribe. This is called the law of exogamy. The institutions of primitive peoples give us the impression that no object was of more vital importance to them than the prevention of incest.

The phenomena described here have remained enigmatic to ethnologists. Not only were they unable to understand the meaning of totemism, and the ceremonies connected with it, but also the significance of exogamy. They attempted to approach these difficult problems as though they were unconnected with each other. An explanation of the inter-related problems of totemism and the incest-barrier, that is, of exogamy, was possible only when they were viewed as a composite whole.

Psycho-analysis approached these questions with knowledge gained elsewhere. It had already recognised that in the life of every child the overcoming of the incest problem represents a psychic achievement of great importance. Furthermore, it had come to recognise an exaggerated fear of incest in the psychology of those individuals with which it was most closely concerned, namely neurotic patients. Freud found in the psychic life of children further analogies with the psychic life of primitive peoples. Very many, if not all, children have in their early childhood a special emotional relationship to one species of animal. This emotional relationship is characterised by its ambivalence. On the one hand the child shows a loving and tender interest in this particular kind of animal, whilst on the other the very same species arouses fear and hatred in him. With present-day children it is the larger domestic animals which most frequently play this part: in towns mainly horses and dogs, and less often cats, chickens, or other creatures. Sometimes a three to five-year-old child imagines itself to be identical to the animal of its choice. Children with a neurotic disposition show such phantastic behaviour to an increased degree. One little boy, for instance, could not be torn away from the chicken run, was interested in nothing but chickens, wanted to hear only songs and poems in which cocks and hens figured, imitated the attitude and the movements of these birds, and for a time even abandoned speech in favour of crowing and cackling. In this case it was love for the chickens which was predominant; in other cases it may be fear of them. Normal children, too, are subject to nightmares in which they are attacked by one particular species of animal, most frequently a dog. It is remarkable that a boy who dreams he is being attacked by a dog, is often accompanied in the dream by his mother. Quite often the child dreams that he talks to the dog, asks its forgiveness, and promises to be a good boy. This in itself suggests that the loved and feared animal has the significance of a parent. The many facts supporting this theory cannot be set out here. It is sufficient to say that such an animal plays the same role in the psychic life of the child as the totem plays in the psychic life of primitive man.

From this individual totemism in the psychology of the child we are able to deduce the way in which his relationship to his parents develops and in particular to trace the origin of his religious feelings and ideas. The phase of the boy's ambivalent attitude to the totem, that is to say, to the father-animal, is succeeded by the phase in which he overcomes his hostile feelings by feelings of tenderness. The early infantile wish to get rid of the father is substituted by the opposite wish. His power is exalted, and he may even be admired as being omnipotent. If at this stage the child is taught his first religious ideas, these ideas will follow the pattern of the previous development. The child, and man in general, cannot imagine a god other than in the image of the father. All religions make use of this comparison.

We have referred to only a few of the many and surprising results of psycho-analytical investigations in the field of the psychology of religion. We may mention that the same methods of investigation have succeeded in explaining hitherto enigmatical phenomena such as the taboos of primitive peoples. We find similar manifestations in the psychology of children and of neurotic patients. Once our science had succeeded in understanding these manifestations, it was able to lift the veil surrounding corresponding phenomena in folk-psychology.

We have briefly surveyed a vast new field of modern research. The wealth of new discoveries has been such that we could only touch on a few points in order to become more familiar with the findings of psycho-analysis, but even this broad outline shows the revolutionary changes brought about by psycho-analytical teachings in every sphere of psychic life. It was psycho-analysis which first discovered the rule of causality in the field of psychic life. It perceived the applicability of the principle of the conservation of energy to the psychic realm and taught us to recognise primitive human impulses in their manifold vicissitudes. Modern biology has shown how the organic development of the individual recapitulates in abbreviated form that of the species. Psycho-analysis has extended this biogenetic law first postulated by Haeckel to the psychic realm. If we compare Freud's theories on the unconscious as the psychic reality, on repression, on the relationship between our psychic life and infantile sexuality, or on his interpretation of dreams, with the theories of other schools of psychology, the difference is striking. At last we have a psychology which equally avoids barren speculation and laboratory experiments which have no relation to real life. Freud's doctrine, as much as any existing inductive natural science, has developed from the observation of living people. Without preconceived ideas, it has fearlessly approached those phenomena of psychic life which previously constituted the 'dark continent' of psychology and, free from false shame or prudery, it has investigated those sides of our personality which academic psychology has been careful to shun as all-too-human.

I fear that some of my readers will be confused, rather than enlightened, by all the new ideas presented to them in this paper. For psycho-analysis demands from everyone who has hitherto subscribed to the theories of traditional psychology the most radical re-thinking. Even a person who is intellectually inclined to make this effort of re-thinking may be emotionally opposed to many of the new ideas. There can be no doubt that Freud's discoveries have dealt to human pride one of those great blows which science has struck it more than once in modern times. The discovery made by Copernicus forced mankind to recognise that the earth is not the centre of the universe, but only one minor planet among many revolving round the sun. This still left man with his belief in his unique position in nature. Then came Darwin to compel man to regard himself as a mere link in a chain of animal species, bearing all the signs of his phylogenetic past upon him. This still left it open for civilised man to feel that he occupied a special position as compared with primitive man, whom he called savage. Freud drove him even from this position, for he teaches that in infancy man is amoral, and that he goes through many stages of development which are entirely similar to the life of the most primitive savages. Such teachings have at all times provoked not merely objective criticism, but also the most passionate emotions and opposition. The opposition to Darwin is still fresh in our memory; the opposition to Freud is remarkably similar to it. One is almost tempted to say 'rightly so', since in the sphere of psychology Freud is the exponent of psychic evolution, as Darwin was of organic evolution.

Gradually, however, the number of those who tend to regard psycho-analysis dispassionately is on the increase. We live in a time of revolution. In the social sphere we are at the beginnings of fundamental changes. Technical progress is rapid. In the realm of art the old ideas have been superseded by new ideas in complete contrast to them. In the sphere of science Einstein's theory demands from us a great re-orientation of our thinking. We can expect of such an epoch that it will not deny recognition to the achievements of psycho-analysis, even though much opposition from academic psychology may have to be overcome.

III

THE DAY OF ATONEMENT

Some Observations on Reik's *Problems of the Psychology of
Religion*

(1920)

THE readers of this journal [1] will be familiar with Reik's earlier
writings on the 'Couvade' and on 'puberty rites'. The author has
put them together with two further hitherto unpublished papers
called 'Kolnidre' and 'The Schophar', in a book which has
recently been published under the name of *Problems of the
Psychology of Religion*.[2] In these new works, which are based upon
careful literary and historical research, Reik applies the psycho-
analytical technique, with surprising success, to two much
debated questions of religious ritual. This paper is designed to
draw attention to Reik's important researches. At the same
time a number of additions to and criticisms of the author's
findings will be made, as a contribution to the psycho-analytical
understanding of the Jewish Day of Atonement and its rituals.

The Kolnidre formula, which is recited in a ceremonious
manner at the beginning of the Day of Atonement, as an introduction to the service for the eve of this day, contains an ante-
cedent annulment of all subsequent promises, renunciations,
curses, vows, and other obligations relating to the period up to
the next Day of Atonement. The meaning of this formula has
often been misunderstood and has never been satisfactorily
explained. It is in irreconcilable contradiction to the usual
significance attributed to promises and commitments in the
Jewish religion. To make this contradiction comprehensible,
Reik investigates the historical development of the oath, and
finds its original form in the so-called 'B'rith', a kind of
covenant such as that which Jahveh made with the patriarchs.
This covenant contains an undertaking by god to protect his
children. On the part of the latter it contains a renunciation of
all violence against the father-god. This covenant becomes comprehensible if we recall the emotional attitude of primitive
human communities towards their totem, which to them is

[1] *Imago*, 6, 1, 1920.
[2] With a Foreword by Professor Freud, *Internationaler Psycho-
analytischer Verlag*, 1919.

equated with the father. Reik here bases himself upon Freud's conception that the origin of religion lies in the guilt-feeling, connected with the 'primal crime', that is, the murder of the father by the horde of brothers. He goes on to explain how the rebellion against the father-god gradually underwent repression, but how it breaks through time and again in the course of the development of human civilisation. Thus the Old Testament is full of the relapses of god's people into idolatry. The constant vacillating between apostacy from Jahveh and returning to him demonstrates most clearly the ambivalent attitude of the people towards the paternal god. In later times large-scale apostacy no longer occurred. The people clung tenaciously and steadfastly to their god, and only single individuals or small groups abandoned their faith under the compulsion or temptation of external conditions. Jewish religion demanded from its followers a special measure of devotion and loyalty to the covenant, and these demands were intensified by the imposition of restrictions of ever-increasing severity. In a manner reminiscent of the process of symptom-formation in obsessional neurosis, religious laws were protected against any possibility of infringement by additional measures enjoining overscrupulousness in every new generation. In post-Talmudic times there was a tendency to abolish all freedom of action by vows and renunciations. We may assume that the burden of such vows, and the painfulness of asceticism provoked a reaction. If we follow Reik's exposition we find just such a reaction in the Kolnidre formula which tries to invalidate for the ensuing year all promises then made. Reik now seeks to prove that the Kolnidre in its wording seems directed against all kinds of self-imposed vows, but that in fact, that is to say, according to its unconscious content, it aims at dissolving or completely destroying the covenant with god. Its motive is therefore the same as that of the primal crime of the tribal horde against the father-god. Reik, who succeeds in tracing the comparison between these religious phenomena and the symptomatology of obsessional neurosis, might well have added that the compulsive thoughts of the neurotic represent a substitute for forbidden actions not carried out. This is exactly true for the Kolnidre, if we continue to follow Reik's exposition. A further analogy with obsessional neurosis is contained in the ambivalence of emotions revealed in the Kolnidre. The tone and manner of its recital show repentance and contrition, in contrast to the rebellion involved in denying the covenant. Reik shows that the Kolnidre formula is to be regarded as a compulsive symptom of folk-psychology, corresponding to certain formulae which neurotics invent as a defence against forbidden instinctual impulses.

To clarify the essential meaning of the Kolnidre, Reik goes back to the most ancient form of the B'rith rite. After referring to Robertson Smith and other authors, and to the relevant factual material, he shows how the original ceremonial consisted in killing, dividing up and eating the sacrificial animal, that is to say, the totem. He points out the strong probability that the Kolnidre springs from such primitive usages in which, according to Freud's analysis, the aggressive attitude towards the father becomes intermingled with penitent feelings. Curiously enough, the fact escaped him that his hypothesis could be supported by even stronger evidence. The ritual of the Day of Atonement shows in the most striking manner the connection between the primitive ceremonial of the totem meal and the Kolnidre. The author, who had otherwise so successfully traced the psychology of the ritual, limited himself to demonstrating the inner connection between the Kolnidre and the prayer formulae immediately following it, and has, if I may say so, omitted to consider those which are further removed from the Kolnidre.

On the day before the feast, that is, only a few hours before the Kolnidre prayer, according to orthodox ritual a ceremony takes place which represents a strange remnant of the old sacrificial cult. For men a cock, and for women a hen, is used as an expiatory offering. The bird's legs are tied together, and whilst a formula is spoken it is swung three times round the head of the person to be expiated. The words sound almost like a form of exorcism. They are: 'This is my expiatory sacrifice; this is my substitute; this cock is to go to its death in my stead.' After the ceremony of swinging it three times, the bird is thrown aside with a gesture of disgust, and later is killed and eaten at the family-table. I will postpone for the present the question why the cock is here taken as a substitute for four-legged sacrificial animals. What is particularly significant for our investigation is the fact that according to the wording of the formula the bird is a personal substitute for the one who makes the sacrifice. The identity of the sacrificer with the totem can also be true in other similar cults. We may say, therefore, that according to old custom, before the beginning of the Day of Atonement and as its introduction, in every house the totem meal is celebrated and thus the primal crime is repeated every year. Since the abolition of the official sacrificial cult the ceremony could no longer be carried out by the whole community. Because of its ability to express the conflicting emotional impulses simultaneously, however, it found a niche in family ritual. We are reminded of the frequent observation that many religious ideas and usages of the pre-Christian era, which have long been abolished by the prevailing religious authority, survive in some form in popular customs and superstitions.

I should like to interpolate here some remarks about the cock as a sacrificial offering. In various cults the totem is in general the chief sacrificial animal. As Reik proves in his subsequent paper on the Schophar, two totem animals can be shown to have existed in ancient Judaism: the ram and the bull. In the sacrificial rules of Leviticus these appear as the most important sacrificial animals. In the same book, however, we already find an ordinance directing the use of poultry for sacrifices prescribed for various occasions. Economic considerations must have made it impracticable to use a valuable four-legged animal for every private sacrifice.

From the time of the ceremonial meal until sundown on the following day the taking of food and drink is entirely forbidden. In other words, the meal with the fundamentally forbidden character is immediately followed by a protracted fast. It now becomes clear why it is the abstention from food which is the appropriate form of atonement. Fasting is conventionally regarded as a self-sacrifice which ethically is supposed to constitute a profoundly important step forward from the killing of an innocent animal. A self-sacrifice is in fact involved in the self-punishment for the killing and eating of the totem, just as in neurotic reaction-formations a repressed sadistic impulse is replaced by an act of self-torment.

After the family meal all members of the community attend a solemn religious service. What happens there, if we accept Reik's account, is nothing less than a repetition of the primal crime; not in deed, but—after the pattern of an obsessional neurosis—in thoughts and word-formulae. This time, moreover, the crime is perpetrated by the whole community and the responsibility for it is shared by the whole community. In the place of the killing of the totem is set the intellectual dissolution of the covenant with the father-god. An accompanying rite is noteworthy: according to the old ritual, the two oldest men of the community step forward and, in solemn ceremonial manner, give permission for the speaking of the Kolnidre. Nowhere else in the whole liturgy is this usage to be found. On the Day of Atonement itself, every Reader, before beginning his allotted chapter of the liturgy, must pray privately at great length.

Curiously enough this is omitted at the service held on the eve of the Day of Atonement. On that occasion the Reader does not ask god's support for the performance of his duties, but obtains his authority from the elders. This shows a different attitude: an autocratic and independent responsible attitude on the part of the gathering. Then the Reader sings the Kolnidre three times, as is often done with the formal parts of the liturgy, raising his voice higher each time.

We find, therefore, in uninterrupted sequence the sacrifice and eating of the totem in the individual houses, and the corresponding ceremony for the annulment of vows in the communal service. This direct sequence leads us to assume an inner connection between the two acts. This lends weighty support to Reik's theory, but the significance of our discovery goes still further.

The question raised by Reik, and only tentatively answered, as to why the Kolnidre was placed outside the rest of the liturgy and at the beginning of the service, can now be easily and convincingly dealt with. The Kolnidre is the substitute for the extreme violence directed against the father-god, for the totem meal, which is followed by the great act of atonement, and must therefore precede the latter.

It is worth while pausing a little at this point. There are other examples of excess preceding a time of repentance and renunciation, for instance, Shrove Tuesday [1] preceding the fast of Lent. A far clearer illustration, however, is provided by certain obsessional neurotics. I had a patient, who, since his boyhood, had succumbed to the compulsion to promise to himself that he would abstain from certain acts. All his previous experience taught him that it would be extremely hard for him to keep these promises. In particular, he would vow to refrain from all sexual activity. After a longer or shorter period of abstention he invariably succumbed anew to the temptation. No sooner had he deviated in the slightest degree from a strict adherence to his resolution, than he would throw himself compulsively into a wild orgy, entirely undoing his intended renunication. When he had given full vent to his impulses, there followed remorse, contrition and the resolution to begin a new life, so characteristic of the psychology of the neurotic. This resolution was nevertheless destined to be broken like all its forerunners.

I should like to illustrate this process by another example

[1] Editor's note: In the German text the example chosen is that of Carnival and the subsequent fast.

from psycho-pathology. A woman suffered from an exceptionally severe cleansing compulsion. At certain intervals she carried out the most thorough cleaning of her home. This invariably culminated in the dusting of a chest of drawers in which she kept her white linen. A whole morning was devoted to this purpose; every speck of dust was removed from the corners of the drawers and from the linen. The patient painstakingly collected every particle of dust on a piece of white paper. Finally, the laborious cleansing process was completed. A state of cleanliness was achieved which gratified the intense preoccupation with cleanliness which dominated her conscious mind, but which was unbearable to the repressed opposing tendency. Thus at the very moment when the utmost cleanliness was achieved, a sudden counter-impulse broke through; with a quick jerk of her hand the patient upset the paper and the dust so laboriously collected was deposited once more in the drawers. Anxiety and depression followed, producing new resolutions of cleanliness, which were reinforced by all kinds of vows, and so the sequence began again without ever coming to an end.

The impulses of such neurotics reveal an ambivalence similar to that which Reik has so convincingly shown to be present in the Kolnidre. With Reik, I should like to draw attention to the fact that in the Jewish religion there was a counterpart to the behaviour of obsessional neurotics in the tendency to reinforce each religious tenet by ever-stricter and more elaborate rules. The Kolnidre is the periodical attempt to get rid of the burden of such obsessions by a single act of violence. Such transgression has then to be followed by atonement and by making the covenant anew.

Our theory about the Kolnidre may be of some assistance in ascertaining the date of its origin. Let us consider the precise wording of the Kolnidre: it cancels in anticipation all self-imposed vows which the members of the community can impose upon themselves within the period of a year. According to the pattern of obsessional neurotics which have here been quoted, we must come to the following conclusion. The formula could only have originated at a time when the tendency to limit and confine life in all directions by vows and renunciations surpassed the endurance of even the most long-suffering. It should be possible to determine when such a tendency reached its climax. The Aramaic wording of the text may point to a particular time of origin, which, however, it is not one of the tasks of the psycho-analyst to fix more precisely. It can merely be postulated here that such a formula could only date from a period in which the compulsive self-limitation coincided with an urge to break the bonds.

The Kolnidre, as Reik has pointed out, also shows traces of 'secondary elaboration', indicating the further working of repression. These are to be found in the Hebrew interpolation in the middle of the Aramaic text: 'From this Day of Atonement to the Day of Atonement which may dawn for our salvation.' It has been proved that in earlier times vows made during the year were retrospectively cancelled. This, incidentally, is clearly evident from the wording of the Kolnidre formula. All the verbs in the assembled formula referring to vows are put into the past tense. The Hebraic interpolation, which refers to the future, appears on close scrutiny almost alien in its context. Between the retrospective and the anticipatory nullification there is certainly a considerable psychological difference. The former appears in contrast to the usual sanctity of the oath, like a malicious breach of the obligation; the latter appears rather like a preventive measure, reminding the psycho-analyst of similar avoidances in obsessional neurotics.

Reik's investigation has taught us that the Day of Atonement is governed by the Oedipus complex. He has, however, overlooked further important facts which reinforce his views. Two of them will be mentioned here, since they enable us at the same time to supplement his findings.

First, we are accustomed to find both in the product of individual phantasy and in myths the two human desires which are invariably found in the closest proximity, and which are clearly illustrated in the Oedipus legend: the son's desire for his mother, and his violent rebellion against his father. If, with Reik, we take the introductory ritual of the Day of Atonement as emanating from the rebellion against the father-god, our views would obtain significant confirmation if we were also to find in the rite of the same festival an indication of the correlated crime of mother-incest. This proves to be the case. To the evening prayer for the Day of Atonement belongs the recitation of Chapter 18 of Leviticus, which is the chapter containing detailed prohibitions against incest,—assuredly a striking fact. As though to emphasise the close relationship between the two main elements of the Oedipus complex in the liturgy, the reading of the law as mentioned above is followed by that of the book of the prophet Jonah. This inner relationship cannot be discovered by superficial observation. It is only recognisable in the light of psycho-analysis. Jonah disobeys an express commandment of Jahveh and flees from him, thus committing a deed similar to that committed by the community in annulling the covenant on the eve of the Day of Atonement. He is swallowed by an animal, escapes with his life, and then appears as a repentant sinner acceptable to god. For those who are familiar from mythology with the widespread phantasy of the god eating his children and with the fact that this phantasy is the counterpart to the killing and eating of the totem, this part of the ritual will have a deeper meaning.

Secondly, the traditional conception of the Day of Atonement implies that as the day progresses the repentant sinner stands before his god with ever-increasing freedom from sin. Accordingly the liturgy increases in solemnity towards the end of the day. Towards evening a ceremony takes place which belongs also to the liturgy of other festivals. The timing of this ceremony for this particular moment, that is to say, its displacement from the morning to the afternoon, cannot be without significance. It is the so-called 'priestly blessing'. All the male members of the community who trace their origin traditionally from the tribe of the priests (the Kohanim), and who therefore enjoy to this day certain privileges in the conducting of divine service in orthodox Judaism, recite the priestly blessing of Aaron to the community.

In his article on the 'Schophar', Reik has provided a clue to the understanding of this custom, again without noticing that he has allowed valuable factual material to escape him. We may here make the comment that this second article concerning the ritual of Judaism surpasses in cogency his first article on this problem. The brilliant conception and execution of his tracing of Mosaic monotheism back to primitive totemism commands our admiration. We will adopt from this exposition certain conclusions concerning the totemistic phase which preceded the Jewish religion, and the earlier history of its priesthood.

It has already been mentioned that in the early history of Judaism there were two totem animals, namely the bull and the ram. The Schophar, or ram's horn, is still used in present-day ritual. According to Reik's description which is convincing but which cannot be quoted here in detail, the blowing of the horn must be regarded as an imitation of the voice of the totem. The sound, in itself unmelodious, is used on high feast-days to summon the worshippers to prayer; it moves its hearers because it represents the voice of god himself. The custom, observed by the strictly orthodox, of averting their eyes from the man who blows the Schophar, is significant. To look upon him is as forbidden and dangerous as to look upon god himself. I make a special mention of this prohibition, because I shall shortly have occasion to return to it. The man who is entrusted with the blowing of the Schophar thus has the task of imitating the totem, and thereby in a certain sense attains divinity. This also holds good for the priestly office in other religions. If the priest also has the duty to eat the sacrificial meat, his identity with the totem is constantly being renewed. In totemistic cults the priests imitate the totem by wrapping themselves in the fur of the sacred animal, by imitating its movements, and by other means. In all these customs the priest's identity with the totem is sometimes revealed and sometimes concealed in varying degrees.

The ceremony of the priestly blessing contains certain detailed instructions of a peculiar kind which we are now in a position to understand. The priestly sect—the Kohanim—wrap themselves in the praying-shawl, pulling it right over their heads. Then entirely concealed from the eyes of the community, they raise their arms in the blessing. A strange position of the hands is prescribed for this part of the rite, which, as far as I know, has not hitherto been satisfactorily explained. The third and fourth fingers must be held together and separately from the other fingers, and must be retained during the whole of the ceremony in this unnatural position. The deep significance attached to this position of the fingers may be recognised from the fact that the religion prescribes that the tombstone of every deceased member of the priestly sect shall bear the identification mark of two hands in this characteristic position. When one considers how strictly Judaism has been avoiding any other pictorial representations, this exception appears very remarkable.

Can we find anywhere a conception which may help us to understand this strange ceremony? We may answer this question in the affirmative, and turn our attention to certain rules of ritual which themselves call for an explanation. Chapter 11 of Leviticus contains laws as to which animals may be used as food and which may not. 'Whatsoever parteth the hoof, and is clovenfooted, and cheweth the cud, among the beasts, that shall ye eat. Nevertheless these shall ye not eat of them that chew the cud, or of them that divide the hoof: as the camel, because he cheweth the cud, but divideth not the hoof; he is unclean unto you. And the coney, because he cheweth the cud, but divideth not the hoof; he is unclean unto you. And the hare, because he cheweth the cud, but divideth not the hoof;

he is unclean unto you. And the swine, though he divide the hoof, and be clovenfooted, yet he cheweth not the cud; he is unclean to you.' Among the few types of four-footed creatures with cloven hoofs which may be eaten—in practice only cows, sheep and goats—are to be found the two which have become known to us as totems, namely the bull and the ram. We here encounter the strange fact that it is precisely the totem animals which are virtually the only ones which may be eaten; whilst among primitive peoples there is mostly a strict prohibition against eating the animal worshipped as the totem, a prohibition which is but rarely waived. We must here suspect a strange process of reversal, but it must be left for later psychoanalytical research to make a detailed investigation of eating rites. Among four-legged animals, the species it is permissible to eat and the species which may be used for sacrifice are the same. If we bear in mind that in many religions the most sacred ceremony consists in the priests wrapping themselves in the skin of the totem animal and imitating its posture, it suggests the following conclusion. In the priestly blessing the Kohanim or priestly sect imitate by the separation of the fingers the cloven hoofs of the totem, the ram. The praying-shawl made of white wool is an appropriate substitute for the wool of the ram. The Kohanim are in this ceremony thus equated with the totem and hence with god. We may also add that the averting of the eyes is prescribed during the pronouncing of the blessing by the priests just as with the blowing of the Schophar. We cannot but recognise in the priestly blessing no less than in the blowing of the Schophar a totemistic ritual. As with primitive peoples the totem is first killed and eaten and subsequently imitated in solemn ceremonial whereby its adherents identify with it, so, too, with the rite now under consideration. Here, however, the action is carried out in two parts. The totem meal, or its intellectual counterpart, the Kolnidre, takes place on the eve of the Day of Atonement; the imitating ceremony takes place on the evening of the Day of Atonement itself, when the unity of the community with god is to be emphasised.

Reik's view that the Kolnidre has the significance of destroying the covenant, is confirmed by the ending of the liturgy for the Day of Atonement which deserves our attention. The solemn closing prayer, the 'N'ilah', ends with a special affirmation of faith by those who pray. The Reader recites the 'Sch'ma' (Hear, O Israel) three times, and three times the community repeats it. After a further sentence repeated three times there follows an emphatic seven-fold repetition of the creed: 'Jahveh is the only god.' This ends the liturgy for the day. The day of repentance therefore begins with a blasphemous annulment of the vows, or rather of the B'rith, the covenant with Jahveh, and ends with an emphatic announcement of his power and uniqueness. The covenant is thus re-established in the most solemn form and the reconciliation of the community with Jahveh has taken place. The deepest meaning of the Day of Atonement is therefore now apparent. The father-god who has been murdered is recognised anew by his sons, and in his turn resumes his obligations towards them.

The main criticism of Reik's theory of the Kolnidre in my opinion is that the author has subjected the Kolnidre to psychoanalytical interpretation in isolation, instead of considering it in relation to the whole of the ceremony. Psycho-analytical experience teaches us that psychological phenomena which are found in close proximity always show a deeper causal relationship. We should always bear this in mind in medical practice not less than in the purely theoretical application of psychoanalysis. If we draw upon psycho-analytical knowledge, as we have done in a summary form in the preceding discussion, we are enabled to understand clearly the reason for the annual Day of Atonement. The covenant with Jahveh with its excessive limitations of instinctual impulses placed so great a burden upon the community that it could only be endured if it could be periodically broken. The fixing of the periods, however, had to be put beyond the arbitrary decision of the individual. On the responsibility of the whole community the B'rith was dissolved once a year, and after a short-lived gratification of the rebellious impulses, was re-established. Without this fresh reinforcement, which could only be effected after abreacting the hostility to the covenant, the covenant would not have been safe from attack either from without or within. Thus originated the Day of Atonement, whose liturgy begins with the sombre sound of the Kolnidre, speaking of heavy guilt, and ends with the proclamation of the uniqueness of the Lord.

Part Three

ESSAYS

DREAMS AND MYTHS

A STUDY IN FOLK–PSYCHOLOGY
(1909)

Contents

I

The Subject-Matter and Theory of Freudian Psycho-analysis

THE theories associated with the name of Sigmund Freud relate to several spheres of psychic life which, at first sight, seem to have little connection with one another. In his *Studies on Hysteria* published in 1895 in collaboration with Joseph Breuer, Freud used pathological psychic manifestations as his starting-point. The progressive development of the psycho-analytical method necessitated the intensive study of dreams.[1] It then became clear that in order to understand these phenomena fully, it was also necessary to make a comparative study of certain other phenomena. Freud was consequently impelled to incorporate an increasing range of psychological phenomena, both normal and abnormal, into the scope of his investigations. In this way, in the 'Sammlung Kleiner Schriften zur Neurosenlehre', he came to collect papers on hysteria, obsessional ideas and other psychic disorders, the monograph on wit which was published in 1905, the *Three Contributions to the Theory of Sex*,[2] and later the psychological analysis of a work of fiction,[3] which together form the first volume of this series. It was Freud's achievement to discern in these apparently unrelated products of the human mind the attributes they share in common. These are their relationship to the unconscious, to the psychic life of infancy and to sexuality. They also share in common the tendency to represent man's wishes as fulfilled and the means used to represent such fulfilment.

Those unfamiliar with the work of Freud and his followers will be amazed that a serious attempt should be made to correlate these phenomena. They will ask what possible relationship there could be between wit and the unconscious. They will question the assumption that an illness from which a patient suffers could contain a wish-fulfilment. They will not comprehend how one can possibly liken an illness to a work of fiction in this respect. They will fail to understand the general interrelationship between the dreams of an adult and the mental life of a child. Above all, they will protest against connecting all

[1] *Die Traumdeutung*, Vienna and Leipzig, 1900 (Second edn., 1909). (*The Interpretation of Dreams*, Standard edn., 4 and 5.)

[2] Now called *Three Essays on Sexuality*.

[3] *Der Wahn und die Träume in Jensens 'Gradiva'*, Vienna and Leipzig, 1907. (*Delusions and Dreams in Jensen's 'Gradiva'*, Standard edn., 9).

these psychological phenomena with sexuality. Freud's teachings therefore appear to be full of contradictions and absurdities. They seem to be indiscriminate in generalising from particular cases. For these reasons one might be inclined to dismiss out of hand a method of research which produces such results.[1]

If I were to attempt here and now to reply to the various objections that will be raised, I should be unable to do so without giving a detailed account of Freud's teachings. I would then be going far beyond the limits of this work. In the course of our investigations opportunites will occur to refer to most of the important problems upon which Freud has worked. For the time being a hint may suffice: the psychic phenomena under consideration are all products of human phantasy. One cannot summarily dismiss the assumption that they may show a certain relationship to each other.

In addition to the products of individual phantasy, however, there are phantasies not to be ascribed to any one individual. Myths and fairy-tales are formations of this kind. We do not know who created them, nor who first recounted them. They were handed down from generation to generation, undergoing many additions and changes in the process. It is in legends and fairy-tales that the phantasy of a nation is revealed. Freud has already done some research in this field and has discovered more than one psychological analogy between legends and the works of individual phantasy. Another author has recently followed in his footsteps. Riklin [2] has carried out the psychological analysis of the fairy-tales of different nations. The present monograph is an attempt to compare myths with the phenomena of individual psychology and especially with dreams. Its purpose is to demonstrate that Freud's doctrines can to a large extent be applied to the psychology of myths and so provide a new basis for their understanding.[3]

[1] This is more or less the attitude adopted by the medical profession towards Freud's theories. Admittedly these theories must appear strange to the uninitiated. It must be emphasised that they are divided from traditional psychology by a wide gulf. This is no reason, however, for dismissing them with a shrug or holding them up to ridicule, as is done by the critics.

[2] The paper by Riklin just published, 'Wish-fulfilment and Symbolism in Fairy-Tales' (Vol. 2 of this series), appeared after this monograph was written. I could therefore only use a short preliminary note by the author (*Psychiatr. Neurol. Wochenschrift*, 1907, Nos. 22–24).

[3] Freud's Work, 'Der Dichter und das Phantasieren', *Neue Revue*, 2nd March, 1908, which was also published after the completion of

II

Childhood Phantasies in Dreams and Myths.
The Application of the Wish-fulfilment Theory to Myths

I will at the outset anticipate some of the principal objections which will be raised against my project. It will be said that myths originate from the phantasies of waking life whilst dreams are produced during sleep, that is, in a state of diminished consciousness. Closer observation, however, shows that this distinction is not fundamental. It is not only during sleep that we dream. There are waking or day-dreams. In these we transport ourselves into an unrealistic situation, moulding the world and our future in accordance with our wishes. It will soon become clear that dreams during sleep have the same tendency. Some people are especially prone to day-dreaming. Their preoccupation is obvious. The transition to a pathological degree of imaginative activity is scarcely perceptible. Children in particular tend to indulge in these dream-like phantasies. A boy will imagine himself the ruler of a great kingdom and victorious in bloody battles, or as a Red Indian chief or in some such role. Pathological degrees of day-dreaming are not infrequently met with in children. This indicates that there is no distinct borderline between day-dreams and the dreams of sleep. Moreover, we know from Freud's investigations that the dream-thoughts are not formed during sleep but during waking life. In the dream they are merely given a shape which differs from that in which we express our thoughts when we are awake.

Another objection, no sounder than the first, may serve as a starting point for pursuing our enquiries further. It will be argued that dreams are products of the individual, whilst myths as it were contain the collective imaginative life of the people. Therefore the comparison will seem false. This objection can easily be disposed of. Even though dreams derive from individual emotions, yet there are emotions common to the whole human race. These are to be found expressed in what Freud calls typical dreams. Freud proved that this group of dreams has its origin in certain wishes shared by all mankind and that these same wishes also form the basis of certain myths.

this monograph, shortly expresses my own basic ideas. There he says: 'Myths are probably the distorted residue of wishful phantasies of whole peoples representing the strivings of early man.' (*Creative Writers and Day-dreaming*, Standard Edn., **9**.)

There are good reasons for using Freud's account of typical dreams as the starting point of our investigations. They give us the opportunity to discuss the wish-fulfilment theory of the dream. We shall, moreover, find them less complicated in certain respects than most other dreams.[1]

According to Freud's theory every dream is based upon a wish repressed into the unconscious. Every human being has undergone experiences the memory of which invariably produces a vivid sense of unpleasure. He tries to eliminate such memories from consciousness. To erase them completely from the mind is impossible. He can only repress them into the unconscious part of the mind. Memories thus repressed and the wishes connected with them then appear to be forgotten: they can no longer be spontaneously recalled. As soon as the functioning of consciousness is in some way impaired, however, and phantasy takes the place of coordinated logical thinking, as occurs in day-dreaming, dreaming and in various pathological conditions, the repressed psychic material is set free. In dreams and in the symptoms of certain psychological disorders the repressed wishes reassert their power. Their fulfilment, originally hoped for but never attained, will be represented in phantasy. That a large proportion of repressed wishes originate in infancy is demonstrated by Freud. To this we shall refer later. For the moment it is sufficient to bear in mind that in Freud's view dreams represent the fulfilment of repressed wishes and that the deepest roots of these wishes are embedded in the dreamer's infancy.

Freud particularly stresses the derivation of typical dreams from infantile memories. Most instructive in this respect are dreams about the death of near relatives. At first sight such dreams seem flatly to contradict Freud's view that every dream contains a wish-fulfilment. Anyone who has dreamed of the death of a near and beloved relative will strongly resent the suggestion that he desired the death of this relative and expressed the secret wish in his dream. He will stress the fact that the dream was accompanied by the most painful feelings, by anxiety and terror, expressing fear and certainly not desire.

This theory, however, does not only take into account present wishes. It strongly emphasises the importance of early infantile impulses. According to Freud's teaching a dream about

[1] Another apparently relevant objection against the juxtaposition of dreams and myths will refer to the gradual development of myths throughout the ages, whereas dreams appear to be fleeting and shortlived. This objection will be answered in the course of this investigation.

the death of a beloved relative does not necessarily mean that the dreamer entertains such a wish at the present time. It may merely mean that he once did so, perhaps in the distant past. Even this, however, will not readily be admitted.

The age at which the infant begins to show altruistic emotions varies considerably. At first he lives in a state of naive egoism. It is erroneous to assume that the infant's feelings towards his parents and siblings are loving from the beginning. On the contrary, there is always a certain amount of rivalry between siblings. The first-born child shows clear signs of jealousy towards a new arrival who receives careful attention on account of his helplessness. It is quite common for a child to begrudge the younger sibling his bottle of milk and to be jealous at seeing the little newcomer on the mother's lap which had hitherto been exlcusively his own preserve. He envies him his toys, he tries to show off his own merits when talking to grown-ups about the new baby. The latter, too, reacts in a similar way as soon as he is capable. He sees the elder sibling as his oppressor and tries to defend himself as far as his weakness permits. Although to a large extent these discordances normally disappear they are never, despite all educational measures, completely eradicated.

One child's hostile impulses against another manifest themselves in death wishes. It will no doubt be denied that any child could be 'wicked' enough to wish another dead. In the words of Freud, 'those who say this fail to realise that the child's idea of "being dead" has little but the words in common with our own.' [1] The child has no clear conception of death. He may hear of some relative having died or being dead. For the child this only means: this person is no longer present. We learn by daily experience how easily the child gets over the absence of a beloved person. He may stretch his little arms in the direction of the disappearing mother, he may cry for a while; then he will find comfort in play or food. He will no longer spontaneously remember the absent mother. Older children, too, of normal psychological constitution, will easily get over a separation. To the small child being dead and being away are identical. When told that someone is dead, the young child is unable to conceive

[1] Editor's footnote: This is a quotation from the first edition of Freud's *Traumdeutung*. It is interesting to note that in the original text, although Freud's name is mentioned as the author of the passage quoted, the reference to the work from which it is quoted is here, as in many other places, omitted. The author took it for granted that his readers would be sufficiently familiar with Freud's writings to make such a reference unnecessary.

that this person will never return. We understand why a child may in all innocence wish for the death of another child or of an adult. If one could get rid of the rival, all cause for competition and jealousy would be eliminated.

Between brothers and sisters this competitive relationship is less intense than between siblings of the same sex. It is modified by the sexual attraction. We shall have occasion to return to this point later.

If we look at the child's relationship to his parents from the same point of view, we meet with new objections. How can anyone assume that the child wishes the death of his father or mother? This possibility might be conceded in cases where children are ill-treated by their parents. It will quickly be added, however, that such cases are fortunately exceptional, and generalisations are therefore not admissible.

The dreams of the death of the father or the mother, occurring as they do in everyone's life, contain the elucidation we need. As Freud points out [1] 'the very great majority of dreams of the death of a parent refer to the parent of the same sex as the dreamer, so that a man generally dreams of the death of his father and a woman of the death of her mother'. Freud explains this behaviour partly as a result of the son's early sexual preference for his mother, and the daughter's for her father. This preference results to a certain extent in rivalry between son and father for the mother's love, or in the case of daughter and mother for the father's love. Sooner or later the son rebels against the father's domination. In some cases this rebellion is overt, in others only latent. At the same time the father defends his power against that of the growing son. A similar relationship exists between mother and daughter. However much civilised man tries to ameliorate or change this competitive relationship by feelings of filial piety or parental love, its traces can never be entirely eradicated. At best, these tendencies are repressed into the unconscious. It is exactly in such cases that they are revealed in dreams. Children who are disposed to nervous or psychic disorders may show an early excessive love for, or rejection of, their parents or of one parent. In their dreams these tendencies appear most clearly and no less in the symptoms of their subsequent illness. Freud gives us very instructive instances of this kind.[2] Among others he quotes the case of a psychotic girl who at first in a confusional state showed a violent

[1] Freud: *Traumdeutung*, First edn., 1900, p. 176; Brill's translation, 1911, p. 303. Standard edn., **4** and **5**.

[2] Freud: *Traumdeutung*, First edn., 1900, p. 179 *et seq.*

repugnance against her mother. When the patient's confusion cleared up she dreamed of her mother's death. Finally she was no longer content with repressing her feelings against her mother into the unconscious. Instead she proceeded to over-compensate these feelings by the formation of a phobia in the form of a pathological fear that something might have happened to her mother. As the patient regained more of her outward composure, so her repugnance was transformed into excessive solicitude over the mother's well-being. I myself have recently observed a very similar case.

It may be added here that the dreams of adults are not infrequently concerned with the death of a child. Pregnant women, suffering from their pregnancy, dream of miscarrying. Fathers or mothers who in their waking state love their child tenderly may, under certain conditions, dream of his death, as for instance where the child's presence prevents the realisation of some ambition.

Typical dreams, then, contain wishes which we do not admit to ourselves in waking-life. It is in dream-life that these secret wishes find expression. These wishes, common to many people or even to all mankind, are also met with in myths. The first point of comparison with which we must deal therefore is the common content of certain dreams and myths. We must follow Freud's exposition still further. As previously mentioned, he was the first to analyse a certain myth—that of Oedipus—from the vantage point gained by the interpretation of dreams. I quote the following passage verbatim from Freud.[1]

'Oedipus, the son of Laius, king of Thebes, and of Jocasta, is exposed when a newly-born child because an oracle had informed the father that his son, who was yet unborn, would be his murderer. He is rescued and grows up as a king's son at a foreign court until, being uncertain of his origin he, too, consults the oracle, and is warned to avoid his birth-place, for he is destined to become the murderer of his father and the husband of his mother. On the road leading from his supposed home he meets King Laius, and in a sudden quarrel kills him. He comes to Thebes, where he solves the riddle of the sphinx, who is barring the way to the city, whereupon he is elected king by the grateful Thebans, and is rewarded with the hand of Jocasta. He reigns for many years in peace and honour and has two sons and two daughters by his unknown mother. Eventually a plague breaks out, which causes the Thebans to consult the oracle anew. Here Sophocles' tragedy begins. The messengers

[1] *Traumdeutung*, First edn., 1900, p. 180 *et seq.*

bring the reply that the plague will cease as soon as the murderer of Laius is driven from the land. The action of the play consists simply in the disclosure, approached step by step and artistically delayed, and thus comparable to the work of psycho-analysis, that Oedipus himself is the murderer of Laius, and that he is the son of the murdered man and Jocasta.'

The Oedipus tragedy is capable of moving us as deeply today as it moved the contemporaries of Sophocles. Yet we do not share their views on gods and fate, nor their belief in oracles. Freud rightly concludes that the legend must contain something which arouses kindred feelings in us all. 'It may be that we were all destined to direct our first sexual impulses towards our mother, and our first impulses of hatred and violence towards our father; our dreams convince us that we were.' [1] In the Oedipus tragedy we see our childhood wishes fulfilled, while we ourselves have in the course of our development replaced our sexual attraction to the mother and our rebellion against the father by feelings of love and piety.

As Freud says, the tragedy itself contains an allusion to the typical dream in which the dreamer becomes sexually united with his mother. Here is the translation: [2]

> 'For many a man hath seen himself in dreams
> His mother's mate.'

The tragedy contains the realisation of two intimately connected childhood or dream phantasies: the phantasy of the father's death and of a love relationship with the mother. We are shown the consequences of the realisation of such phantasies in all their horror.

The same conflict between father and son is represented in the myth concerning Uranus and the Titans. Uranus tries to rid himself of his sons, fearing they might encroach upon his power. His son Kronos retaliates by castrating his father. It is just this form of revenge which points to the sexual aspect of their rivalry. Kronos in turn seeks to safeguard himself in the same way against his own children. He devours them all with the exception of his youngest son Zeus. Zeus takes his revenge upon Kronos by forcing him to disgorge his children again and then banishes him with the other Titans to the Tartarus. According to another version Zeus also castrates his father.

---

[1] *Traumdeutung*, First edn., 1900, p. 182.

[2] Editor's note: Translation from the Greek text. The author was a Greek scholar.

III

Symbolism in Language, in Dreams, and in other Phantasy-Formations

The story of Oedipus and that of Uranus and his offspring have an inner relationship to one another as well as a significant similarity in their external forms. Both stories are almost entirely lacking in the disguise of symbolism. We hear the events told in stark words. It is notable that this is also true of the typical dreams we have made use of to elucidate these myths. Here, too, as Freud remarks, the symbolic disguise is strikingly thin.

In interpretating dreams we repeatedly encounter a psychic agency which Freud called censorship. This will occupy much of our attention later. Here only its most important features need be mentioned. The censorship does not tolerate the appearance in the dream of our secret wishes in their original and undisguised form. The true purport of the dream must be obscured by 'dream distortion'. To circumvent the censorship extensive 'dream work' is carried out. We shall study this process in detail later. For the moment only one type of dream distortion, that of the symbolic disguise of wishes, need occupy our attention. The dreams of the father's death and of sexual union with the mother, discussed above, are a striking exception in that the wish which in a waking-state would certainly appear repellent to us, is quite openly and without symbolic disguise represented as fulfilled. Freud bases his explanation of this upon two grounds. First, we believe ourselves to be further removed from such wishes than from all others. Censorship is therefore unprepared for such enormities. Secondly, the wish may very easily be concealed behind a solicitude for the life of the beloved person. It is therefore most interesting that both the Oedipus legend and the legend about Kronos and Zeus are also very poor in symbolic means of expression. In waking consciousness man believes himself infinitely far removed from the horrors of Oedipus and those perpetrated by Kronos against his children and his father.

For the moment we may say that remarkable analogies exist between certain myths and certain dreams. Whether these analogies can claim general validity will need further investigation. The analysis of most myths, as of most dreams, is rendered more difficult by the symbolic disguise of the intrinsic content. It is precisely because this complication is absent in the Oedipus legend and in the typical dreams whose content is related to it

F

that it is particularly suitable to serve as an introduction to the problems which interest us.

If most myths show a symbolic mode of representation, their true content or meaning must differ from their outward presentation. Like dreams therefore they require interpretation. The Prometheus myth may serve as an example of the symbolising myth. We shall subject it to an interpretative procedure similar to a dream analysis. Further elucidation of the comparison between dream and myth will be carried out by means of this example.

I realise that my attempt to interpret the myth upon the model of dream interpretation and the statement that the same symbolism is employed in both will meet with opposition. It is Freud's great merit to have investigated this symbolism. Through his investigations we have come to understand important connections between the psychic formations repeatedly referred to. The value of this understanding, gained by painstaking research, has been entirely and often passionately denied by Freud's critics. Opponents of his teachings condemn symbol interpretation as phantastic and arbitrary. They maintain that Freud and his followers are victims of self-delusion and construct everything according to pre-conceived notions. The especial displeasure of the critics has been aroused by the assumption that the symbolism of dreams and similar formations serves to express sexual images. None of Freud's teachings, however much they may diverge from current schools of thought, has been so violently attacked as that on the interpretation of symbols. Yet this is of the greatest importance for our further progress. Before embarking on the analysis of a particular myth, therefore, I want to construct the broadest possible basis for this part of my investigations. For this purpose I shall seek to prove that the symbolism studied by Freud is deeply embedded in everyone and has always been so embedded in all mankind. We shall find that this symbolism is for the most part sexual and is used to express sexual phantasies. The following arguments are partly based upon Kleinpaul's [1] valuable work. This author, too, was compelled to make a stand against critics with moral prejudices. To quote a remark of Kleinpaul [2] in reference to this: 'We would point out that such (i.e. sexual) phantasies belong not only to patriarchal times when they were accepted as natural, but that they are still active at the present

---

[1] Kleinpaul, 'Leben der Sprache', **1**, *Die Rätsel der Sprache;* **2**, *Sprache ohne Worte;* **3**, *Das Stromgebiet der Sprache.*

[2] *Sprache ohne Worte*, Leipzig, 1890, p. 490.

day although they are branded as depraved.' Sexual symbolism, I assert, is a psychological phenomenon, accompanying man through time and space. It is most clearly visible in the infancy of our culture. In a less crude but still distinct form it is to be found in the psychic life of man down to the present day. Kleinpaul thus appropriately sums it up: 'Man sexualises the whole universe.'

Let us begin by considering the origins of the plastic arts. In this field we come across human genitalia depicted in an infinite variety of ways, sometimes in more hidden forms, sometimes too clearly to admit of any doubt. Sometimes their outline can be traced in ornamentation; elsewhere vases, urns and other receptacles are fashioned in the shape of genitalia. In the crafts of the most diverse peoples we find objects bearing the name of the prototype on which they are modelled. Egyptian, Greek, Etruscan and Roman vessels and implements bear clear testimony to the sexual symbolism which is ever active in the human race. So, too, do the arts and crafts of culturally backward peoples, unless we close our eyes to obvious facts. Here is a large and fertile field of research in the realm of aesthetics, for observations of this kind are scattered throughout literature.

In the religious observances of all peoples sexual symbolism is of even greater importance. Innumerable rituals have a symbolically sexual significance. Fertility rites, widely diffused among many peoples, give rise to the most prolific symbolism. This symbolism is sometimes, though not always, expressed in some blatantly obvious form such as that of a phallus.

We do not need to wander far afield. Our language itself provides the best evidence of the important part which sexuality has always played in the thoughts of men. All Indo-Germanic and Semitic languages have, or had in former times, 'genders'. This fact has generally been lost sight of. Let us stop to ask ourselves why nouns and adjectives in the German language are of male or female gender. Why does the German language attribute masculinity or femininity to inanimate objects? Some of the Indo-Germanic languages have yet a third gender. Into this gender fall all those objects which find no place in the other two categories, either because imagination has sought in vain to find a sexual analogy, or because there is some special reason for stressing the fact that they are sexually neuter. It must be admitted that the reason why a particular object has been given one gender rather than the other may be by no means easy to discover. It should also be noted that some nouns may be of different gender in two kindred languages. A close investigation into this most interesting problem of philology would take us too far afield. A few rules particularly applicable to the German language may be indicated here.[1] In German all diminutives are of neuter gender. In the imagery of folk-lore they are likened to small human beings. A young child is often referred to as 'it', and is treated as neuter. In some places even grown up girls are referred to as 'it' as long as they remain unmarried. 'Mädchen' and 'Fräulein' are after all diminutives and therefore 'neuter' until they are married. Animals may bear completely different names according to their sex. Other animals are listed under one of the three genders irrespective of their sex. In some cases the reason is obvious. Of the animals, those reproducing male characteristics such as strength and courage, are of masculine gender. That is why beasts and birds of prey belong to the masculine gender. Cats are generally spoken of as females. Their suppleness, grace and agility suggest feminine qualities.

Even more remarkable is the fact that in all languages inanimate objects are sexualised. In various languages a particular gender is regularly or at any rate preferably allotted to a given object. This must be due to a sexual symbolism prevailing among different peoples. In the German language ships usually belong to the feminine gender. The names given to ships are mostly used in a feminine form even where such names are normally masculine. Even the English language, which retains only the rudiments of sexual differentiation, treats ships as feminine. Only the battleship is assimilated to the valiant male and is called 'man-of-war'. It is consistent with this that the ships' bow is often decorated with a female figure. 'In the sailor's eyes the ship has shoulders and buttocks, she is like the ark containing the seed of life, and like the mystical little box which at the feasts of Demeter and Dionysus was carried in procession by the women. She is like the wife of the Indian God Siwa crossing the oceans of the world with a mast as with a phallus' (Kleinpaul). Another phantasy may also play its part here. The sailor is often separated from his wife for long periods and for such periods he is tied to his ship. He lives with his ship as a man on land lives with his wife and family. Thus the ship figuratively becomes the sailor's wife.

The pupil of the human eye, which appears as a round black

[1] Editor's footnote: The points here made, though true of Old English, are, except for a few survivals, not applicable to Modern English.

spot, is sexualised in the same way in the most widely varying languages. In Latin 'pupilla' means a young girl; the Greek χόρη, the Spanish 'niña' and the 'kanna' in Sanskrit all have the same meaning. In Hebrew there are two expressions, one of which again means 'young girl', whilst the other means 'manikin'. The delicate little mirror image we see in the other person's pupil has, according to most investigators, given rise to this name. Kleinpaul, however, objects to this poetic explanation and offers a more prosaic one: unsophisticated phantasy likens the round spot in the centre of the iris to a hole, treating it, as the ear is treated, as the crude symbol of female sexuality. Whichever explanation may be the correct one, the fact of the sexualisation of an organ, in itself completely asexual, remains.

In certain German dialects hooks and eyes are called manikins and wifies. Expressions containing the word female or mother, such as female screw and matrix and patrix, are to be found in many trades. Such expressions always describe a hollow or cavity and a complementary projection fitting into it. In Italian there are male and female keys according as they fit by means of a solid or a hollow end into the corresponding part of the lock.

We are wont to speak of towns or countries as of female persons. Most trees are feminine to us; [1] fruit-bearing clearly is the point of comparison. It is noteworthy that in Latin it is a strict rule that trees are of feminine gender.[2]

I will confine myself to a few significant examples. If one begins to study German, one meets this sexual symbolism on all sides. Kleinpaul's monograph 'Das Stromgebiet der Sprache' offers abundant material which bears this out.

Human phantasy thus attributes sexuality even to inanimate objects. This indicates the enormous importance of sexuality in human phantasy. It goes to show further that man's relationship to inanimate objects is by no means purely objective; this relationship is a distinctly subjective and personal one originating in his sexuality. Man's need to personify the objects around him is deeply rooted in his nature: the child will scold and strike the table it has knocked against. Man is not content, however, to attribute life to inanimate things; he also sexualises them. This leads us to an understanding of Kleinpaul's opinion,

[1] Editor's footnote: i.e. in German.
[2] German students of Latin commit this to memory by means of the mnemonic:

> Die Weiber, Bäume, Städte, Land
> Als feminina sind bekannt.

quoted above, that man sexualises the whole universe. It is most remarkable that linguistic and medical research lead to the same conclusion on this point.

As Freud [1] has proved, man's sexual instinct is, in an early phase, auto-erotic. This means that he knows as yet no object outside himself on which to concentrate his libido. Only gradually is libido directed on to other objects. When this process takes place, however, it embraces not merely human and animate objects, but inanimate objects also. It is intended to deal in detail in another publication with the ramifications of sexuality and in particular with deviations in this realm which are of far-reaching importance for the understanding of certain mental disorders.

We have established the fact that man has always attached great importance to sexual differences. Human sexuality is impelled to range far beyond the bounds of direct sexual satisfaction. Man permeates his whole environment through and through with his sexuality and language shows how constantly active and prolific is his sexual phantasy. In view of these facts it seems very strange that Freud and his followers have been upbraided for over-rating the role of sexuality in normal and abnormal psychic life. It seems to me that the danger of under-rating it is much more real. Moreover, it is often argued against Freud that the instinct of self-preservation governs human life to a much greater extent than does the sexual instinct. To place the latter in the forefront is, in their view, to exaggerate its importance. The path of investigation first explored by Freud is said to delight in bringing sex into everything. In consciousness the instinct of self-preservation and its derivatives may often enough take precedence. Freud's opponents, however, err in taking only conscious events into consideration. Freud himself has never ascribed to conscious sexual images an unqualified predominance. It is the unconscious repressed images which exert the strongest influence upon phantasy.

We need only look closely at our mother [2] tongue in order to dispel the criticisms levelled against Freud's theory of sexuality. Language springs in a unique way from the innermost being of a people. It gives expression to a people's phantasy. It becomes apparent in the many metaphors and similes of which we are now scarcely conscious. We do not utter a single sentence which does

[1] See his *Three Contributions to the Theory of Sex.* Editor's note: Now known under the title: *Three Essays on Sexuality*, see Standard edn., **7**.

[2] Editor's note: i.e. German.

not contain symbolic expressions. This symbolism, however, is to a large and important extent of a sexual character. I should like to mention again the fact that in German there are words of masculine and feminine gender and neuter words. If Freud's opponents are right, that is to say, if it is really the instinct of self-preservation and not the sexual instinct which plays the predominant part in man's psychic life, then it is very surprising that language differentiates things according to sex. Why does language not differentiate things according to whether or not they serve the instinct of self-preservation? Why does it differentiate between masculine, feminine and neuter objects instead of between edible, potable and, as a third possible category, things unfit for human consumption?

A number of objects and activities have from time immemorial been in the service of sexual symbolism. We find them used in this sense over and over again in the Bible, the Vedas, in Greek mythology and Nordic sagas, in the poetry of historical times and in dreams. Here belongs for instance the serpent as a symbol of the penis. In Genesis the serpent tempts Eve. Again, in German and Nordic fairy-tales we find that the serpent has the same symbolic meaning.[1] In the dreams of women, the serpent plays a large part: the meaning of the symbol is usually transparent. The superstitious fear of snakes is certainly connected with the same phantasy.[2] Psychotic women frequently tell us that they are being attacked by snakes which crawl into their genitalia or into their mouth. We know well that in this connection the mouth is merely a substitute for the vulva. This illustrates Freud's concept of 'displacement upwards'.[3]

Another very popular symbol is the apple which stands for female fertility. Eve tempts Adam with the apple.[4]

How deeply sexual symbolism is rooted in man is shown in a most instructive way in the association experiment. A person is given certain stimulus-words to which he has to associate other

---

[1] Riklin: *Psychologie und Sexualsymbolik der Märchen*.

[2] See footnote on p. 203.

[3] Cf. the paper by Riklin.

[4] The pomegranate is clearly a symbol of fertility, evidently on account of its many seeds. It is therefore the emblem of Juno, the Goddess of Marriage. The poppy, full of seeds, is an attribute of Venus. In one myth Venus changes into a carp. The female carp's abundance of roe was proverbial in ancient times. In some countries rice is thrown at the bride and bridegroom at weddings. Similar customs are well known in many parts of the world; they are supposed to represent fecundity. See Kleinpaul, *Sprache ohne Worte*, p. 27.

words at random. The choice of responses, as well as certain manifestations which accompany the reaction, indicates that in many cases the stimulus-word has by way of association touched upon a 'complex' of a sexual kind in the subject of the experiment.[1] The readiness to correlate the most innocuous word to the complex and to connect it symbolically with it is often very great. The subject of the experiment is entirely unaware of this tendency whilst giving the response. In some cases the subject can himself elucidate the connection between response and sexual complex. In the process of doing so, inhibitions of varying strength have to be overcome. In other cases considerable analytical efforts on the part of the investigator are needed to uncover the connection. Those who have some experience with the technique of the experiment, and with psychological analysis will find sufficient indications in the response and the accompanying manifestations to direct their questions appropriately. In the Zürich Psychiatric Clinic a list of one hundred stimulus-words is in use. With very many persons the application of these words has yielded interesting results relating to the sexual symbolism of the unconscious. These results coincide entirely with those Freud obtained by other methods.

A few examples may serve to illustrate this. A stimulus-word provoking with great regularity striking psychic phenomena is the word 'plough'. Used as a stimulus-word, it arouses in the subject of the experiment all those manifestations which experience has taught us to recognise as signs of emotion, such as delayed reaction-time, non-comprehension, or repetition of the stimulus-word, hesitation in pronouncing the response or gestures betraying embarrassment. Obviously the subjects of the experiment conceive 'ploughing' as a symbolic representation of the sexual act. It is interesting to note that in Greek and Latin as also in Oriental languages, the verb 'to plough' is quite commonly used in this connotation.[2] Other stimulus-words such as 'long', 'mast', 'needle', 'narrow', 'part' are invested with a sexual meaning with astonishing regularity. It

---

[1] In the papers published by the Zürich Psychiatric Clinic (especially in the *Diagnostische Assoziationstudien* published by Jung) the word 'Komplex' is used for a constellation of ideas strongly charged with emotion, which has a tendency to split off from consciousness and to be repressed into the unconscious.

[2] Kleinpaul, *Rätsel der Sprache*, p. 136. Editor's footnote: Shakespeare used the word in this sense in *Antony and Cleopatra*, Act II, Sc. ii, line 233: 'He plough'd her, and she cropped.'

seems that we are apt to attach a sexual significance to isolated words casually thrown out to us. In cases where a powerful sexual complex is active this tendency is particularly noticeable.

In the light of these facts it seems clear to me that symbolism, and particularly sexual symbolism, is the common property of all mankind. The objection that symbolism and the importance ascribed to it exists only in the imagination of a few biased theorists is untenable. Kleinpaul [1] expresses his opinion on this point emphatically and incisively: symbols are not made, they just exist: they are not invented but merely recognised.[2]

I do not intend to confine myself merely to a reference to Freud's work on symbolism, and to the dreams analysed by him. I shall relate here a fragment of a dream analysis as far as is necessary to explain the meaning of symbolism omitting, for the sake of brevity, the rest of the dream-material. The dream, reported to me by a friend—a woman—was as follows:

'I am alone in a longish room. Suddenly there is a noise underground. This, however, does not surprise me. I remember at once that from a certain part of the floor a subterranean canal leads directly into the water. I therefore lift a trapdoor in the floor and immediately a creature appears, clad in a brownish fur and looking rather like a seal. It throws off the fur and turns out to be my brother. Breathless and exhausted he asks me for shelter as he has absconded, swimming the whole

[1] Kleinpaul: *Sprache ohne Worte*, p. 26.

[2] Freud's critics disdain to pay serious attention to symbolism and its nature. Recently, for instance, Weygandt ('Kritische Bemerkungen zur Psychologie der Dementia Praecox', *Monatschrift f. Psychiatrie und Neurologie*, **22**, 1907) tried deliberately to misinterpret the symptoms of a twilight-state in a most absurd manner. By this means he sought to demonstrate that Freud's method of interpretation was arbitrary and nonsensical. Here the fundamental fallacy of such critics is clearly revealed. They believe symbolism to be an arbitrary invention, capable of being consciously produced. Freud's works, however, show symbolism to be rooted in the unconscious. Whenever the dominion of consciousness is wholly or partially abandoned, as in sleep, in twilight-states or when attention is distracted, repressed phantasy-material emerges. This material appears in veiled form; it makes use of symbolism. According to Bleuler ('Freud-sche Mechanismen in der Symptomatologie der Psychosen', *Psychiatr.-neurol. Wochenschrift*, 1906) symbolism is based upon a lower form of associative activity which uses vague analogies instead of logical sequences. In clear consciousness and with our attention alert we are incapable of this kind of associative activity. Symbolism can therefore be no arbitrary invention.

way under water. I make him lie down on a couch in my room and he goes to sleep. A few moments later a renewed and much louder noise is heard at the door. My brother jumps up with a cry of terror: "They are after me, they think I am a deserter." He slips into his fur and tries to escape by way of the subterranean canal, but he returns immediately and says: "It's no use now, they have entered the passage from the waterside." At that moment the door bursts open and several men rush in and seize my brother. Despairingly I call to them: "He has done nothing wrong, I will plead for him."—At that moment I awake.'

The dreamer has been married for some time and is now in the early stages of pregnancy. She is awaiting her confinement with some anxiety. On the previous evening she had asked her physician to explain to her various points concerning the development and physiology of the foetus. She had been instructed by reading, yet was found to have formed some misconceptions. She had, for instance, failed to appreciate the significance of the amniotic fluid. She also imagined the fine hair (lanugo) on the foetus to resemble the thick fur covering a young animal.

The canal which leads directly into the water stands for the birth passage. Water stands for the amniotic fluid. From this canal emerges a hairy animal, like a seal. The seal is a hairy animal living in the water just as the foetus lives in the amniotic fluid. This creature, representing the expected child, appears immediately, signifying quick and easy delivery. It turns out to be the dreamer's brother. In fact this brother is considerably younger than the dreamer. After the mother's early death she had to take care of him. Her relationship to him was rather maternal. Even now she likes to call him 'the little one' and to refer to both her younger siblings together as 'the children'. The younger brother therefore stands for the expected baby. She longs for his visit for she lives far away from her family, and therefore expects both her brother and the baby. This is the second analogy between brother and child. For a reason which does not concern us here she wants her brother to leave his home. Therefore in the dream he 'deserts' his home; that home is by the water and he very often swims there—the third analogy with the foetus. Her home is also by the water. The small room in which she finds herself in the dream overlooks the water. In this room there is a couch which can also be used as a bed. It is used as a spare bed if a visitor comes to stay. The visitor she expects to stay in the room is her brother. This provides a fourth analogy: this room is to become the nursery; the baby is to sleep there.

The brother is breathless when he arrives. He has been swimming under water. The foetus too, after having left the birth canal, has to fight for breath. The brother goes to sleep at once, just like a child soon after birth.

Now follows a scene in which the brother is very frightened. He is in a situation from which there is no escape. Just such a situation, imminent for the dreamer, is her confinement which has been frightening her for some time. In the dream she passes on this fear to the foetus or to her brother who stands for the foetus. She makes him lie down because he is so exhausted. After her delivery she will be exhausted and will rest. In the dream she is active and makes her brother lie down. She has yet another way out of the situation. Her brother is a lawyer and has to act as defending counsel; he has to 'plead'. She takes over this role from him, she pleads for him. In return she passes her fear on to him.

The dream contains symbols which may be regarded as typical. Between a child and a seal, between a subterranean canal and the birth canal there is only a vague analogy. Yet in the dream one is substituted for the other. The dreamer's brother takes the place of her child although he has long since grown up. For her, he is still just 'the little one'. Such equivocation is common in dreams.

Some of the wish-fulfilments in this dream are obvious: the wish for an easy delivery which one need not fear and the wish to be able to take care of her brother. This dream, the interpretation of which is incomplete, may contain further concealed elements of wish-fulfilment.

I will now give one example to show that the same symbolism is made use of in certain psychopathological states. The hallucinations of psychotic patients bear a striking resemblance to dream-images. This applies, whether such hallucinations are of many years standing or are only transitory, such as those occurring in twilight-states. The analysis shows that this resemblance is more than superficial.

A girl aged ten was ravished by her uncle, a drunkard, in a barn near her parents' house. He had threatened that if she resisted him he would set fire to the house. Intimidated by these threats, she had yielded to him several times. When, some time later, a mental illness broke out, the memories of the sexual assault and the self-reproaches which followed upon her surrender formed the main content of her psychosis. In other words the memories determined the pattern of the symptoms. These memories concealed themselves behind sexual symbolism, which is in conformity with dream symbolism. From a detailed exposition of this case, given in an earlier publication,[1] I quote here the relevant passage: the patient suffered for many years from nocturnal visions, in which she would see the barn in flames. This scene is obviously doubly determined: the uncle had used the threat of fire and had ravished her in the barn. In addition she had frightening dreams. Once she dreamed of a flight of owls. The birds fixed their eyes upon her, flew at her, tore off the bedclothes and her nightdress and screeched: 'shame on you, you're naked!' Obviously this is a recollection of the assault. Later, when awake, she had a vision of hell, in which the scenes were of a markedly sexual character. She saw 'transformed creatures',—'verwandelte Geschöpfe'—half-animal, half-human, and serpents, tigers and owls. Drunken men appeared, changed into tigers and attacked the females.

The wish-fulfilments contained in these visions and dreams can only be understood in the light of the whole case-history. Here it is sufficient to understand the symbols. Of special interest are the 'transformed creatures'—a combination of drunkard and tiger—which represent the patient's uncle. Thus the uncle's drunkenness and animal brutality are unified in one symbol. The serpents appearing in a clearly sexual scene can have no other meaning than that which we have already met with. Certain kinds of animals are important sexual symbols in dreams and psychoses. A very erotic patient, well-known to me, and suffering from hebephrenia, has given the animals figuring in her hallucinations the name of 'beauty-beasts'—a euphemism not wholly devoid of an erotic meaning. Riklin has collected excellent examples of this kind of symbolism from the fairy-tales of different peoples. Finally I should like to draw attention to the symbolism in the novel by Jensen analysed by Freud.[2]

[1] 'Über die Bedeutung sexueller Jugendtraumen für die Symptomatologie der Dementia praecox.' *Zentralblatt f. Nervenheilk.*, 1907. See 'The Experiencing of Sexual Traumas as a Form of Sexual Activity', *Selected Papers*, p. 47.

[2] *Der Wahn und die Träume in Jensens 'Gradiva'*, 1907.

IV

The Analysis of the Prometheus Myth

The most variegated human phantasy-formations are permeated with the same essentially sexual symbolism. I now turn to the analysis of a myth. In the structure of the myth we shall observe not only symbolism, but also other important analogies with the dream.

According to Greek mythology Prometheus created man and then stole fire from the gods, to give it to his creatures. The idea that man is created by a higher being is met with amongst a great variety of peoples. However familiar it may appear to us, it yet demands elucidation. The story that the creator of man, who is not a true deity nor yet a man, steals fire from the gods and thus enters into conflict with Zeus, also needs further explanation. The origin of the myth concerning the descent of fire was elaborated by Adalbert Kuhn, the founder of comparative mythology. A number of fundamental studies on various mythological figures were undertaken by Kuhn. His starting point was the fact that certain myths, which are common property amongst the Indo-Germanic peoples, are contained in the Indian Vedas, but in a much less elaborated version than that known to us from Greek and other sources. Kuhn thus succeeded in tracing the figures of Athene, of the Centaurs, of Orpheus, of Wotan and of other gods and heroes of Greek and Germanic mythology back to Vedic sources. In this way he explained the true meaning of these myths. His voluminous treatise *Über die Herabkunft des Feuers und des Göttertranks* (1859, new ed. 1886) became of the greatest importance for mythological research. Other research workers such as Delbrück, Steinthal, Cohen, Roth, Max Müller and Schwarz soon followed him. I shall here give only the most important results of Kuhn's investigations, confining myself, for technical reasons, to the myth concerning the descent of fire. In this I am following, in the main, an extract of Kuhn's work, made by Steinthal [1] in the course of a critical review. I have also made use of Cohen's [2] commentaries on Kuhn's work. Within the limits of the present monograph, it is of course

[1] Steinthal, 'Die Prometheussage in ihrer ursprünglichen Gestalt.' *Zeitschrift für Völkerpsychologie und Sprachwissenschaft*, 2, 1862.

[2] Cohen, 'Mythologische Vorstellungen von Gott und Seele.' *Zeitschrift für Völkerpsychologie und Sprachwissenschaft*, 5 and 6, 1865 and 1869.

impossible to adduce all the evidence to be derived from comparative philology and mythology in support of each individual point of the analysis. I would therefore refer the reader to the original work of Kuhn as well as to the two papers by Steinthal and Cohen mentioned above.

Such investigations as have hitherto been made indicate that all Indo-Germanic peoples originally produced fire by friction. We can trace this method into historical times; even the technical terms pertaining to it are known to us. In some culturally backward peoples we still meet with the same procedure. How man first came to produce fire by friction remains an open question. According to Kuhn nature was man's tutor: he may have seen in the primeval forest how a dry shoot of a creeper, moved to and fro by the breeze, rubbed against the hollow of a branch, thus catching fire. Peschel [1] cast doubts upon the likelihood of this explanation. He believed that drilling and similar mechanical activities must have revealed to man how two objects can produce heat by friction, without a similar process in nature having been observed.

The primitive implements of fire consisted of a rod of hard wood and a disc of soft wood containing a hollow. The wood was kindled by turning and drilling movements of the rod in the hollow. It is a property of the fire thus produced soon to go out again. Then it has to be rekindled. Man made the self-same observation with another fire—the celestial fire. By day the fire of the sun shone upon him from above, shedding warmth and light upon him. At times he also saw streaks of fire coming down from heaven, lighting and burning. This celestial fire, too, would go out after a while. Therefore in the sky, too, something must burn and become extinguished. According to the ancient imagery of Indo-Germanic peoples, cloud formations were regarded as a tree, the ash-tree of the universe—Yggdrasil—which we come across in many myths. The wood of the ash-tree served man for kindling fire. When he saw the fire in the sky he thought that the wood of the ash-tree in the heavens was burning. Lightning flashing from heaven to earth was fire descending from Yggdrasil. Hence it came to be thought that the fire on earth had come down from heaven. The rapidity with which lightning passed across the sky was reminiscent of the flight of birds. This gave rise to the further belief that a bird, nesting on the celestial ash-tree, had borne the celestial fire to earth. In the myths of various peoples and at various times this role has been ascribed to the eagle, the hawk and the wood-

[1] Peschel, *Völkerkunde*, Sixth edn., Leipzig 1885, p. 141.

pecker. Certain kinds of trees bearing red berries, such as the mountain-ash, or thorns or leaves shaped like feathers, were thought to be transformations of the fire-bird. Such characteristics were believed to represent the bird's colour, claws and plumage.

To the fire in heaven and on earth the imagery of the Indo-Germanic myth adds a third kind: the spark of life. Here we meet with the same analogy which led to the identification of celestial and terrestrial fire. The spark of life, too, must be kindled. Whilst it dwells within the body, the body remains warm. This, too, like all other fires, must go out. The most striking analogy was that between the creation of life and the kindling of fire. As the boring-rod kindles the fire in the wooden disc, so human life is kindled in the womb. Many illustrations of this analogy are to be found in mythology and in language. I note in passing that the two essential components for producing fire by primitive means often bore the names used for the male and female genitalia. This shows how deeply this notion had taken root in the people's mind. Moreover, the same analogy is to be found in Semitic languages. In Hebrew the words for 'masculine' and 'feminine' mean literally perforator and perforated.

So, too, the igniting of the spark of life, the creation of man is displaced upwards to Yggdrasil. Man, as well as fire, takes his origin from it, and thus both man and fire are brought to earth by a bird; hence the stork which brings children.

A later epoch depositing, so to speak, a new layer on the myth, creates gods resembling human beings. It retains the old analogy between fire and life, but simply gives it a new form. The god of fire is also the man-god. In the Vedas we meet a god Agni: agni the equivalent of the Latin ignis, meaning fire, who personifies fire, light, sun and lightning. At the same time he is also the first man. In the myths of various peoples Agni is also the fire-bird. In the oldest Latin myths, Picus, the woodpecker, stood for the fire-bird, for lightning and for man. According to a later version of this myth he was the first king of Latium and also was the god who watched over women in childbirth and over infants, that is to say, the god of life.

With the increasing personification of gods, everything in nature became a product or attribute of the gods. Thus fire no longer was a god but was produced by a god. In the morning god would rekindle the dead fire of the sun by boring into the sun's orb. He produced lightning by driving a wedge into a thundercloud. Like the heavenly fire, earthly fire also needed constant rekindling. If the fire went out it meant that Agni had disappeared. He must have hidden himself. As in the sky he was hidden in a cloud, the cloud-tree, so on earth he was hidden in the wooden disc from which he could be induced to emerge by the processes of boring and rubbing. Here we meet with a new figure of mythology whose oldest name, in the Vedas, is Matharichvan. Matharichvan brings Agni who hides in clouds, or in wood, back to earth. According to another version he finds Agni in a hole or cave. To mankind he brings the light and warmth necessary to sustain life. His name means 'he who swells or moves inside the mother', that is, lightning or the boring rod. Prometheus in the Greek myth corresponds to Matharichvan, the fire-bringer. In historical times the name of Prometheus, which had undergone various transformations, was interpreted as 'the provider'. Among older forms that can be traced is 'Pramantha'. This name is ambiguous. It means first of all 'he who produces something by friction'. By friction he produces fire and creates man. Here it should be noted that 'matha' means the penis. The second meaning of Pramantha is the fire-thief. Alongside the conception that Prometheus-Pramantha produces fire there is the other that he, like Matarichvan, brings or steals fire from heaven. He hides the fire sparks in a Narthex shrub, one of the varieties of wood used to produce fire.

In mythology we come across a threefold representation of fire: as fire and as fire-god, as fire-creator or producer or bringer, and finally as man. In mythology man is also identified with fire, in that the first men have their origin in fire and because man contains within himself the spark of life.

V

Infantile Traits in Individual and Folk Psychology. Wish-fulfilment in Dreams and Myths

The short exposition presented in the previous chapter gives but an incomplete idea of the number of sources which merge to produce the Prometheus myth. The tracing of these sources was of great scientific importance. It led to the overthrow of the traditional assumption that myths are the allegorical expression of philosophical or religious ideas. Kuhn tried to show that every myth is based upon the observation of some natural phenomenon. He demonstrated that every myth has one meaning which is clearly apparent from its wording, and in addition a latent content concealed behind the veil of symbolism.[1] Those familiar with Freud's dream interpretation and and with the theory of dreams based upon it will discern far-reaching analogies between Kuhn's interpretation of the Prometheus myth and Freud's interpretation of dreams. The fact is that both dream-formation and myth-formation display important external differences. If therefore the same method of investigation can be applied to both, this fact may be regarded as confirmation of our assumption that behind these external differences there lies an internal relationship. The example of the Prometheus myth may serve here to establish the psychological relationship between dreams and myths.

The Prometheus myth can, for our present purposes, be told in a few words. The interpretation revealing the true meaning of these few words takes up much more space. Just such proportions are to be found in the dream. Even a short dream contains far more than might be thought from its simple narration. What Freud established for dreams also holds good for myths. Behind the manifest content a latent content lies hidden. To discover the latter we need a method of interpretation. As with dream interpretation, such a method must uncover all the images and emotions expressed in the myth.

Owing to the varying importance of the differences between latent and manifest dream-content the dreamer is but rarely able to understand his own dream. He himself declares it to be nonsensical or absurd. He may even deny that the dream has any meaning at all. If he actually tries to fathom the meaning of his dream he will give an incomplete explanation based only on the manifest content. This is also true of peoples. They do not understand the latent content of their myths. They give them an inadequate explanation. This can easily be shown by a few examples. Dreams of the death of a near relative, which

[1] Kuhn was not afraid to speak frankly of the sexual character of this symbolism. We have recently had ample experience of the way in which such theories are attacked as unscientific and unethical. In the paper quoted in the previous chapter (page 173), Steinthal took it upon himself to defend Kuhn against both these lines of attack. I cannot refrain from quoting his words here, for they seem to be directed against the opponents of Freud's teachings with prophetic insight: 'A method in which every argument is weighed with judicial scrupulousness and care and expressed in simple and impartial language and in which inferences are drawn only with the utmost caution, deserves both scientific and moral recognition.'

have already engaged our attention, are invariably misinter-
preted by the dreamer. In the same way the ancient Greeks
failed to discern the true meaning of the Prometheus myth. They
misunderstood even the meaning of the name 'Prometheus'. We
shall return to this point later.

The fact that the attitude of a people towards the myths they
have created is the same as that of a dreamer towards his dreams
calls for an explanation. Freud gives us the solution to this
problem. His dream theory culminates in the sentence:
'Dreaming is a fragment of the superseded psychic life of the
child.' [1] This statement is incomprehensible without further
elucidation. Freud arrives at his concept in the following way.
Our memory retains far more impressions than those normally
accessible to our recollection. We are especially apt to 'forget'
those memories connected with a painful emotion. They are
not, however, effaced completely. It is merely that they cannot
be recalled by an effort of the will. We have already encountered
this process of repression into the unconscious. Because they are
tinged with painful emotion, we are particularly prone to expel
from consciousness and to obliterate from memory unattained
or unattainable desires. Dreams draw the largest and most
essential part of their material from these repressed ideas. Only
a small and insignificant part of the dream-content is taken from
present day or recent material. The same happens where pathological processes interfere with conscious mental activity. Here,
too, old memories emerge from deep repression. We can observe
this particularly clearly in cases of hysteria and of dementia
praecox. The concept of repression is indispensable for the
explanation of the most diverse pathological symptoms. The
repressed memories can belong to any phase of life. Painstaking analysis, however, succeeds in proving that the ultimate
basis of a dream or of a symptom of any such disorder is always
a childhood memory. In the child not only repressed desires, but
also current, unrepressed desires, so far as they are unattainable,
are expressed in waking- and in dream-phantasies. At a later
age this phantasy activity mainly occurs during sleep. In
dreams the adult retains not only the pattern of infantile
thinking but also its objects. Desires and events from childhood
days, which seem to have been forgotten, remain in the depth of
the unconscious. Here they lie in waiting, as it were, until an
experience corresponding to an incident in childhood is encountered. Then the later experience is assimilated to the
earlier one. In this way the infantile memory is reinforced in the

[1] Freud: *Traumdeutung*, First edn., vii, p. 334.

unconscious. Once it has reached a certain degree of intensity it makes itself manifest in the dreams of healthy persons and in the symptoms of neurotics or psychotics. For this, two conditions must be fulfilled. There must be a lowering of conscious activity as occurs in dreams and in certain morbid states, and there must be a precipitating cause. Few will be prepared to agree with Freud and myself in attributing such far-reaching effects to infantile wishes and experiences. It will be objected that in later life infantile interests are suppressed and replaced by interests of a totally different kind. As will be shown, however, this objection is fallacious. Until the publication in 1895 of the *Studies on Hysteria* by Breuer and Freud the importance of infantile impulses and memories was never sufficiently appreciated. To these authors credit is due for having drawn attention to the importance of infantile memories. In subsequent years Freud further elaborated this theory. The views on the significance of infantile experiences have undergone essential modifications, but have never been abandoned. It is clear to us why early infantile memories exert so much influence on the psychic development of the individual. Although many of the child's experiences arise from external causes and are thus not rooted in his personality, others derive from his own individual make-up. In two shorter papers [1] I have attempted to prove this for certain sexual experiences of childhood. We can here formulate the conclusion reached as follows: the child owes part of his experiences, and probably the most impressive part, to his innate impulses. Moreover, in early infancy the child has not yet learned to subordinate his own wishes, on ethical grounds, to those of others. His feelings are not yet moderated but are receptive to all impressions and he is therefore prone to react with great and uninhibited intensity.

To childhood memories later memories are assimilated. To the repressed infantile wishes those of later life are added. An example of this is the infantile preference of the son for his mother and his rivalry with his father, and the wishes deriving from these impulses. A recent event may reawaken these infantile memories, which then find expression in a dream. This single example may suffice to elucidate what Freud means when

[1] Abraham: 'On the Significance of Sexual Trauma in Childhood for the Symptomatology of Dementia Praecox.' *Zentralblatt für Nervenheilkunde und Psychiatrie*, 1907; (see this vol., Part I, p. 13) and 'The Experiencing of Sexual Traumas as a Form of Sexual Activity', published in the same journal. See *Selected Papers*, p. 47.

he calls the dream a fragment of the superseded psychic life of the child.

It is in dreams, therefore, that the child's imaginative activity and the objects of that activity retain their vitality in adult life. The analogy between myths and dreams now becomes clear. The myth survives from a remote period in the life of a people which we might call its infancy. Such an analogy is not difficult to justify. In his *Interpretation of Dreams* Freud uses an expression which aptly illustrates the position. He designates that period of infancy of which our memory is vague as the pre-historic period in the history of the individual. Even though our recollections of that period may be very indistinct, we have not lived through it without its leaving some traces behind. The wishes which were dearest to us at that time and which at best we remember imperfectly have not been completely eradicated; they have merely been repressed. They live on in our dream phantasies. This also holds good for myths. They come from the pre-historic period in the life of the people, of which no definite traditions have been handed down to us. They contain memory traces dating from the infancy of the people. Can the wish-fulfilment theory of dreams also be applied to myths?

I maintain that it can, and in terms of Freud's theory of dreams formulate my views as follows: the myth is a fragment of the superseded infantile psychic life of the people. It contains, in veiled form, their infantile wishes originating in pre-historic times. We have already become familiar with important evidence for this view in comparing certain myths with 'typical' dreams. We recognised that in the Oedipus myth, just as in certain dreams, infantile sexuality finds expression. The son's sexual desires for the mother give rise to wishes which, like many others, are subject to repression. Our upbringing consists in an enforced and systematic repression of innate impulses.

In the early stages of a people's development, where more natural conditions prevailed and where convention had not yet assumed rigid forms, such impulses could be carried into action. At a later stage they were suppressed by means of a process which we can compare with repression in the individual. They did not become completely extinct, but were preserved in the myth. Owing to this process, for which I should like to suggest the name 'mass-repression', the people are no longer able to understand the original meaning of their myths, just as we fail to understand our dreams.[1]

[1] The fact that a people no longer understands its own myths cannot be due to their being partly taken over from other peoples. A

It seems as if a people expresses in the myths dealing with the period of its earliest infancy those wishes usually most strongly repressed. Let us consider the biblical descriptions of Paradise. Freud has strikingly summarised them thus: 'Paradise is nothing but the collective phantasy of each individual's infancy.' [1] In Genesis the fact that Adam and Eve were naked and not ashamed of their nakedness is particularly stressed. We know that Jewish law strictly demanded the covering of the body. An infringement of this rule is always explicitly condemned in biblical stories. To the mass-phantasy about the nakedness of the first men we find a parallel again in a typical dream. We all dream at times that we are walking about with little or nothing on, even moving about among other people who, however, take no notice of our appearance. The feeling of anxiety usually accompanying this dream corresponds to the strong repression of the infantile wish to exhibit oneself naked before other people. Freud has shown in detail that this dream contains infantile exhibitionistic phantasies (*Traumdeutung*, page 166 *et seq.*). He reminds us how much children enjoy showing themselves naked to other children or to adults, or showing off before them. In some people this infantile aberration of the sexual instinct is retained to an abnormal degree. It may completely supersede normal sexual activity. Such people become exhibitionists.

Jewish morality, so strict where sexual matters were concerned, demanded that the collective phantasy of human nakedness must be transposed into the earliest infancy of mankind. The Greeks, being far less ashamed of their nakedness, had no need to transpose this phantasy into so remote a period. Freud has pointed out that the myth of Odysseus and Nausicaa deals with the same theme. It is therefore a parallel to the dreams about nakedness already discussed.

The Greek myth concerning Prometheus corresponds to the biblical story of the creation of Adam and Eve. As we have already seen, it differs from it in that the phantasy of nakedness or its equivalent is missing. It contains, however, the story of the stealing of fire, for which there is no equivalent in the biblical version. We have to examine the Greek account of the origin

people can only take over myths from other peoples because it finds that they contain its own complexes. These complexes, however, are under repression. Moreover, as every people varies the myths it takes over, one would expect that it would at least understand the meaning of such variations. But this is not the case.

[1] *Traumdeutung*, First edn., V.d, p. 169.

of man and especially the story of the stealing of fire. This will enable us to discover the repressed collective phantasies and wishes contained in it. To do this we must first direct our attention to certain general characteristics of the myth. For the interpretation of these characteristics we must turn once more to Freud's dream-theory.

Freud asserts that all dreams are self-centred. We have all had to learn the necessity of suppressing our selfish impulses. We had to repress these impulses for the sake of the majority, for social, family, and other reasons. If, however, the unconscious achieves expression, as happens in the dream, then the repressed impulses make their way to the surface. It is true that they have to use a careful disguise. Their undisguised appearance is prevented by the censorship. The self-gratifying nature of the dream is apparent from the fact that the dreamer himself is always the central figure of it. This does not mean to say that the dreamer always sees himself as the central figure of the events taking place in the dream. The dream often seems to be like a play of which the dreamer is a mere onlooker. In such a case, however, he himself is represented by the actor who plays the leading role. This role is played by a person sharing some characteristic or experience in common with the dreamer. The dreamer identifies himself with the central figure of the dream. This makes it appear as though the whole dream revolves around the person playing the leading role. In fact this identification stands for an 'as if' (Freud: *Traumdeutung*, page 216). Dream language, however, knows no such phrases as 'as if'. In a dream the only way in which comparisons can be made between different persons or things is by drawing analogies between them. We have already stated, in connection with Freud's thesis, that the purpose of the dream—a wish-fulfilment —is completely self-centred. In the same way the other psychic formations which we compared with the dream are likewise self-centred. It would take us too far afield to demonstrate this in the case of hysterical twilight-states. The position is clearer in the case of chronic mental disorders accompanied by hallucination. The psychotic state is also completely self-centred. The patient is always the central figure of his hallucinatory system. He is the victim of intrigues, injuries and persecutions of all kinds which are being engineered against him on all sides. His workmates want to get rid of him; an army of detectives is spying upon him. He is the one and only isolated and just man, against whom an unjust, malicious world is waging war. He takes up arms against the whole world. Thus grandiose ideas form an essential part of any persecutory psychosis. Psychiatry speaks of megalomania when only one definite delusion of grandeur is being expressed. It is preferable, therefore, to use the more general term grandiose complex. To hear a mental patient recounting his delusional system is reminiscent of the structure of the legend-cycles which have formed around certain figures of mythology. The delusional system of the mental patient is like a myth in which he extols his own greatness. There are mental patients who maintain that they are some historically famous person such as Napoleon or Bismarck. Such a patient, having discovered any one analogy between himself and Napoleon, readily identifies himself with Napoleon, just as we are wont to do in dreams. The psychosis, like the dream, lacks the 'as if'. If we go more closely into details we find abundant justification for the comparison. Mental patients tend, for instance, to transpose their delusions, especially their delusions of grandeur, to their infancy. I refer in particular to the delusions of high birth, because they are of special interest for the further analysis of the Prometheus myth. Such cases are known to every alienist. A patient may say, for instance, that the people whose name he bears are not his real parents; that in fact he is of royal birth but had to be got rid of for some mysterious reason and was therefore handed over, when a child, to foster-parents and that his enemies are trying to maintain the fiction of his lowly origin in order to defeat his rightful claims to the crown or to a great fortune.

These delusions of high birth again remind us of the childhood phantasies in which the little boy is a prince or king who eclipses all others by his victorious battles. The wish for greatness is satisfied by this phantasy of royal descent. For in childhood phantasies a prince is without doubt predestined to arouse the admiration of the whole world. A mentally active child ardently longs to be big in both senses of the word. It seems to me that whoever attains success in adult life, whether in reality or in imagination, must have harboured within him a complex of grandeur. The phantasies woven in childhood are forgotten. The complex nurtured by those phantasies, however, lasts as long as life itself. If at a later age his ambitions are not realised then even the healthy person will often displace his wish-fulfilment back into childhood and start praising the good old days.

This complex of grandeur is characteristic of the childhood of a people no less than of an individual. Nor does it completely disappear in the 'historical' age of a people, where it can still be traced just as in the individual adult. In the myth, too, an identification takes place. The people identify themselves with the hero of the myth, for to them, too, the 'as if' is still unknown.[1]

All peoples have woven a myth around their origin. Such a myth reminds us to a surprising extent of the delusions of high parentage found in some mental patients. All peoples claim to be descended from their principal god and to have been 'created' by him. Creation is nothing more than procreation stripped of sexuality. This emerges with wonderful clarity from Kuhn's interpretation of the Prometheus myth. Prometheus 'creates' man; but if we investigate his history, he is found to be the driller, the creator, the god of fire. From the Vedas we learn about various priestly families who serve the fire-god Agni and who trace their descent from the fire. The names of these priestly families (such as Angirases and Bhrgus) actually mean fire or flame. Hence man traces his descent from gods of his own creation, from the fire he exalted to a deity, from Yggdrasil, whence the fire came down to him. Askr, the ash-tree, is in the Nordic saga the progenitor of the human race. Thus in ancient times man projected his grandiose complex heavenwards. What insignificant successors are our mental patients who are content to imagine themselves the descendants of some great human figure, or we ourselves who did likewise in our childhood phantasies!

In other respects, too, the Prometheus myth abounds in examples of identification. One need only remember the identification of driller, lightning and man. If man is procreated by a god it follows that either man is divine or his god is human. Man identifies himself with his god. Thus it is in the earlier version of the Prometheus myth. A later age replaced procreation by creation.

The history of creation contained in the Old Testament is an apparent but not a real exception. Admittedly, in the Genesis story man does not descend from his divine maker. God creates man in his own image. Here, in the manifest content of the story, identification has been replaced by assimilation. Israel's descent is traced from the patriarchs. Studies in comparative mythology, however, show these patriarchs to be figures taken over from a pagan theocracy. Thus originally Israel also traced its descent from a divine being. Later this view had to be

---

[1] Steinthal: 'Die Sage von Simson', *Zeitschrift für Völkerpsychol. und Sprachwissenschaft*, **2**, 1862, states that this expression 'gleichwie' ('as if') has wrought the most profound change in the intellectual development of mankind.

adapted to monotheism. Now the original gods had to become subservient to the one and only God. National pride had to content itself with bringing the patriarchs into a specially close relationship to their God. God enters into personal relationship with the patriarchs, speaks to them and even makes a covenant with them which is to be handed down to their descendants. These in turn come to feel themselves to be in a specially close relationship to their God.

VI

The Effects of Censorship in Dreams and Myths. The Process of Condensation

We are already familiar with the concept of censorship. Although the repression maintained during the waking state is relaxed in the dream, yet the unleashed wishes are prevented from appearing quite openly. The repressed images are prevented by the censorship from attaining clear unequivocal expression. It forces them to assume strange trappings. By this dream-distortion the real, latent dream-content is transformed into the manifest dream-content. As Freud has shown, the latent dream-thoughts are already formed in advance during the waking state by means of unconscious thought-processes. The dream does not form new thoughts; it merely transforms thoughts already formed during the waking state in accordance with the demands of the censorship. Freud distinguishes four ways in which this process is achieved. We now have to investigate whether similar processes are to be found in the myth, whether censorship is also active here, and whether the myth, like the dream, makes use of such means of representation to evade the censorship. Here, too, we may use the Prometheus myth as a typical example. In certain instances, however, we shall have to draw other myths into the range of our observations.

The first component of the processes of dream-work to be considered is that of condensation. We have already met with it in the Prometheus myth, but did not investigate it closely. It struck us that the Prometheus myth, which at first sight seemed so simple, expresses a large number of ideas in very few words. As we have already seen, these ideas constitute the latent content of the myth. One element of the manifest dream-content very often contains not one but several dream-thoughts. This is also true of the myth. If the few words in which the myth is told really contain all the thoughts which Kuhn's work has revealed to us, then each word must be 'over-determined' just as in the case of the dream. Dream interpretation is able to show that a person appearing in a dream may stand for several real persons. One often finds, for instance, that one of the dream figures has the face of one person known to the dreamer while the rest of his body is that of another. The dreamer thereby establishes a relationship between those two persons, perhaps because they have one important attribute in common. Each event in the dream can also stand for several events. In dream analysis we must therefore always consider this equivocation. Every word of the dream-story can comprise a double or manifold meaning.

Just as the elements of the dream are over-determined so, too, are the elements of the myth. The Prometheus myth owes its form to a vast condensation process. The figure of Prometheus himself is, as we have learned from the analysis, condensed from three conceptions. According to the first of these he is the fire-god, according to the second he is the fire, and according to the third he is man. The myth concerning the stealing of fire has been condensed from these three elements. Steinthal [1] has summed up this important result of Kuhn's analysis in one telling sentence: 'The god of fire, having descended from heaven in the shape of a human being, brings himself to earth in the form of a god or a human being and in the form of a god or the divine element, gives himself as divine element to himself as a human being.'[2]

The inner relationship of dream and myth arises from the process of condensation common to them both. This becomes particularly illuminating to those familiar with Freud's technique of dream analysis. They will recognise in the apparently insignificant details of the myth examples of the process of condensation already met with in the dream. Kuhn's analysis adduces evidence of the manifold determination of practically every element of the Prometheus myth, and even for each individual symbol occurring in it. I merely recall how, in the case of the heavenly bird, for instance, the most variegated symbolical functions are condensed.

[1] Steinthal: *Die Prometheussage in ihrer ursprünglichen Gestalt*, p. 9.
[2] Editor's footnote: This is the best we can make of this quotation, which seems to us far from clear: 'Nachdem der Feuergott als Mensch vom Himmel herabgekommen ist, holt er als Mensch oder als Gott sich selbst als Gott oder als göttliches Element auf die Erde und schenkt sich als Element an sich selbst als Menschen.'

It is to the work of condensation that we owe the strange
neologisms of the dream. Freud (*Traumdeutung*, page 202 *et seq.*
and elsewhere) gives interesting examples of this process
together with their interpretation. Neologisms of a very similar
kind are produced by mental patients.[1] Normal persons, too,
produce them in the waking state in slips of the tongue.
Examples of this are mainly to be found in Freud's *Psychopathology of Everyday Life*, from which I will quote but one.[2]

'Ein junger Mann sagt zu seiner Schwester: Mit den D. bin
ich jetzt ganz zerfallen, ich grüsse sie nicht mehr. Sie antwortet:
Überhaupt eine saubere *Lippschaft*. Sie wollte sagen: *Sippschaft*,
aber sie drängte noch zweierlei in dem Sprechirrtum zusam-
men, dass ihr Bruder einst selbst mit der Tochter dieser Familie
einen Flirt begonnen hatte and dass es von dieser hiess, sie habe
sich in letzter Zeit in eine ernshafte, unerlaubte *Lieb*schaft
eingelassen.'

The same process of word condensation, which takes place
in the slips of the tongue and the dreams of normal people, and
in the neologisms of the mentally abnormal is also to be found
in the Prometheus myth. By rubbing, Pramantha (i.e. Prometheus) creates fire and—man. According to another concept
he steals fire in order to give it to man. These two concepts are
condensed in the name Pramantha. Pramantha means 'he who
rubs', and also 'he who robs'. This condensation is made possible
by the similarity of sound of the noun matha, meaning the male
genital organ (mentula in Latin), and the verbal root math,
meaning to take or to rob. In addition the double meaning of
rubbing is noteworthy.

VII

Displacement and Secondary Elaboration in Dreams and Myths

Many of the differences between the latent and the manifest
content of dreams and myths are to be explained by the phenomenon known as condensation. Another process made use of by
our unconscious for the purposes of dream-distortion is that to
which Freud gave the name displacement. This component

---

[1] Jung: *Psychologie der Dementia Praecox*, Halle 1907.

[2] Editor's footnote: This example (Second edn., 1907, p. 30 *et
seq.*) is untranslatable because of its play on similar sounding words.)
It is, therefore, not included in Brill's translation and is reproduced
here in German.

of dream-work also has its counterpart in the myth. I shall, for reasons which will soon become apparent, discuss displacement in conjunction with the third element of dream-work, namely secondary elaboration.

At the outset of our enquiry into the analogies between dreams and myths we had to justify the assumption that such an analogy exists. Two objections against this assumption were dealt with at once, whilst a third was provisionally left unsettled. To this we must now return. According to the findings of later investigations it may be argued that the myth has undergone important transformations before assuming the form in which it is handed down to us, whereas the dream is an ephemeral creation of the moment. This, however, is only apparently the case. In fact the dream-content, too, is produced by a protracted process. In comparing the life period of man and of a people we found that dream and myth originate in pre-historic times. We saw that the constituents of the dream were pre-formed already in waking life. We may now add that the dream-process is not finished at the moment the dreamer awakes. The contest between dream-forming images and censorship still continues. Even whilst we attempt to recall a dream to memory, especially whilst telling it to another person, censorship still effects further changes in order to make dream-distortion more complete. Freud called this secondary elaboration.[1] It is merely a continuation of the process of displacement which goes on during the dream. Both processes are identical and serve the same purpose. They displace both the content of the dream and the emotion accompanying it. Those elements which are of pre-eminent importance in the dream-thoughts are relegated to a secondary place in the dream. Subordinate elements are elaborately spun out. The effect produced in the dream is called by Freud 'the inversion of all values'.[2] The least important is substituted for the most important and is transposed into the focal point of interest. The emotional stress

[1] I am considering here only those manifestations of secondary elaboration which appear when an attempt is made to recount the dream. These are of special significance for the comparison with the myth. I am not going into the other effects of secondary elaboration which already influence the structure of the dream during its formation.

[2] Editor's footnote: Freud took over this expression—Umwertung aller Werte—from Nietzsche. In translating it the play on sound is lost. To render it as 'the revaluation of all values' would retain the assonance, but at the expense of accuracy.

connected with the dream-thoughts is displaced from the important on to the unimportant. Both processes are repeated during secondary elaboration. It is precisely the most poignant parts of the dream which on awakening are most rapidly and forcibly repressed. This makes it more difficult to recall them. The accompanying emotion once again undergoes a modification similar to that which has already taken place.

If the dream was based upon a complex of strong emotional significance, then that complex will reassert itself, during the same or a subsequent night, in further dreams. Such further dreams tend to contain the same wish-fulfilment as the first. They merely incorporate new means of expression, other symbols and different associations. A powerful complex can manifest itself for many years in the shape of a recurring dream. In this respect one need only remember the typical dreams previously discussed in detail, for instance the typical infantile dream of nakedness. Again, typical dreams provide the connecting link between the dream and the myth. The psychological process by which a particular dream accompanies a dreamer through the varying phases of his life, changing gradually by the incorporation of new elements, corresponds to the process by which the myth undergoes gradual modification in the course of the life-periods of a people.

The length of time, however, over which a myth develops is naturally much longer than for a dream. Moreover, we can ask a person whose dream we want to interpret for information on doubtful points. To analyse a myth is very much more difficult, for we have to make use of comparisons and associations to enable us to understand a psychological structure created thousands of years ago. After such a lapse of time we shall succeed only in a few favourable cases in finding out which part of the process of displacement occurred when the myth first took definite shape, and which part occurred at later periods in the course of oral transmission from generation to generation. New generations had new ideas. Wherever a tradition was no longer in conformity with its ideas a later generation undertook a secondary elaboration of the myth. Nor should we forget the far-reaching influence exerted upon the mythological traditions of a people by the myths of their neighbours. For all these reasons we should be straining the facts if we attempted to make an artificial separation between displacement and secondary elaboration in the myth. In dealing in the next chapter with the process of displacement in the myth I leave open the question whether primary or secondary displacement is involved.

VIII

The Effects of the Process of Displacement in the Myths of Prometheus, Moses and Samson

In the course of our researches we have repeatedly come across the effects of the process of displacement in the myth without giving them particular attention. The Greek version of the Prometheus myth bears distinct traces of this process. As we have learned from Kuhn's investigation this myth originated in an age which did not yet worship the forces of nature as personified in anthropomorphic gods. Gradually, as the personification of gods took place, Agni and Matharichvan emerged. Agni represented fire, he was the fire-god; Matharichvan was the god who produced fire by boring, he who could summon forth Agni when Agni concealed himself. The two figures were not originally separate. On the contrary, the name of Matharichvan is used as an alternative to Agni. Only later does Matharichvan become a separate entity.

Matharichvan, who corresponds to Prometheus in Greek mythology was, strictly speaking, the fire-bringer. In the Greek version of the myth he becomes the fire thief. He brings fire from heaven to earth against the will of the gods, and is punished for doing so. Prometheus must subordinate his will to that of Zeus. This constitutes the most important displacement in the myth. In the original myth Matharichvan-Prometheus brings back Agni. In this version the emotional tone of censure for his temerity is absent, whilst the Greek version of the myth here shows emotional displacement. Thus Prometheus, who sins against the gods, becomes the representative of man, who so often rebels against divine ordinances. Through this transformation of the myth the original meaning of the name Prometheus—Pramantha—became lost. In a by-gone, less sophisticated age, he had been called the procreator or the driller. This conception was subjected to repression until the original meaning of the name had been entirely forgotten. It underwent some degree of modification in that way and acquired a secondary meaning, that of the 'provider'. Had he not provided fire for his creatures and thus justly earned this name? This transformation of the name Pramantha into Prometheus and the change in meaning associated with it are highly instructive examples of displacement.

The process of displacement in the Prometheus myth gains

added interest if we now turn our attention to that part of
Kuhn's work which we have hitherto omitted from the discussion. In conjunction with the myths concerning the descent
of fire Kuhn deals with the closely related myth of the descent
of nectar. I cannot enter here into the details of their common
origin without digressing too far from our theme. Let it suffice
for me to suggest that the common origin of lightning and rain
from the thundercloud may have led to the assumption of a
common origin of fire and of nectar in the myth. We are here
most concerned with one particular finding of comparative
mythology, namely that the Moses of the Bible corresponds to
the Prometheus of Greek mythology and indeed of Indo-
Germanic mythology in general. If we compare the law-giver
Moses of the Old Testament with the Aeschylus version of the
fire-bringer Prometheus we find the two figures have very little
in common. The story of Moses, however, like that of Prometheus, shows traces of considerable displacement. We must
distinguish between the Moses of mythology and the Moses of
the Bible. The Biblical Moses, like Prometheus, ascends to
heaven and, as Prometheus brings down the fire, so Moses
brings down the law. He ascends to the accompaniment of
thunder and lightning. Here again the thunderstorm comes in.
It is hardly by chance that the law is called fiery.[1] Moses is
usually depicted as a trusted servant of the one God. Whereas
Prometheus comes into conflict with the gods through stealing
the fire, Moses receives the law from the hands of God, so that
no conflict can arise. The rebellion of Moses against God is to
be found elsewhere. The figure corresponding to Moses in the
pagan myth calls forth water from the cloud by means of
lightning. Moses is provided with the equivalent of the lightning
or the driller of the pagan myth in the rod, a symbol found repeatedly in countless legends. With this rod he smote the rock
in the wilderness and it gave out water, in disobedience to the
Lord's command (see Numbers, Chap. 20). Moses is punished
for his disobedience by being forbidden to enter the promised
land. Thus Moses does not steal water; he merely smites the
rock and brings forth water from it. According to God's
ordinance he should have spoken to the rock. He was so
carried away by his impatience that he struck the rock. Here
the displacement is unusually extensive. Moses, a simple man,
becomes a servant of the Lord. He does not even commit a
theft, like Prometheus. He merely brings forth the promised
water prematurely. Thus Moses' fault is displaced on to a

[1] Deut. Chap. 33. ii.

comparatively trifling wrong. At the same time God's power is exalted by his punishing even a relatively trivial sin.

This throws an interesting sidelight on the origin of certain pathological ideas. A very similar process of displacement, which Freud called 'transposition', is to be found in the aetiology of obsessional ideas. According to Freud's investigations, obsessional ideas derive from the patient's self-reproaches over some forbidden sexual activity. The patient attempts to make restitution for what he regards as sexual transgression by observing the strictest rectitude in other spheres, as though it were in those other spheres that his fault lay.[1]

I have recently [2] drawn attention to a closely related process found in such mental disorders as dementia praecox and melancholia. The delusional feelings of sin in patients suffering from such disorders can often be traced back to self-reproaches of a sexual character. These patients tend to displace their guilt feelings from their sexual memories on to some minor shortcoming of another kind. They cannot be deflected from these thoughts. If one considers such mental states from the Freudian standpoint this type of behaviour becomes clear: it is an attempt to avoid guilt feelings.

Displacements such as those demonstrated in the story of Moses are frequently met with in the Old Testament. There we come across many originally pagan myths which were taken over by the new religion as the people gradually adopted monotheism. In the course of this development they had to undergo considerable modifications. The transition to monotheism occurred only very slowly and after violent struggle, as all the historical books of the Old Testament bear witness. The gods and godlike beings of the ancient myths had to descend from their pedestals and to content themselves with the role of mortals and to become subject to one god. In some cases this displacement goes so far as to make the former god, now a man, into a particularly devoted disciple and the elect of the one true god. The figures of the patriarchs and of Moses are products of this process of displacement. For the study of this process the story of Samson is particularly suitable. Steinthal's [3] elaboration

[1] I cannot here embark upon a detailed account of Freud's teachings on this subject, and refer the reader to *Sammlung Kleiner Schriften zur Neurosenlehre*.

[2] Abraham: 'The Experiencing of Sexual Traumas as a Form of Sexual Activity' (1907), see *Selected Papers*, p. 47.

[3] Steinthal: 'Die Sage von Simson', *Zeitschr. für Völkerpsychol. und Sprachwiss.*, 2, 1862.

of this theme is masterly. I mention here a few of its main features, because it has led to results similar to those produced by the analysis of the Prometheus myth.

Samson is, as the etymology of his name clearly shows, the sun-god of ancient Semitic paganism. He is the counterpart of the Hercules of Indo-Germanic mythology. Hercules, too, is originally the sun-god or sun-hero. The Hercules myth resembles that of Samson in several important traits. Samson is the sun-god with long hair, like Apollo. He is the god of warmth and procreation, the beneficent giver of light. In summer he attains the zenith of his powers. Winter and darkness are therefore his natural adversaries which are personified in the moon-goddess. In the evening when the sun goes down the sun-god, according to a widely held belief, flees from the pursuing moon-goddess. In summer, whilst his power is at its height, he cannot enjoy it, for after the solstice it will wane. He is vanquished by the goddess of winter and darkness, as a strong man may be vanquished by a woman. According to the version in the Book of Judges, Samson the creator and sun-god showed himself weak towards a woman. Delilah most probably represents a metamorphosis of the goddess of winter and darkness. Samson loses his strength when he loses his locks, that is to say, when the sun-god loses his rays. Just as the sun regains its strength when winter is past, so Samson's hair grows again and he regains his strength, albeit only for a short time. He seeks death and finds it at the feast given by his enemies the Philistines in honour of their god Dagon. Dagon, however, is the barren god of the sea and desert, the mythological counterpart of the sun-god and therefore a hostile power.

Samson, both as hero and as sun-god, slays himself. This element, too, is to be found in other myths. In the Bible Samson's suicide is also related as having occurred elsewhere than at the feast of Dagon, although in this second version it is more difficult to recognise. The sun-god unites within himself two opposing tendencies. He is on the one hand the warming, vivifying god, and on the other the scorching, destroying, consuming god. He is represented in his more forbidding aspect by the symbol of the lion; in summer the sun reaches its zenith in the zodiacal sign of the lion. Just as Agni and Matharichvan were originally a unity which later became divided into two opposing forces, so the consuming heat of the sun, in the sign of the lion, is split off from the beneficent sun-god. The first heroic deed of Samson, like the first labour of Hercules, was to defeat a lion. The benevolent sun-god slays his

G

malevolent counterpart in the shape of a lion, thereby slaying himself.

A strongly distorting process of displacement has transformed the sun-god into Samson, the consecrated hero. Only a few traces of his original characteristics remain which, standing apart, are incomprehensible: the strength residing in his locks, his weakness towards a woman, and his end by suicide. Samson, because of his long locks, became in later myths 'Nasir', the betrothed of the Lord, who delivers his people from bondage. Here the identity of Samson and Hercules with the Phoenician Melkart, the protector of his people, plays a decisive part. How the sun-god of pagan times becomes the consecrated hero is not clear in all its details. That such a transformation took place, however, can be confirmed from many sources. Israel had to wage war against the Philistines for centuries, in the course of which it lost its freedom. The ancient sun-god, once the god who gave life and protection from the consuming fire, became the national hero, thus representing a wish of the people as fulfilled. Having become the national hero he then had to fulfil yet another wish. Like Moses, he is changed from a god into the servant of the one God, and is chosen by God to help his people. He does not appear at the head of an army, but always alone, just as the sun makes its way alone across the sky. Alone he slew the Philistines with the jawbone of an ass. Even when blind he faced thousands of Philistines alone and took them with him into death.

IX

The Means of Representation in the Myth

Having rediscovered in the myth the work of condensation and displacement characteristic of the dream, one more aspect of dream-work or its counterpart in the myth remains to be investigated. The dream does not easily find means of representation for all images and the same is true of the myth. There is, however, one difference: the dream takes the form of a play, whilst the myth takes epic form. Yet both must consider the technical possibilities of representing their material. The dream must find pictorial means of representing abstract ideas. For this purpose linguistic terms are apt to be used in a literal sense. For instance, in a dream communicated by Freud, the dreamer wants to express the idea that a musician she loves 'towers far above all others'. In the dream she sees him standing on the top of a tower in the concert hall, conducting from there. Similarly the links of logic contained in our language cannot be represented in the dream. We have already learned that the dream represents the very important relation 'as if' by identification, and that the same process can be found in the myth. Another such relationship, namely 'either/or', may be expressed in the dream in several ways. One method, for instance, is to arrange the various possibilities side by side; that is to say, each is depicted in turn and then placed alongside the others, as though for selection. Another method has recently come to my attention. The dreamer represents the various possibilities, normally expressed by 'either/or', in several dreams. According to our experience the dreams of one night invariably serve one and the same wish-fulfilment. My own experience tends to show that a number of dreams occurring in one night usually serves to state the various possibilities of wish-fulfilment. In this way the alternative possibilities represent an 'either/or'. In one case this explanation seemed particularly illuminating. A lady whose marriage was about to take place, but who had reason to fear strong opposition in several quarters, once told me five dreams, all of which occurred in one night. With the help of my exact knowledge of her circumstances I could assert that the five dreams all served to envisage the various possibilities of her future. In each of these dreams the dreamer concealed herself or her fiancé behind another person of her acquaintance who had been in a situation similar to that envisaged in the dream. It was particularly interesting to note the abundant use of infantile material. The people do exactly the same in their myths. They represent the same wish in different myths. Here we learn to understand one of the causes for the close relationship between the contents of many myths. If a wish is especially strong it finds expression in several myths. Each single representation takes up a new position with regard to the wish, showing it from a new angle. We need only refer here to the two biblical versions of the Genesis story existing side by side.

A close relationship between two elements of a dream is often expressed by putting these two elements or their symbols closely together in the manifest content of the dream. We observe the same in the myth. In the Prometheus myth we always find the driller in close proximity to the disc or to the wheel. In Genesis we find serpent and apple equally close to one another. The Prometheus myth further serves to demonstrate clearly how one person can be concealed behind several symbols:

Prometheus is both driller and lightning. We have met with a particularly interesting example of this kind in the story of Samson. The suicide of the sun-god Samson is represented by showing how Samson the sun-hero kills the sun-lion.

The greatest demands upon the technique of representation are called forth by the necessity of circumventing the censorship. We have already referred to symbolic disguise in general. In the myth concerning the descent of fire we meet disguise in symbols, notably of the male procreative organ, and of the procreative function. This reminds us of dream-symbolism. The driller, the rod or other similar instruments are often used in the dream as symbols representing the penis. Dreams in which women are stabbed by men are transparent wish-fulfilments. In other dreams a sword, a tree, or a plant whose shape lends itself to such representation is used as a male symbol.

The correlative part of the female anatomy is also to be found in the myth. It is the sun-disc or sun-wheel, or the cloud inside whose cavity Pramantha or the lightning or the thunderbolt moves. It also appears as the cave in which Agni is hidden.

In the Prometheus myth we have encountered fire in three forms: as fire from heaven, as fire on earth, and as the spark of life. In dreams fire often symbolises sexual ardour, the fire of love. As Prometheus is the life-giving god, the fire of love might be considered as a fourth variety of fire.

X

Wish-fulfilment in the Prometheus Myth

Now that we have established that dream-censorship and dream-work are completely identical with processes found in myth-formation, we will return to the question of wish-fulfilment in the Prometheus myth. We must ascertain what lies concealed behind the symbolic disguise of the myth. It will be shown that in this part of our work, too, we cannot do without the help of Freud's method of dream-interpretation.

The Greeks themselves made one attempt in this direction. They no longer understood the inner meaning of the myth, but the hero's name was readily adapted so that some meaning could be discerned in it. Thus Pramantha became 'the provider'. Such a demi-god was, as it were, a very useful figure in meeting a universal wish of mankind: the wish for a protector. There is no doubt that the interpreting of the name as 'provider' expresses a wish. We know, however, that this was a secondary meaning ascribed to the myth, and that the symbolism of the Prometheus myth does not accord with this interpretation. All this reminds us of precisely similar observations in dream psychology. It sometimes happens that even at the most superficial level a wish expressed in a dream is instantly recognisable. In these cases the dreamer is quite prepared to admit the existence of such a wish. This wish is always perfectly harmless. The question then arises, what purpose the dream-work serves, since the wish which was to be disguised by it is perfectly apparent. If, however, one undertakes a more detailed dream-analysis it will be found that behind the obvious wish another, which is repressed but connected in some way with it, is hidden. The obvious wish forms the top layer of the dream. Underneath another repressed wish lies concealed. This, however, does not conclude the work of interpretation. Sometimes it is possible to uncover with certainty yet a third layer. In dreams, as in psychosis, the deepest layer is always formed by the memories of infantile wishes.

Such stratification can also be demonstrated in the Prometheus myth. We know from Kuhn's investigations that the oldest layer of the myth represented the identification of man with fire and of man's origin with the origin of fire. The second layer corresponds to a later conception which postulated the existence of personal gods. At this level of the myth the fire-god is also the man-god who procreates man. At the third and most recent level, Pramantha is no longer the procreator but the creator of man and his 'provider'.

The wish-phantasy clearly apparent in this most recent layer has already been discussed. According to the analogy with the dream, we may expect each of the two earlier layers also to express a wish. We already know the wish contained in the second layer. Man derives his origin from a divine being and thus becomes divine himself. He is identified with Pramantha. We were able to demonstrate a similar tendency in the infantile phantasies of individuals. We traced this tendency back to a complex of self-aggrandisement. The wish of the second layer of the Prometheus myth could then be formulated thus: we want to be made by a god-like being and so to be godlike ourselves. Each of us is a Pramantha. I would point out here that this phantasy has an unmistakably sexual component. If, then, sexuality forms a relatively subordinate component in the second layer, we find in the deepest layer a purely sexual content, that is to say a wish-fulfilment of obviously sexual character. The second layer differs from the earliest by its highly developed sexual repression.

The symbolism of the earliest layer is unmistakably sexual. It gives expression to a complex of sexual grandeur. Man identifies his procreative potency with the ability of the driller to kindle fire in the wooden disc and in the heavens in the form of lightning. The most ancient version of the Prometheus myth is an apotheosis of man's procreative powers.

We have already sought to prove that sexuality forms the innermost kernel of man's being. It is an old and widespread error to assume that all young children are wholly indifferent where sexual matters are concerned. I am not here dealing with cases of abnormal sexual precocity. It is mainly owing to Freud's investigations [1] that we have come to accept the view that sexual activity exists in early infancy. The child is admittedly not conscious that this activity is sexual; it differs vastly from the sexual activity of the mature normal individual. The child's sexual scopophilia awakens at a very early age and with it the curiosity about sexual differences, procreation and other matters. All children sooner or later ask the question: where did I come from? What the child learns about this provides rich food for his imagination. In the growing child interest in sexual processes creates greater tension than does anything else. An explanation in this sphere received unexpectedly often causes a violent emotional upheaval. The first physiological signs of sexual maturation which the child notices in himself may equally produce anxiety and repugnance.

We have repeatedly seen pathological phantasy-formations derived from infantile phantasies. We have also found specific similarities between these pathological formations and myths. The physician who uses psycho-analytical technique to penetrate into the psychic life of neurotic and psychotic persons often meets with phantasies produced by infantile scopophilia and curiosity. I would here refer to Freud's analysis of a case of paranoia.[2] In the realm of obsessional psychic manifestations sexual curiosity is of very special significance. This applies patricularly to the so-called brooding mania. Patients suffering from this particular disturbance are compelled, much against their will, to brood over transcendental things such as the origin of god and of the universe, or they must rack their brains

[1] *Drei Abhandlungen zur Sexualtheorie. Three Contributions to the Theory of Sex*, now published under the title: *Three Essays on Sexuality;* see standard edn., **7**.

[2] Cf. *Kleine Schriften zur Neurosenlehre*, p. 124. Standard edn., **12**.

for reasons why things are as they are and not otherwise. A case I myself observed and which I will briefly describe here will serve to elucidate the role of infantile sexual scopophilia for the understanding of such states in persons with neurotic tendencies.[1]

The patient discerned in himself two kinds of obsessional manifestations: firstly the compulsion to pray and secondly the compulsion to examine every object most meticulously and then to brood over its origin, construction and design. He reported that he had been subject to this compulsion since childhood, and although it might diminish for shorter or longer periods of time, it inevitably recurred. Analysis showed that as a boy he had repeatedly tried to undress people with whom he shared a bedroom or bed. His whole interest was concentrated on seeing genitals and buttocks and on finding out about the details of conception and child birth. His curiosity was undoubtedly of pathological intensity and the lengths to which he went to try and satisfy this curiosity led to severe self-reproaches. As a result, he began to pray to God to make him grow up to be a good man. This praying rapidly became obsessional in character. He covered sheets upon sheets of paper with prayers and read them over as often as possible. He was terrified of omitting a single word. As the praying increased so the compulsive scrutinising of all objects increased along with it. It could be shown that the patient had substituted the study of all kinds of emotionally neutral objects for the scrutiny of certain parts of the body, as he considered such scrutiny sinful. His special interest was directed to the reverse side of these objects and the way they were made. By brooding over the origin of emotionally neutral objects he sought to offset his brooding over the origin of man. As is usual in such cases, the emotion of anxiety was transposed [2] on to emotionally neutral objects. The subject which preoccupies all growing children, and which preoccupied this boy to an abnormal extent, also forms the basis of that branch of the study of myths called anthropogeny.

The procreation of man, the coming into being of a new life, is an enigma. For this reason alone it is not surprising to find that it has always aroused particular interest in man and has played a large part in the formation of myths. To an age so far removed from that of the scientific study of natural processes, procreation must have appeared as magical. Strong support

[1] See this vol. Part I, p. 36.
[2] Cf. *Sammlung kleiner Schriften zur Neurosenlehre*, p. 118 *et seq.*

can be provided for this assumption. The magic wand plays an important role in myths and miracle stories. For reasons which cannot be discussed here it is beyond doubt that this magic wand is merely the symbolical representation of the penis. A very similar symbol is the rod boring into the wooden disc, around which the oldest version of the Prometheus myth is woven. There is one remarkable feature of the Prometheus myth to which I have not previously referred, namely that it is an exclusively masculine myth. Man as the procreator, Pramantha, appears in the myth both undisguised and in symbolical form. Woman is only represented by the symbol of the wooden disc and is mentioned only incidentally in the myth. We had already arrived at the conclusion that the oldest layer of the Prometheus myth is an apotheosis of procreative power. This view is now fully confirmed. The oldest form of the Prometheus myth serves to proclaim masculine procreative power as the main principle of life. This aggrandisement of the masculine aspect of sexuality persists to the present day.

XI

The Analysis of the Myth of the Descent of Nectar

The myth of the descent of fire, which we may now properly call a myth concerning procreation, is closely connected with the myth of the descent of nectar. We have already indicated this connection, but we have not so far undertaken an analysis of this myth. Our previous experiences lead us to expect that two closely related myths will possess the same underlying ideas. For the analysis of the nectar myths Kuhn's writings may once again serve as a starting point. At a certain stage, however, we shall have to branch out on our own.

In the oldest Indian sources the name for nectar is amrta; later it is called soma and in the Zendavesta haoma. The names nectar and ambrosia are familiar to us from Greek mythology. Various miraculous and mysterious effects are attributed to nectar: it vitalises, inspires, and confers immortality. This latter quality is clearly expressed by the word 'amrta' and its etymological equivalent 'ambrosia'. Nectar, too, has a similar meaning.

All peoples of whom we have any knowledge have produced intoxicants whose consumption induces the familiar deceptive sensations. They make man feel vitalised, inspired and elated. At the same time they give him an increased feeling of warmth and arouse his sexual desire. The Dionysian revels are invariably erotic in character. Drink thus induces in man two kinds of fire: bodily warmth and the fire of passion. Man obtained intoxicating drink from the juices of certain plants. In myths these plants are called soma. Of these the ash or rowan tree is of particular interest to us. This is a tree whose wood was used to kindle fire. From its branches the juice soma was extracted.

In addition to this earthly soma a celestial soma is known to mythology. Both are identified with each other, just as are terrestrial and celestial fire. On earth soma and fire are derived from the ash tree. Just like the celestial fire in the Prometheus myth, celestial soma comes from Yggdrasil, the ash or cloud tree. It is produced by drilling into the wood of Yggdrasil, that is, into the cloud. Earthly soma is thus celestial soma which has descended from the celestial ash tree. A bird nesting in its branches brought it down to earth. The analogy with the fire-myth is striking. Just as celestial fire represents the heat of the sun and lightning, so celestial soma represents more than one element. It stands for both dew and rain, and hence for the nectar of the gods. In some myths the cloud-tree is described in greater detail. It has its roots in the lakes; from beneath it fountains rise which descend to the earth as rain. From its branches falls the dew.[1]

We have previously asserted that in the oldest layer of the Prometheus myth the kindling of terrestrial and celestial fire serves merely as a symbolical substitute for the process of procreation. We may rightly assume that terrestrial and celestial soma are likewise symbolical representations of a third substance, which we have not so far discerned. Though the interpretation is obvious, Kuhn has overlooked it. Our analysis must therefore go beyond that of Kuhn to the third and most

---

[1] In another image traceable in Indo-Germanic mythology clouds were visualised as a galloping horse. Dew was supposed to fall from its mane to earth. From this cloud-horse, carrier of the inspiring soma, the winged horse Pegasus of the Greek legend took its origin. In another version the rushing clouds represented the avenging Erinyes. The Germanic legends about the wild chase have the same derivation. The idea of one cloud pursuing another, trying to catch it, is to be found in a modern painting, entitled *Hay-making*, by Segantini. It is noteworthy that the phantasy of an artist whose works represent the idea of the unity of nature has a pattern similar to that of the phantasy of pre-historic peoples.

important meaning of soma, most important because revealing its original meaning.

Celestial soma is won by drilling into the cloud, that is to say by a symbolical act of procreation. It seems to me an obvious conclusion that soma stood symbolically for human semen. Semen has both a vitalising and an immortalising effect, for it serves procreation. It fertilises as does celestial soma falling upon the earth as dew or rain. We can now comprehend the close connection between the myths concerning the descent of fire and of nectar. The organ of procreation and semen are natural correlatives.

Just as with the fire-myth, over this oldest layer of the myth, whose sexual significance clearly emerges, a second stratum was deposited. The second version differs from the earlier version in that it personifies natural phenomena. Anthropomorphic gods make their appearance and there is intense sexual repression. We come across a semi-divine being called soma. Soma is the quintessence of potency and fertility. Our hypothesis as to the true nature of soma is here fully confirmed. In certain myths Agni, whom we have already encountered, takes the place of Soma.

It is of great interest to mention here a Greek myth in which the image of the creation of nectar by drilling has been preserved. It helps us to understand the most recent layer of the soma myth. Zeus desires to reach Persephone who is concealed in a bank of clouds. He therefore changes himself into a serpent and bores his way into the cloud. The sexual symbolism is transparent. The result of the union of Zeus and Persephone is Dionysus, the god of wine and the personification of nectar. Dionysus is suckled by the Hyades who, as goddesses of rain, are a further personification of celestial soma. Their constellation dominates the rainy seasons.

The Zeus of Greek mythology corresponds to Indra. In Indian mythology Indra is the god of the serene cloudless sky. He also plays an important part in the soma tale. He becomes the soma-thief. As in the third layer of the Prometheus myth Matharichvan brings back Agni, so Indra brings soma from a cave where it is guarded by the Gandharves.[1] Indra perpetrates this theft in the guise of a hawk. In some myths, however, the theft of soma is ascribed to Agni who also takes the shape of a bird. We have previously met with Agni as the bird who

[1] In a monograph on this subject Kuhn has shown that the Centaurs of Greek mythology originated from the demonocracy of the Gandharves.

steals fire. We now meet him again as the thief of soma and are thus faced with a remarkable identification. The hawk has to fight the Gandharves for the possession of soma. In this fight he loses a feather which falls to earth and changes into the soma-plant. We have already come across a similar story in the course of our analysis of the Prometheus myth. As with this latter myth, the soma-myth is so much distorted in its third version that sexuality is completely absent from its manifest content.

On further investigation of the soma-plant, we shall find additional proof of the identity of soma and human semen. The branch of the soma-tree (a symbolic substitute for the penis) is said to possess a miraculous quality. Not only does it yield the soma fluid, but it enters into the most variegated rites and ceremonies. From the mountain ash, for instance, is cut the divining-rod used, among other purposes, for finding subterranean water. According to an ancient custom herdsmen would beat their cattle with a staff from the mountain ash to increase fertility and yield of milk. The branch of the soma-tree is also represented by the magic wand, by the staff borne by Hermes and in the Thyrsus-staff, a wand used by Dionysus to bring forth wine from the rock. The bible story in which Moses smites the rock with his miraculous rod to bring forth water has already been mentioned. The symbolical significance of this rod becomes still clearer if we remember that it turned into a serpent before Pharaoh's eyes.[1]

Among the many functions of the ash tree in myths and rites there is one which deserves our special attention. The churn-staff used in butter-making was fashioned from ashwood. The reason for this was that the ash was said to give protection against all kinds of witchcraft. During butter-making one was believed to be particularly exposed to the influences of witch-craft. According to the sources at our disposal, there can be no doubt that the process of churning butter, like that of kindling fire, is likened to the act of procreation and is its symbolical substitute.[2] The butter thus produced was compared with, or rather identified with semen as well as with soma. A story by Mahabharata describes the origin of soma in a way which is

[1] The process of erection has obviously stimulated phantasy activity to an extraordinary degree. The turning of the rod (phallus) into the serpent stands for the return of the erect penis to the flaccid state.

[2] Editor's footnote: It is interesting to recall in this connection the taboo against making butter whilst menstruating.

reminiscent of the process of butter-making. I here follow Kuhn's version [1] and relate it in abbreviated form. The gods, who desire amrta, and the asura, which are evil spirits, use the mountain Mandara as a churn-staff for swirling the ocean. Indra coils the serpent Vasuki like a cord around the mountain and gods and asuras then begin to pull. As they pull smoke and flames erupt from the serpent's gorge and thick clouds gather, causing lightning and rain to descend upon the gods. At the same time the swirling of the mountain causes the trees growing on its summit to be rubbed against each other and to burst into flames. The fire thus kindled envelops the mountain like lightning illuminating a dark cloud. Indra puts out this fire with cloud-water and the sap from all the gigantic trees and plants flows into the sea. These waters, composed of the most exquisite juices, change into butter to form soma. In the myth this soma is identified with the moon and from it various other mythical beings originate. At last Dhanvantari emerges holding a white jug containing the amrta. Gods and asuras engage in combat to possess it, the gods being victorious.

The old Indian epics contain some other descriptions of the winning of amrta. None of them is inconsistent with the interpretation of soma which I have adopted. Each of the three layers, which we could discern in the myth, contains a wish-fulfilment analogous to that contained in the corresponding layer of the Prometheus myth. Just as in the Prometheus myth procreation and the organ serving it is the object of apotheosis, so here semen is deified. By repressing the sexual content of the myth, semen is gradually turned into nectar. It becomes the gift of a benevolent god to mankind. Thus the soma myth undergoes a transformation similar to that of the Prometheus myth and likewise ends in a non-sexual in place of a sexual wish-fulfilment.

XII

The Wish-fulfilment Theory of the Myth

I have tried to formulate a theory of the origin of the myth on the basis of psychological observations and to support this theory by a detailed analysis of examples. The time has now come to discuss the relationship between the views put forward here and other theories concerning mythology.

[1] Kuhn: *Die Herabkunft des Feuers* (1886), p. 219.

The oldest and, as I believe, the most popular theory to this day assumes the myth to be the metaphorical expression of philosophical and religious ideas. According to a widespread view such ideas are supposed to be the basis of the psychic life of mankind. I cannot subscribe to this view. Children do not bring with them into the world a code of altruistic ethics, nor can it be assumed that pre-historic men were endowed with a fund of philosophical or religious ideas which they subsequently symbolised in myths. An extremely lengthy process of repression was necessary before such ethics became the firmly established acquisition of a people. This process of repression must be repeated in an abbreviated form with every human being. Our analysis of the Prometheus myth has shown that the only element of that myth which has the appearance of a moral or religious idea, that is the conception of Prometheus as a provider, is of an incidental and secondary character, whilst ideas and wishes of a very different kind were revealed as the true basis of the myth. What Freud has shown to be true for the Oedipus myth, I believe I have shown to be equally applicable to the Prometheus myth. That is, that the origin of these myths is not to be traced to ethical, religious or philosophical ideas but springs from the sexual phantasies of mankind. I consider the ethical and religious components of the myth to be the results of subsequent accretions, the product of repression. Other myths, too, which I could not deal with in such detail, appear to lend support to my theory.

Fifty years ago, when Kuhn originated the science of comparative mythology, this new branch of learning broke with the earlier views concerning the origin of myths. Delbrück [1] concisely expressed this change of opinion. He maintained that every myth originates from some process in nature and that it is an unsophisticated attempt to explain natural phenomena. The myth came to be regarded as having undergone a gradual process of development and various myths were compared with similar myths found amongst other peoples.

One modern theory asserts that all myths of Semitic and Indo-Germanic peoples have a common origin in the observation of the stars. More recent research has shown that the original home of astronomy was Babylon and that many myths can be traced to Babylonian sources. This is the so-called Astral

[1] Delbrück: 'Die Entstehung des Mythus bei den indogermanischen Völkern', *Zeitschr. für Völkerpsychol. und Sprachwissenschaft*, **3**, 1865.

Theory. For details of this theory reference should be made to a short paper by Winckler.[1]

If one assumes natural phenomena to be the origin of every myth and looks upon the myth as an expression of astronomical concepts, such a hypothesis is, in one respect at least, unsatisfactory. It fails to provide insight into the motives of myth-formation. It does not take into account the essential ego-centricity of all human phantasy-formations. Astronomical concepts may well have had a powerful influence upon the elaboration of myths, but their importance can be no more than secondary. The dream, too, incorporates into its material observations made by the dreamer in his waking life. Indeed, if one omits to make an exact analysis of a dream, such observations may appear to constitute its most essential content. The dreamer makes use of such material because it evokes a response from something within his own personality. It enables him to disguise his phantasy wishes under the cloak of symbolism. For just such a purpose a people makes use of astronomy.[2] They project their phantasies heavenwards. The people themselves form the central point of their own myths and in those myths they experience the fulfilment of their wishes.

The wish-fulfilment theory of the myth can easily be extended to include religion. The original identification of man with his god has, both in myth and in religion, been lost sight of. By a protracted process of repression the monotheistic peoples have achieved submission to God as their creator. If slow but far-reaching changes have led to the recognition of the one and only God as the father of mankind, though no longer in the sense of the procreating but of the providing father, this again is due to a wishful phantasy originating in infancy. It is the same wishful phantasy which led the Greeks to look upon Prometheus as the provider. Man wishes for a providence to take care of him. He projects his wish heavenwards where must dwell the father who takes care of all men. The cult of the adoration of the Madonna just as clearly derives from an infantile wish-phantasy. The adult, confronted with all the exigencies of human existence, craves the ministering mother who took care of all his needs in childhood. Hence he projects his surviving childhood phantasies on to the queen of heaven. All ideas of a life after death, whether depicting a here-

[1] Winckler, 'Himmels- und Weltenbild der Babylonier als Grundlage der Weltanschauung und Mythologie aller Völker'. *Der alte Orient*, Leipzig 1902.

[2] Editor's footnote: This of course refers to pre-scientific astronomy.

after in the Christian sense or as a place of sensual pleasure in the Islamic sense, are no more than the fulfilment of wish-phantasies.

I have explained the origin of the myth and its transformations in the light of the wish-fulfilment theory. I must now say something as to its disappearance. The fact that myths dis- · appear is well known and to us this fact provides yet another analogy with the dream. Every dream undergoes regressive changes, sometimes at a rapid rate, at other times more slowly. No absolute forgetting ever occurs, but the dream-thoughts with their associations relapse into repression. In the same way a time comes when a people forgets its myths. Every people reaches a phase in which it discards its traditions and where a realistic mode of thinking takes the place of the earlier phantasy-formations. This development is accelerated by progressive understanding of natural phenomena and also by the attainment of increased mastery over reality, which goes some way towards satisfying the grandiose aspirations of a people. Other collective phantasy-formations participate in this regressive process, not least among them being the symbolism of language. The process of sexual symbolisation in the language comes virtually to a standstill, whilst existing symbolism falls into desuetude. The English language has progressed, or rather regressed, furthest in this respect. Here only slight traces of sexual differentiation survive. Linguistic and mythological symbolism obviously provide an inadequate vehicle of expression for a modern-minded people like the English. Practical success makes it possible to discard wishful-phantasies. A people whose attainments fall far short of its grandiose aspirations behaves very differently. The Jewish people provide a good example of this. Through long periods of time they have preserved the wishful-phantasies of their early history, such as that of being the chosen people and of inheriting the promised land.

Modern science regards as a fundamental principle of bio-genetics the fact that the development of the individual recapitulates the evolution of the species. Over long periods of philo-genetic development manifold physical changes have taken place in every species. The individual must undergo similar development changes. A corresponding process takes place in the psychic sphere, where philogenetic development is likewise recapitulated. The most important illustration of this is that in pre-historic times the people moulded their wishes into phantasy-formations which survived into historical times in the form of myths. In exactly the same way the individual, in his 'pre-historic period', moulds his wishes into phantasy-formations which persist in the dreams of his 'historical times'. Thus the myth is a surviving fragment of the psychic life of the infancy of the race whilst the dream is the myth of the individual.

XIII

Determinism in the Psychic Life of the Individual and the Community

The principles of analytical research embodied in the work of Freud comprise the phenomena of both normal and ab-normal psychic life and the psychology of the individual and of whole nations. In all these spheres psycho-analysis is able to demonstrate that every psychic phenomenon is determined by specific causes. At the present time the belief in divine inspiration has already become discredited. Psycho-analysis must direct its attack to another quarter. The belief is still widely held, even in scientific circles, that the sphere of psychic life is under the rule of chance. There is a refusal to recognise that all the multi-farious incidents of everyday life, thoughts, mistakes and lapses of memory, the contents of dreams and the individual symptoms of mental disorders are determined by specific psychic factors. Men cling to an outworn dualism. They assign to psychic events a unique position by excluding such events from the sphere of scientific determinism. The theory that psychological events are due to coincidence is entirely barren as it can never account for the specific phenomena of psychic life. This is the basis of Freud's teaching. It regards every psychic phenomenon as the effect produced by a specific psychological cause and it therefore searches for that cause. The principles of determinism operative in the realm of the psychic life form the subject-matter of this line of research.

The child comes into the world endowed with its constitution as a primary determinant of its later psychological behaviour. The aspect of this constitution which is most important for the understanding of all phantasy-formations is the psycho-sexual aspect. In childhood, before the process of repression sets in, this psycho-sexual constitution is revealed in its most undis-guised form. When the child begins the transference of his libido on to certain animate and inanimate objects and its withdrawal from other objects, the influences of his education and environment produce their effect upon him. These influences force him to repress part of his natural impulses and particularly his sexual impulses. The repressed infantile sexual impulses exercise a determining influence second only in importance to that of the inborn constitution. Infantile psychic material is to be met with over and over again in all phantasy-formations. Memories of later life are added as a third factor. They, too, are largely subject to repression. Memories which cannot be recalled by an effort of the will are generally regarded as non-existent. Freud was the first to recognise the decisive effects of the repressed psychic material and to attach due weight to it.

Nowhere in the whole psychic realm is there such a thing as chance. What at first sight appears to be the result of chance will be found to have its causes deep in the inborn constitution and in infantile sexual repression. Incidents occurring after childhood are like tributaries flowing into the main stream. To attach such overriding significance to the determining forces of sexuality is not to overestimate its importance. Throughout organic life the preservation of the individual is subordinate to a higher principle, that of the preservation of the species. The drive serving the preservation of the species must of necessity be the more powerful; otherwise the species would perish.

Analytical research as practised by Freud is still in disrepute. It shares this fate with a branch of philology, namely etymology, of which it was once said that it is characterised by the fact that vowels play no part in it and consonants but a small part. A scientific method of interpreting words has a future before it. The word 'etymology' comes from $\epsilon\tau\upsilon\mu\sigma\varsigma$ meaning true. It is thus the science of the true meaning of the basic elements of the language. The teaching of Freud is an etymology of psychic phenomena. It, too, has a future before it, though doubtless one in which it will have to make its way against prudery and the prejudices of modern science.

II

GIOVANNI SEGANTINI:
A PSYCHO-ANALYTICAL STUDY [1]
(1911)

Preface to the Second Edition

THE first edition of this essay was welcomed by some and adversely criticised by others. In the thirteen years which have elapsed since its publication my psychological experience has increased, but I have found no cause to alter the views there expressed. It is satisfactory to note that after so long an interval all that was previously said may be allowed to stand. At the same time I welcome the opportunity of incorporating certain recent psycho-analytical findings into the study written in 1911, as a further contribution to the understanding of the artist. In recent years I have made a particular study of depressive states, and I believe I can now contribute to our further understanding of Segantini's melancholic tendencies. Such additions as I have felt able to make in this respect are set out at the end of this work.

Sils-Maria, *June*, 1924   KARL ABRAHAM

Preface to the First Edition

We possess a number of short essays on the life and art of Giovanni Segantini, and a large work by Franz Servaes consisting of an account of his life and a critical appreciation of his art. This is included in the special edition of the works of Segantini published by the Austrian Government as a memorial to him, and it has also appeared in a popular edition.[2] Servaes

---

[1] Abraham, Karl: *Giovanni Segantini, ein psycho-analytischer Versuch. Schriften zur angewandten Seelenkunde*, H. XI, p. 65. Vienna, Deuticke, 1911. First published in German in 1911. Revised edition published in German in 1925. First published in English in the *Psycho-analytic Quarterly*, October 1937.

[2] Servaes, Franz: *Giovanni Segantini: Sein Leben und sein Werk.* Leipzig, 1907. All references in which the number of the page is given in the text refer to this edition.

gives us a description of Segantini both as an artist and as a man which is excellent in every way. It is not, therefore, the purpose of the present essay to improve on this author's study of the artist, but to consider problems of a different kind. Nor is it intended to give yet another descriptive account of Segantini's individual characteristics but rather to explain them psycho-logically.

The psycho-analytical researches of Freud and his school throw a new light on the general and individual manifestations of psychic life. Starting from investigations into the unconscious, these researches led to important discoveries concerning the laws governing artistic creativeness. One of the more recent works of Freud, entitled *A Childhood Memory of Leonardo da Vinci* has, apart from its other results, thrown important new light on the artistic individuality of this master. No one, however, has yet undertaken the comprehensive study of the life and special mental make-up of a creative artist from the psycho-analytical point of view, or tried to demonstrate the effect of his unconscious drives upon his artistic creativeness.

Among the creative artists of our time Giovanni Segantini stands out as a powerful and independent personality. His development, his external and inner life, his artistry and his works are all so highly individual that they constitute in themselves a whole series of unsolved psychological problems. The purpose of this paper is to consider these problems from the psycho-analytical point of view.

It may seem surprising that a physician should attempt to use this new method to analyse the psychic life of an artist. The reason for this lies in the development of psycho-analytical research. Psycho-analysis is a method whose original aim was to seek for the unconscious roots of morbid psychological conditions, of nervous disorders or 'neuroses'. It soon extended beyond this limited field and was found to be a fruitful method of investigation into the most diverse spheres of psychic life. Owing to the purpose for which it was originally devised its exponents have hitherto been, in the main, medical men. The physician who, with the help of analysis, has become familiar with the unconscious of the neurotic, has a definite advantage over other observers. In the artist he meets with a number of psychological qualities with which he is already familiar in the neurotic. These are traits connected with conscious or unconscious phantasy life.

There is an important difference, however, between the purpose of this essay and that of the medical application of psycho-analysis. The psychotherapist who practises this method joins with the patient in a common task. Gradually he gains deeper insight into the patient's unconscious, and so is able with the latter's help to fill in gaps in the patient's associations. The situation is different where one seeks to analyse the psychic life of one who is no longer living. In such a case one has to use such evidence as is available and to interpret it with the help of knowledge obtained from other similar cases. The material left to us by Segantini in his works, his notes and his letters, or that has been collected by others, is naturally incomplete.[1] I am therefore quite aware of the fact that this analysis will not provide an answer to every question. Is this a reason for not attempting it? Segantini's rich personality offers too much that is rare and attractive to allow one to abandon the task.

We who were Segantini's contemporaries owe it to an artist of such genius, to so great a man, to explore his personality and to try to understand it. We shall not be disappointed in our expectation that as a result of our efforts we shall gain a better understanding of the psychology of the artist. The attempt itself may show how far Freud's method enables us to achieve our aim.

1

Segantini died on September 28th 1899 at the height of his creative activity. Only ten days before his death he had climbed the Schafberg near Pontresina for the purpose of completing on its summit the centre panel of his Triptych of the Alps. This last work, conceived on a grand scale, was more to him than a mere glorification of the mountains. According to him, the task of painting was not merely to produce a true likeness of reality; it was to give expression to the most personal ideas and feelings of the artist. For this reason he depicted the bounty of nature, the mother with a child at her breast, and beside her a suckling animal; he painted the break of day, the awakening of nature after her winter sleep, the life of man; he painted all living things at the height of their being, and finally he painted the dying day, nature frost-bound, and the death of man. In his last work he expressed more forcibly than he had ever done before the kinship with nature and the common fate shared by every living thing.

[1] *Notes and Letters of Giovanni Segantini*. Edited by Bianca Segantini. Leipzig, Klinkhart und Biermann.

Segantini had already portrayed all these subjects individually and in many different combinations, representing them in never-ending variety. In this way he produced his immortal master-pieces: *The Mothers, Springtime in the Alps, Ploughing in the Engadine, The Homecoming,* and many more. Yet he still felt the urge to paint one more work, destined to be his last. In this symphony of life he wished to express all that for him represented the essential meaning and value of life.

It is not only from the artist's pictures that this intention can be learnt; he has also clearly avowed it in his writings. On several occasions he exchanged the brush for the pen in order to uphold his interpretation of the essence of art against other opinions. A year before his death he composed an answer to Tolstoy's question: 'What is Art?' In this he laid great stress on the importance of the moral idea underlying any work of art. Art is for him a dedicated activity, serving to glorify and trans-figure labour, love, motherhood, and death. Segantini himself thus indicated the sources from which he constantly derived his artistic inspiration.

Other artists have of course also drawn inspiration from the same sources. It is characteristic of Segantini's individuality that for him all these springs flow into one main stream, that for him apparently widely diverse groups of ideas are inseparably inter-woven. A glance at Segantini's life shows that it was governed by the same principles as governed his art. We may ask ourselves what determined the direction of his artistic creativeness and the pattern of his life. We may be sure that parental example and education played no positive part, for by the time he was five Segantini had already lost both his parents. The circumstances of his youth can have assisted neither his spiritual nor his moral development. He grew up without proper schooling, al-most illiterate, and neither the years which he passed alter-nating between the homes of his stepbrother and stepsister nor those spent in a reformatory can have exercised a refining in-fluence upon him. His youth was dark and dismal, a continual struggle against hostile authorities. He had to forge his artistic ideals, his character, and his philosophy almost unaided. Only the psycho-analytical method of investigation can explain his development, since this method alone takes the instinctual drives of infancy as its starting-point. To justify the application of this method I can appeal to no less an authority than Segantini himself. 'You enquire', he writes in one of his letters,[1]

[1] *Notes and Letters of Giovanni Segantini.* Edited by Bianca Segantini. Leipzig, Klinkhart und Biermann, p. 82.

'how thought and art could have developed in my almost savage life in the wilds of nature. I hardly know how to answer you; to obtain a satisfactory explanation one would probably have to descend to the very depths, and in that way study and analyse every emotion of the soul right down to the first, the very first stirrings of childhood life.'

I will follow the artist's hint and turn to his childhood.

The most momentous incident in Segantini's childhood was the early death of his mother. He was scarcely five years old when he suffered this loss.

A son can seldom have cherished the memory of his mother so lovingly as did Segantini, and this love grew ever greater with the years. The mother gradually became idealised into a goddess, and the son's art was devoted to her cult.

He who had become an orphan so early in life knew no loving care during the whole of his youth. Was it because of this deprivation that he became the painter of motherhood? Did he, in his art, make an ideal of that which in reality had been denied him? However obvious this explanation may seem, it will soon prove to be completely inadequate.

Many children in their tender years suffer the same misfortune as this artist. They scarcely comprehend the extent of their loss, are soon comforted and only think of the lost one when adults say something to revive memories. Sometimes these childhood memories and feelings are harder to efface. With Segantini, however, the picture of the mother is never erased; on the contrary, it develops in his phantasy until it becomes the centre of his whole inner world. The negative factor alone, the lack of motherly care, cannot explain the sovereign power of the mother-ideal. Segantini himself has given us a clear indication where we are to seek the roots of this power. He says at the beginning of his autobiography:

'I carry my mother in my memory, and were it possible for her to appear at this very moment before my eyes I would still easily recognise her after thirty-one years. I see her in my mind's eye, her tall form walking wearily. She was beautiful, not like the dawn or like noon, but like a sunset in spring. When she died she was not yet twenty-nine years old.'

In these words of the mature man there is no single mention of motherly love or care. When we read his description of the sad period which began for him with his mother's death, we look in vain for any comparison to show how well he was cared for by his mother, and how badly he was treated later. Of this we find not one word.

Segantini speaks of totally different things: of the beauty, the form, the movement, the carriage, and the youthfulness of his mother, whose picture is ever before his eyes. If one imagines the two words 'my mother' omitted from the above quotation, these lines might well be those of a lover speaking of his lost beloved. Only thus can the depth of feeling in his words be comprehended.

We hear in the words of the adult an echo of the eroticism of the child. The science of psycho-analysis has already made us familiar with the view that the first expressions of eroticism in the boy are directed towards his mother. These erotic feelings, the character of which in early childhood, until about the age of five, is obvious to the unprejudiced observer, alter their characteristic appearance gradually during the further course of childhood. The primitive eroticism of the child is purely egoistic. It is directed towards the unlimited possession of its object, and is resentful if others also obtain pleasure from the proximity of the loved one. It shows manifestations of hate as well as of love. At that period of yet untrammelled impulses and instincts a boy's love is coupled with an aggressive, even cruel, element.

The study of neurotic minds has shown that in some people these impulses are of abnormal strength. The extreme cases are those of children who in later life fall victims to so-called obsessional neurosis. The outstanding characteristic of the instinctual life of such children is that feelings of love and hate are continually intermingled and this gives rise to severe psychological conflicts. In such cases one regularly finds signs of an exaggerated love for the parents alternating rapidly with signs of hatred culminating in death wishes.[1]

In normal people as well as in neurotics the damming-up of these instincts through the process of repression and sublimation takes place during the next phase of childhood. In this way are formed the socially important inhibitions which reduce these instincts quantitatively. Alternatively, in certain cases the manifestation of such instincts is completely inhibited, or is directed towards different, altruistic ends. According to the mental disposition of the individual, some of this sublimated sexual energy is transformed into intellectual, scientific or artistic activity. The greater the original strength of the

[1] Cf. Freud: '*Observations on a Case of Obsessional Neurosis.*' *Jahrbuch für psychoanalytische und psychopathologische Forschungen*, **1**, 1909 (Standard edn., **10**), see in particular p. 413. Something similar can be observed in people liable to depressive states.

instincts, the deeper and more comprehensive the sublimation necessary before the individual can submit completely to the demands of the social pattern.

Contrary to conventional opinion, we now accept that the primitive feelings towards the parents, just like other expressions of love and hate, arise from infantile sexuality. The individual must obey the moral exhortation to honour his father and his mother. It is noteworthy that the commandment does not order one to love one's parents, for this would only forbid feelings of hate; the commandment is directed equally against love and hate, for both in their respective ways are manifestations of the sexual instinct. Both run counter to the prohibition against incest, and from their common sublimation arise feelings of reverence which are free from any sexual flavour.

Is it the supreme spiritualisation of his feelings for his mother that gives to Segantini's works their characteristic stamp? Should we regard this mother-worship as resting on a sexual basis?   The discoveries of psycho-analysis permit us to answer this question emphatically in the affirmative. It is true, as mentioned above, that most of this information was gained from the study of so-called neurotics, so that a short justification is required if we wish to apply it to the personality of Segantini. Artists and neurotics have much in common in their psychic disposition. In both, the instinctual life is of originally abnormal strength and has undergone a complete change through a particularly intensive repression and sublimation. Both live partly outside reality, in a world of phantasy. In the neurotic the repressed phantasies are elaborated into the symptoms of his illness: in the artist these phantasies find expression in his works, although not exclusively there. Every artist shows neurotic tendencies. He is never completely successful in the sublimation of the repressed instincts, which are partly transformed into nervous manifestations. This is certainly true of Segantini.

As we learn from the psycho-analysis of neurotics, the process of repression produces in the feelings of the boy a change which is of great consequence. In his conscious mind the exaggerated erotic attraction towards his mother, who cares for him, is replaced by gratitude and reverence. As the incestuous wishes become strongly repressed, over-emphasis is laid on the qualities of motherhood.[1]

This compensating over-evaluation of motherhood is excep-

[1] Other consequences connected with this process will be discussed later.

tionally marked in Segantini, just as it is in neurotics. From this, and from other manifestations shortly to be discussed, one may conclude that in his childhood Segantini's libido was directed towards his mother in the form of overpowering impulses of love and hate, which were later subjected to vigorous sublimation. This feeling was, as I see it, spiritualised in the cult of motherhood, in a profound veneration for Mother Nature, and in a selfless, altruistic love which embraced all creation.

Just as in the case of the neurotic, we find in Segantini occasionally a breaking through of the repressed instincts. The original eroticism of the child could not be completely sublimated; now and again it shows itself, although in a much milder form. One cannot overlook the erotic element in the description which Segantini has given of his mother, although it has undergone a remarkable etherealisation. He used his art to spiritualise the figure of his mother and to exalt her above all earthly feelings. A number of Segantini's most beautiful works depict a mother absorbed in tender contemplation of her child. In each of these pictures we are enchanted by the woman's slender, youthful figure, by the slightly bent posture and the lovely delicate features.

These pictures were painted about the artist's thirtieth year, when he was living at Savognin in the Grisons. About this time he created various pictures entirely from his phantasy. Two of them have a peculiar history, which for us is of the greatest interest.

Segantini himself tells us that the sight of a rose once aroused in him a sensual feeling which would not leave him. As he was slowly pulling the petals from the flower, he was overpowered by the vision of a rosy youthful face. This vision moved him to paint over an earlier picture of a woman dying of consumption, so as to represent a young woman in full health.

We can understand this incident better when we consider a second and similar one, the description of which I have taken from Servaes' biography.

'Segantini himself relates that one day when he was climbing the topmost peak of a mountain he saw, when only a few paces from the summit, a large flower which seemed to stand out distinctly from the bright blue sky and was clearly silhouetted against it. It was a flower of great beauty and radiance, the like of which he felt he had never seen before. Lying flat on the slope he gazed at the wondrous sight, as it stood there alone in the full light of day. Then it seemed to him that the flower grew to a gigantic size before his eyes, and that it took on, in his imagination, attractive human forms. The large stem turned into a bent branch, and upon it reclined gracefully the seated form of a blonde and rosy young woman, holding a naked child in her lap. The child held in its hands a dark red apple, corresponding to the robust pistil that rose out of the flower. Segantini then painted this vision, calling it *An Alpine Flower*. Later he renamed the picture *The Fruit of Love*.'

The artist immediately associates the beauty of a flower with the beauty of his long dead mother. From this moment the flower and his mother are identical to him. In front of his eyes the flower changes into the picture of a Madonna.

The erotic basis of this phantasy becomes especially clear to those who recognise certain symbols occurring here, which recur in all human phantasy-formations.

Servaes rightly remarks that the figure of the child in the picture *The Fruit of Love*, with its vigorous health, is in striking contrast to the delicate mother. It is of great interest to explain this feature of the strange picture. Has the artist depicted himself as the joyous child beside the mother? The fact that when Segantini was born he was so weak that he had to be baptised before the appointed time seems to speak against this. Yet another circumstance confirms our hypothesis. In the autobiography he says: 'My birth resulted in a weakening of my mother's health, which killed her some five years later. To recover from this weakness she went to Trient in my fourth year, but the cure did her no good.' The young wife did not recover; she gradually became worse, whilst the child, who had sapped her strength, thrived and outlived her.

The words quoted here deserve attention for yet another reason. The thought of having caused the death of a beloved person is encountered very frequently in neurotics.

As already mentioned, the childhood libido of a neurotic is characterised by strong feelings of hatred. These express themselves in phantasies of the death of the loved person or, if the latter really dies, in feelings of satisfaction, even of cruel pleasure. Later, when repression gains in power, guilt-feelings arise against which the neurotic is powerless to defend himself, although in his conscious mind he finds no grounds for such self-reproaches. He accuses himself of responsibility for the death of his father or mother, although in fact his childhood crime consisted in no more than forbidden phantasies and feelings. These self-reproaches are followed by attempts at making reparation for such crimes, which take an exaggerated form in obsessional neurotics. The memory of the loved person is cherished with excessive fervour and becomes sanctified. Alternatively an attempt may be made to repress the fact of the death into the unconscious, and in phantasy to resurrect the dead one.

An event in his childhood which Segantini himself recounts [1] shows clearly that for him mother-worship was a form of reparation for hostile or cruel emotions in his childhood. 'The first time that I ever took a pencil into my hand to draw was when I heard a woman tearfully say to her neighbours: "Oh, if I only had her picture; she was so beautiful." As these words were spoken, I saw the beautiful features of a young despairing mother before me and was deeply moved. One of the women present pointed to me and said, "Let this boy make a picture; he is very clever." The beautiful tear-filled eyes of the young mother turned towards me. She said nothing, but went to her room, and I followed her. In a cradle lay the body of a tiny girl, who could not have been much more than a year old. The mother handed me paper and pencil, and I began. I worked for several hours, as the mother wished me to draw the child as if she were still alive. I do not know whether my picture was an artistic success, but I remember that for a moment the poor woman looked so happy that she seemed to forget her grief. The pencil, however, remained at that poor mother's house, and it was not till many years later that I took up drawing again. This incident may have been the seed from which the thought developed that I might use this medium to express my feelings.'

It would be very simple to trace the boy's first artistic achievement to a noble and compassionate impulse, especially as we know that as a man Segantini was particularly susceptible to such feelings. To do so, however, would be to allow the really remarkable aspect of this incident to pass unnoticed.

At that time Segantini could not have been more than twelve years old. That being so it seems amazing to me that he could stay for hours alone with a dead body without feelings of fear and horror. These reactions of fear, horror and compassion only develop gradually in the course of childhood by means of sublimation of the sadistic impulses. If the latter are unusually strong, there is a change-over to a particularly strong feeling of compassion with the sufferings of others and fear and apprehension of death. In later life both these characteristics were particularly pronounced in Segantini. At the time he drew the dead child, however, the process of sublimation had made but little progress in this direction, and it may therefore be

[1] In a letter to the poetess Neera. *Collection of Bianca Segantini*, p. 84.

concluded that even after his twelfth year a particularly strong component of cruelty had successfully resisted complete sublimation.

In the scene just described, the sadistic impulse finds satisfaction in the contemplation of the child's dead body, and of the mother's grief. On the other hand his compassionate impulses are satisfied by drawing the picture to please the beautiful young mother and to alleviate her sorrow.

Twice in recounting the incident Segantini mentions the beauty of the young woman in a manner which closely resembles the description of his own mother. As she stands before him she replaces his mother in his imagination and by the process of transference [1] stimulates his artistic faculties. For the sake of a mother he becomes an artist. If we assume that, like the neurotic, he tries to make amends to a strange mother for the wrong he has done to his own mother by his death wishes, we shall find confirmation in another part of the story. Segantini states that the reason for staying for hours beside the corpse was to represent the dead child as living, in accordance with the wishes of the grief-stricken mother. So there was an art by which one could, as it were, summon the dead back to life. Later he often used his art to bring back to life the memory of his mother. Therein lay, as we can now understand, an act of atonement which the adult imposed upon himself for the sins of his childhood. This behaviour is extraordinarily reminiscent of the obsessional neurotic who, although in a different form, imposes upon himself acts of penance.

After this first groping effort years passed during which Segantini, under the pressure of wretched circumstances, had to relinquish the idea of drawing. At last he succeeded in gaining admittance to the Brera Academy in Milan. The first pictures he painted there, relying upon his own phantasy for inspiration, were so closely linked with his earliest childhood attempt at drawing that it seemed as if no more than a single day had passed. Death and motherhood were his themes.

The pictures of death will be discussed separately later. Here we will consider the first picture which Segantini painted and exhibited at the Academy: it was a head of Niobe. It was said to have so touchingly represented the grief of the mother for the death of her children that it created a sensation.

[1] From the psychology of the neuroses we are familiar with the process by which feelings relating to the original infantile sexual object can be transferred to a new person by identifying this latter in phantasy with the original object.

At this time Segantini was in a phase of physical and mental development. We know that this age stirs in the human being all that has lain dormant through repression and sublimation in the second period of childhood.[1] The adolescent must now take up a definite position towards his earliest love-objects. He must now decide whether he will persist in his original attachments, or whether he will free himself from them and transfer his feelings on to new objects. During this period the extent to which he will ultimately repress and transform his instincts is determined.

In Segantini the transference of the love impulses on to the mother, long since dead, only now showed itself in its full strength. Such fixation of the libido was bound to lead to a tremendous sexual repression, the effects of which can be recognised everywhere in Segantini's life and works.

From the reports of that period of his life we hear nothing of those love affairs which common opinion expects of a young artist. On the contrary, his attitude towards the female sex was reserved and shy. He differed from his contemporaries in his great sensitiveness, and his avoidance of every objectionable word in conversation.

We see from this that Segantini's instinctual life was inhibited; this can only be explained on the basis of a libidinal fixation to his mother.

Not until he was twenty-two years old did he experience what is usually called first love. From his earliest childhood upwards he had been completely dominated by his actual first love, his love for his mother. The strength of this first love was still manifest. We find in Segantini an unusual limitation of choice of sexual objects. He was not able, as young people usually are, to form relationships and dissolve them again; his choice, once made, was final. This monogamous trait, which we also meet in neurotics, showed itself in a remarkable manner in Segantini.[2]

In his twenty-third year, in 1881, Segantini painted his first picture which had an erotic subject, and it remained, with the exception of a few pastoral pictures executed during the next few years, the last of its kind. Segantini enquired of his friend, Carlo Bugatti, whether the latter's sister Beatrice would sit for him. He painted her in the costume of a noblewoman of the

[1] Editor's footnote: In present-day psycho-analytical nomenclature we would call this the latency period.

[2] See also my paper: 'The Significance of Intermarriage between Close Relatives in the Psychology of the Neuroses.' *Jahrbuch für psychoanalyt. Forschungen*, Bd. I, 1909. This vol. Part I, p. 21.

Middle Ages; a falcon sits on her left hand and with her right hand she feeds it. The picture bears the title *La Falconiera*. Servaes rightly draws attention to the fact, which is indeed obvious, that the painter is enamoured of her. In fact Segantini fell in love with, and soon afterwards married, his beautiful model.

His love for Beatrice, Bice as she was called in the family, was as ardent and unchangeable as his love for his mother. His married life bore not the remotest resemblance to the usual idea of an artist's marriage. This is not to say that Segantini was a good family man. To the end of his days he was passionately in love with his life's companion. The letters which he wrote to her, when from time to time they were separated, bear testimony to this. They sound like the transports of a young man in love. Their feeling tone is reminiscent of those passages in the autobiography which deal with the artist's mother.

Segantini's early marriage shows the unusual phenomenon of epitomising the whole of his love-life. It is, however, clear that the extremely powerful instincts of the artist could be confined in this manner only if they were allowed in their sublimated form to reach out to an infinite number of persons. Whilst Segantini was strictly monogamous in his love-life, he directed his spiritualised love towards all nature and all mankind.

Here we must pause for a moment. We are about to subject to analysis the workings of these instincts in the art and the life of the adult man.

Before we leave his youth, however, we must examine the importance of his father as well as of his mother.

2

In the artist's autobiography we read very little of his father. We learn that his father left his home in the village of Arco with the five-year-old Giovanni after the early death of Giovanni's mother. He went to Milan to his grown-up children by an earlier marriage. When he could not make a living in Milan, he suddenly decided to emigrate to America with one of the sons of his first marriage, leaving Giovanni behind with a stepsister. From that time the artist never heard from his father again.

It is remarkable that though Segantini lost both parents within a short space of time he writes about his mother lovingly and at great length but tells us little more of his father than the bare facts given above. Whereas he uses his highest art to glorify motherhood and raises a fresh memorial to motherhood in every one of his works, one looks in vain for any positive expression of the feelings linking him with his father. In those of his pictures in which one finds a father as well as a mother, the father is never the central figure of the picture.

It would seem almost as though his father had had no effect on his development or on his work and as though he were quite indifferent to him. Segantini's silence is, however, eloquent; it arises, as will now be shown, from the repression of the most violent hostility towards his father.

Owing to the bisexual disposition of human beings the erotic feelings of the boy reach out to both parents. At an early age a preference for the mother can be observed. As a direct result of this, feelings of jealousy and enmity towards the father develop. When Segantini's mother died he had no further need to be jealous, and normally the boy's whole love would have turned towards his father. At this moment his father took a step which inevitably killed all the love of the child for him, and increased the feelings of hostility; he took the imaginative boy, whose emotional needs he overlooked, from the paradise on Lake Garda to the dreariness and misery of the city, handed him over to a stepsister who gave him neither her time nor her love, after which he forsook him completely. Thus the feelings of affection for the father were stifled at the outset, and hence we fail to find in the young Segantini any of those substitute formations which normally arise from the sublimation of the son's love for the father.

During puberty one normally finds a more or less extensive detachment from paternal authority; but even after puberty one can still see signs of it in expressions of filial piety and affection. The sublimation of a lasting, positive relationship to the father makes itself felt throughout the whole course of life, in the desire to lean on someone stronger, in a tendency towards submissiveness and in an anxious clinging to convention. Even after adolescence it may occur that a son still maintains an attitude of childish dependence on his parents. The conservative tendency may then be particularly pronounced and progressive activity markedly lacking.

Segantini is the exact antithesis of this latter type; he may be said to go to the other extreme. He is completely devoid of the submissive attitude, the conservative trait. Somewhere he writes: 'Every development, whether it be social, religious or of any other type, has as its first aim the sweeping away of what already exists, nihilism and destruction.' Here Segantini gives expression to truly revolutionary tendencies. He is taking revenge on the paternal authority against which he must have rebelled in his earliest childhood and in particular, revenge on his father for abandoning him to misery after his mother's death. Segantini was not content with this negation of the existing order of things; his desire was to make way for the new by destroying the old. Not only did he advocate this attitude in theory; he acted in accordance with it long before he proclaimed it in words.

We can therefore say that Segantini's father had a purely negative significance for him. As his love for his mother flows out in a sublimated form to the whole of nature, so his hatred, originally focussed on his father, is turned against everything which restricts his will. It is true that the aggressive impulses directed against his adversary are attenuated through sublimation. Thus they provide Segantini with the energy which sustains him against all opposition and helps him to win through. From childhood onwards Segantini's life is a living protest against all authority attempting to encroach upon his personality.

However much this energy may be turned against the paternal authority, one must not overlook the fact that it is just in this that Segantini identifies himself with his father. To the boy the father is the natural model, on account of his superior size, strength, vitality and knowledge. His rivalry with the father, more than anything else, must evoke in him the wish to equal him in all these attributes. This provides an important impetus for the child's phantasies of grandeur.

The rebellion against paternal authority and the wish to become self-sufficient, independent, and grown-up are to be found in the young Segantini to an unusually marked degree. These character-traits help us to understand his development as a man and his career as an artist.

It is deeply moving to read, in the artist's biography, how at the age of six he had to spend his days from morning till night alone, locked up in a narrow, bare room. For a time he endured this fate, as long as these monotonous surroundings aroused his curiosity and stimulated his phantasy. Then he writes: 'One morning, as I was looking drearily out of the window without thinking of anything in particular, the cackling of some neighbouring women came to my ears. They were gossiping about someone who, as a young man, had tramped from Milan to France, and done great things there. . . . For me this was a revelation. It was possible, then, to leave this tenement and to wander far away . . . I knew the road; my father had shown it to me as we walked by the palace. "That," he said, "is the gate through which the victorious French and Piedmontese troops entered. The triumphal arch and the road were built by Napoleon I. The road is said to lead through the mountains straight into France." And the idea of going to France along this road would not leave me.'

The women's words reminded the boy of an impressive tale told by his father in which he, too, had spoken of France and of a man's great deeds. This was enough to awaken his childish longing for greatness, and his impulsive energy demanded immediate action. The six-year-old boy runs away, takes with him a piece of bread, walks through the triumphal arch, and takes the road of the great Napoleon.

Not long before, his father, too, had left Milan one day without saying much. The little one does the same. He is not satisfied with the phantasy of all boys, to equal his father. He wants to be like the man whose greatness compels even his father's admiration.[1]

The rest of the artist's childhood story, as he tells it himself, is rich in strange vicissitudes, so rich that we must doubt whether it really can all have happened. Could it not be possible that the extravagant phantasy of the child and of the adult has invented some of it, or at least transformed it, so that his own judgement was later no longer able to separate phantasy from reality?

Justification for such an assumption is to be found in our knowledge of certain phantasies which are produced by so many persons in a surprisingly uniform manner that we have to recognise in them something typical, common to all mankind. The same ideas will be found in mass-phantasies, that is to say in the myths of the most diverse peoples and times. In my study entitled 'Dreams and Myths' [2] I have proved that myths, in their form and content, show the greatest conformity with the childhood phantasies of the individual. More recently Rank has dealt in particular with the myth of the birth of the hero.[3] Every people in its myths attributes to the birth and childhood of its hero wonderful happenings which are in full conformity

[1] Persons whose aggressive impulses are inhibited by strong repression like even now to identify themselves in their phantasy with Napoleon. This is the most important unconscious source of the Napoleon cult.

[2] 'Dreams and Myths, A Study in Folk-psychology.' *Schriften zur angew. Seelenkunde* and this vol., Part III, p. 153.

[3] Rank: 'Der Mythus von der Geburt des Helden.' *Schriften zur angew. Seelenkunde*, Part V. (The Myth of the Birth of the Hero: a Psychological Interpretation of Mythology.)

H

with the childhood phantasies of individuals. Segantini's child-hood story reminds us in a striking way of these heroic legends.

The stories of Moses, Sargon, Cyrus, and Romulus and Remus all have a common feature in that the son of noble parents has for some reason to be got rid of. He is saved in a miraculous manner, saved from drowning, for instance, or found by chance by strangers of humble birth. He is brought up as their son and has to perform menial tasks. Even in his youth, and in contests with his rivals, he shows special qualities which single him out from his surroundings and prove him to be destined for higher things. When he is grown up he learns the secret of his origin, takes revenge on his oppressors, performs heroic deeds, and finally wins all the honours that are his due.

Let us now return to Segantini's account of his childhood.

The boy ran on along the highway, until at nightfall he sank down exhausted at the side of the road and fell asleep. He was oblivious to the fact that rain soaked him to the skin. He was awakened by some country-people who were passing along the road. They took charge of him, put him into their cart, and carried him home with them. On the way he fell asleep again and only awoke when he had reached the house of his rescuers. When he was dry and warm they asked him about himself. Here his autobiography goes on to say: 'I remember how I recounted a long story, with many details, about an accident which once occurred to me and which made a deep impression on me. One day, when I was about three or four, I crossed a small wooden bridge which led from the main road to a dye-works. It went over a mountain stream which had been dammed up so as to drive many mills with its power.' On the bridge, Segantini goes on to say, he had met a bigger boy who had accidentally pushed him into the water. A soldier had jumped in after him and had saved him as he was being swept towards a mill-wheel.

Then follows the end of the story. As the country folk heard from the little Segantini that he did not want to go back to his sister at all they said: 'We will keep you with us, you poor little orphan. What you need is the warmth of the sun. But we are not rich, and therefore if you wish to stay with us and become one of us you will have to make yourself useful. . . .' 'The next day the woman cut off my long hair which fell to my shoulders in rich curls. Another woman standing by said: "Seen from the side he looks like a son of the king of France."

'That same day I became a swineherd; I was not yet seven years old.' The boy was only allowed to stay for a few weeks in his new surroundings, where he experienced far more kindness than from his sister in Milan. This short episode is described by Segantini with great exactness and fond attention to detail. We find in this story all the essential elements of the myth of the birth of the hero: the separation from the parents' home, even though it takes place in a manner different from that in myths, followed by the miraculous rescue by peasants who take pity on the child and who are prepared to bring him up as their own. Into the story of this rescue Segantini weaves a second rescue story. As a child of three he was saved from drowning. Like so many heroes of mythology he, who in appearance resembles a royal prince, has to do the humble work of a swineherd for his foster-parents.

It is not possible, in this childhood story of the artist, to draw a sharp line of demarcation between fiction and fact. Those who know the extent to which incidents of childhood are subjected to the transforming influence of phantasy will not fail to recognise the traces of that influence here. I will give only one example. Segantini remembers hearing at the age of six that he looked like a son of the king of France. It is not very likely that he remembered the words which were said at that time. What he recalls, however, is identical with the boy's typical phantasies of high parentage. The father, as the proto-type of all power and greatness, is often, in the child's phan-tasies, exalted to the level of a king or an emperor. This is repeated in the dreams of adults, in which the father not in-frequently appears as a king. Hostile impulses against the father reveal themselves in the boy's phantasy of dethroning him, becoming himself the son of the imaginary king, and making his real father a mere foster-parent. To be a prince is among the most usual childhood phantasies of grandeur. It is very probable that the little Segantini merged these phantasies with what he had heard about the king of France, so that this idea, by reason of its wish-fulfilling character, assumed in his memory the guise of an actual event.

The whole moving story of Segantini's childhood is very like an individual myth. People with strongly developed ambitions often surround their childhood with such myth-formations. That these are in Segantini's case so largely identical with the myth of the birth of the hero goes to show that he draws upon material which lies buried deep in the human mind.[1]

[1] We cannot believe that Segantini was influenced in his phantasy-weaving by a knowledge of mythology. His education was not sufficient for that.

As already mentioned Segantini had soon to leave his refuge and return to his sister. Our information about the ensuing years is but scanty. We only know that Segantini was compelled to go first to one and then to another of his stepbrothers and stepsisters. For a while he lodged with a stepbrother who had a cooked meat shop in Val Sugana and then went back to the stepsister who had in the meantime married an innkeeper. Such were the surroundings in which the boy had to live. In his phantasy he certainly dwelt in far-off lands, and several times he actually ran away, in the firm belief that by so doing he would make his fortune like the heroes in fairy-stories. When in the end no-one felt able to manage such a runaway and ne'erdo-well, he was got rid of, and sent to a reformatory school in Milan. There he was employed as a cobbler.

Not even the discipline of this institution, however, could break the spirit of the twelve-year-old boy. He rebelled against the authority of the church, as he had rebelled against every other form of authority. When the time came for him to go to communion he stubbornly refused. He was punished by detention, and ran away when released. He was caught and brought back again, and this time remained in the institution until he was fifteen years old. His masters had to try to adjust their methods of education to his personality: by so doing they got on with him more easily. In the end he achieved his long-cherished desire to be apprenticed to a house-painter.

The fifteen-year-old apprentice was now faced with a new authority, a decent enough man, but one who had an exaggerated opinion of such little skill as he possessed. He was no more successful than his predecessors in forcing his opinions upon his apprentice.

As a result Segantini did not stay with him for long. He resolved to leave his master, and having done so entered the Brera art school, and tried in the face of great difficulties to eke out a small living. In various ways he attempted to make a little money, but often he did not earn enough to buy sufficient food.

Because of his exceptional gifts and his outstanding personality he quickly won recognition from his fellow-students. He soon became the leader of those art pupils who were in revolt against artistic traditions and conventions, and in that way he incurred the displeasure of his teachers. After the young revolutionary's initial success at the Milan exhibition, he was on the next occasion allocated a very unfavourable place in which to hang the picture he exhibited. This aroused all Segantini's anger. A scene followed which Servaes describes thus: 'He went there, pulled down his work, and tore it to pieces. This was not all. When he met in the street the professor whom he believed to be the cause of the injustice he had suffered, he questioned him angrily, and found it so difficult to control his temper that he clung to a lamp-post and shook it so long and so violently that the glass broke.'

This made it impossible for Segantini to stay there any longer, and at the age of twenty, unable to submit to any authority, he took a bold step towards independence. Struggling constantly against extreme poverty, he went his way with unflagging energy. He has summed up the fate of his youth in eloquent words: [1] 'With the body, in which my soul was fated to be a prisoner, I had to fight many battles. Abandoned and orphaned when but six years old, I was cast out, alone and loveless, like a mad dog. In such circumstances I could only run wild and unruly, constantly in rebellion against established authority.'

The strongest expression of his hatred of all obedience was soon afterwards given by the young Segantini in an action which Servaes omits to mention. Segantini, who was an Austrian subject, evaded military service. The fact that he was not deterred by the possible consequences from taking this step shows how strongly he was dominated by his urge to be free. His punishment was that he was unable to return to his native land for a long time. He suffered deeply through this enforced exile. When he died he was near to the fulfilment of his heart's desire, to see once again the homeland he loved so much.

This action seems out of character in a man of such strong moral scruples as Segantini. The analysis of his unconscious mind makes it comprehensible to us. In loving his native land he expressed his love for his mother; in hating the government of his native land he expressed his hatred of his father.

3

In Segantini's mind, and no less in his emotional life, mother, home, and nature form an indivisible unity. By virtue of their inner relationship they merge, as we usually say, into an 'emotionally-charged complex'.

The unusual power of this complex can be explained in the light of Segantini's childhood story. When he lost his mother he also had to leave his home and the countryside. With one blow he was deprived of all that was most dear to him; in his memory, therefore, these three remained inseparably bound up.

[1] *Collection of Bianca Segantini*, p. 72.

His father took him away from the surroundings he loved: the big city, in which he remained isolated, offered him no emotional satisfaction. In consequence he hardened his heart against his father and against the city. Because they starved him of love he turned away from them for ever. His intensified love for his mother, home and countryside must have derived particular reinforcement from this reaction.

In the darkest period which Segantini had to endure as a youth, he seized every possible opportunity to escape from the city to the countryside which, according to the evidence of his friends, he passionately loved. When he had succeeded in finding in his Bice a substitute for his mother, he could no longer bear to stay in Milan. He felt irresistibly drawn to the country. He had also to replace the home he had lost so early in life. He went with his young wife to live in Pusiano in the Brianza, the region lying between the two southern arms of Lake Como. There he became the painter of his simple rural surroundings.

At that time Segantini was still far from the zenith of his artistic powers. As Servaes rightly remarks, his art was confined within narrow limits. He painted scenes from village life in a narrative manner. Some of these pictures show that he had not yet completely emancipated himself from academic influences. It was when he depicted men and animals side by side that he approached most nearly the style of his later works. All these scenes contain but little movement; there are dreaming herdsmen, a shepherdess quietly saying her Ave Maria, a mother leaning sorrowfully over an empty cradle. All these pictures were painted in dark tones. At that period Segantini painted dim interiors, the glimmer of moonlight, the darkness of stormladen skies; he was particularly fond of painting the soft glow of sunset.

The works of this period often show one particular feeling tone: man's kindness and sympathy for animals. In the little picture called 'Uno di piu' the shepherdess, full of motherly tenderness, holds a newborn lamb in her arms. In another picture called 'Sheep-shearing' a shepherd bends lovingly and tenderly over the animal whose fleece he shears.

To this period belongs the first conception of a picture devoted to a subject which he subsequently took up and fully worked out. It was called 'Ave Maria a trasbordo'. A languid peace pervades it. The boatman rests on his oars; the woman with the child in her arms seems to be sunk in slumber; the herd of sheep filling the ferry press towards the foreground, yet their bodies seem almost motionless. Over it all lies the light of the setting sun and the stillness of the evening.

This picture contains all the features characteristic of the Brianza period, and is possibly its best example—a real Segantini. During this period the artist underwent a change; he ceased to underrate the technical aspect of painting and no longer looked upon the emotional content of a work of art as the only thing that mattered.

Servaes [1] describes this as a period of free-flowing activities. His output was great. He gave free rein to his need to find artistic expression for his emotions ('sentimenti').

In his autobiographical notes Segantini writes: 'Nature had become for me an instrument which gave musical expression to all that my heart had to say. It sung the quiet harmonies of sunset and the innermost being of nature. Thus was my spirit imbued with a deep sadness which reverberated in my soul with infinite sweetness.'

We must stress two aspects of Segantini's psychic life at this period: his tendency to depression and his sympathetic love and compassionate kindness towards all creatures. It is particularly important to note this because later on Segantini underwent a remarkable change in both these aspects.

We must remember that during his adolescence the artist's sexuality was subject to extensive inhibition. If, as has been shown, the active, masculine element was largely repressed, one would expect this to lead to a reinforcement of the opposite component. An element of passivity is thus brought into the whole psychic life, which in more than one respect is reminiscent of the psycho-sexual behaviour of women. The submission to suffering is preferred to active aggression. In this way arise the frequent depressive moods so characteristic of neurotics which regularly, though not always consciously, contain alongside their suffering an element of pleasure. Segantini speaks of this 'sweet melancholy' not as of an evil, but as of a rich source of artistic inspiration. In the pictures of this period the passive element, the sadness, finds symbolical expression in grave tranquility and subdued tones. The sunsets which Segantini so often portrayed at this time suggest to us those thoughts of death which are inseparable from moods of depression; they also indicate the focal point of all his phantasies, which was his mother. 'She was as beautiful as a sunset in spring', he later wrote of her. Death phantasies once referring to his mother, and

[1] The description here given of this phase follows closely that of Servaes.

later turned back on to himself, found their sublimation in the works of this time.

His love of nature and his compassion for every living thing derive, as we have already shown, from the repression of aggressive instinctual impulses. Thus his own suffering and compassion served the aim of instinctual sublimation.

Then came the great change in the psychic life of the artist. The weary melancholy ceased to be the dominant mood; it gave way to an exuberant joy in creative activity. Later, however, and particularly towards the end of his life, the sombre mood frequently regained the upper hand.

This process is well known to us from the study of neurotic patients. In them, too, puberty usually brings with it an intensity of repression far beyond the normal. As a result the sexuality of the neurotic shows a remarkable degree of femininity. Neurotics, too, frequently display from the beginning of sexual maturity until the third decade of life, or even longer, a listlessness and passive acceptance of their suffering. Only gradually do they overcome this phase and achieve a positive attitude towards life, and a normal or even exaggerated capacity for work.

Segantini was fortunately now able to convert his aggressive impulses, which up to that time had been paralysed, into a great surge of creative activity. Such activity, essentially masculine, became his main driving force and as a result his concept of nature and the character of his art also changed.

From the Brianza Segantini went for a short while to Caglio, which lies high above Lake Como. There he painted the first of his pictures conceived on a grand scale, *Alla stanga—Milking time*—a vast landscape bathed in the light of late afternoon. It depicts a herd of cows by a gate, some in the foreground, some further back, and in between men busy about their farm work. This was no mere sketch of rustic life; it was a bold attempt to comprehend the whole of nature by his art.

Soon afterwards Segantini went with his wife into the high Alps, in search of a place in which to settle. After wandering about for a long time he finally, in 1886, chose the village of Savognin in the Grisons. This virgin spot seemed to satisfy most completely his feeling for nature. In the quiet mountain village, almost unknown in the great world outside, he found a new home. There with his wife and children he shared the life of the mountain dwellers.

The ascent from the foothills of Brianza to the high Alpine valley of Savognin is a milestone in Segantini's development.

What attracted him to the heights was first of all the proximity of the mountains, which were here as near to him as they had been in his old childhood home. Furthermore he wanted, as he says in one of his letters, to gain a thorough knowledge of nature. To the eye of the artist the clearness of the air, the brightness of the sunlight, the luminance of the colours all held a powerful attraction. Above all, the ascent to the heights symbolised for him, the solitary worker, his striving upwards towards perfection, and signified his constant longing to out-grow his own limitations by his unceasing activity and the wish to conquer the whole of nature as an artist, so that he could rule it as a king. 'There,' he writes in his autobiography, 'I directed my gaze more boldly towards the sun, whose rays I loved, and wanted to capture.'

The work of the following years was anything but an easy giving of himself. It was a harnessing of all his powers which gratified the sublimated desire for aggression. Segantini himself confessed that he was gripped by an agitation which made work seem effortless. Everything within him impelled him to his work which he called 'the incarnation of the spirit in matter', and an act of creation.

What a changed outlook on life! The man who for years had turned his back upon life in weary melancholy now saw himself in daring flights of fancy as a creator or a ruler of nature. He found himself by reverting to his childhood phantasies of grandeur.

The gentle, compassionate love of nature was transformed into a burning lust, an ardent wish for possession. Segantini describes it in glowing words, from which the following passages are taken.

'I am a passionate lover of nature. On a beautiful sunny spring day in these mountains which have become my home ... I am filled with infinite elation; the blood courses in my veins as it did in my youth when I was with my beloved.'

'I am intoxicated by this love, which is insatiable, and bending low I kiss the grass and the flowers. . . .

'I am athirst, O earth, and bending down to the purest everlasting springs I drink of thy blood, O earth, which is blood of my very blood.'

We can translate these thoughts into scientific language thus: the sight of nature intoxicates the artist's senses in a way which he himself likens to sexual excitation. The sublimated drives clamour urgently for satisfaction; and this demand is directed towards no less than the whole of nature. In the sensual love for

Mother Nature, his love for that mother who was 'blood of his own blood' is resurrected.

The first year of Segantini's sojourn in Savognin saw the production of works which are numbered among his greatest.[1] Some of them take up the older themes of the Brianza period. It is just these which show most clearly the development of his power. First there is the *Ave Maria a Trasbordo*. In a masterly way Segantini made a few changes both as regards the composition and the light effects in the picture. More important still, he experimented for the first time with a new technique, the disintegration of colours, a subject to which we shall shortly return. From the same period dates the charming picture *The Girl Knitting at the Gate*. When he painted the same subject for the first time in the Brianza he produced nothing but dull, dim lights. Now it is flooded with dazzling sunlight.

In this period of change there was but one constant factor in Segantini's art: the mother complex. Whatever thoughts and feelings pertained to this did not seem to be subject to any change or variation, as is clearly shown in the following characteristic trait. Segantini would not allow the young peasant girl who had been his model for the *Girl Knitting* to leave him again. 'Baba', as she was called, had to move into his house. She remained there throughout the following years as his only model, in addition to which she became the trusted companion of himself and his family. Having found in her the type he needed for his pictures of motherhood and work, he had no need for change, and kept to her as his only model.

In the following period he represented the idea of motherhood in a great masterpiece of overpowering strength, *The Two Mothers*. A young girl is seated on a stool in a cowshed; her head sinks in slumber as she holds her sleeping child in both arms. Close by one sees the massive body of a cow, with a young calf at her feet. A hanging lamp throws a mild, reddish light upon the woman and the child, and upon the hindquarters of the cow. The rest of the picture is hidden in a dim half-light. A solemn tranquility lies over the group: one can only agree with Servaes' discerning remark that the artist emphasises, through the peace common to all the figures in the picture, the essential similarity of the two mothers. This effect is heightened by an equally simple means—the direction of the lines. Servaes here says: 'The cow stands with straight back, bending her head over the trough; where the cow's back ends the head of the young

[1] In the following passages the description again closely follows that of Servaes.

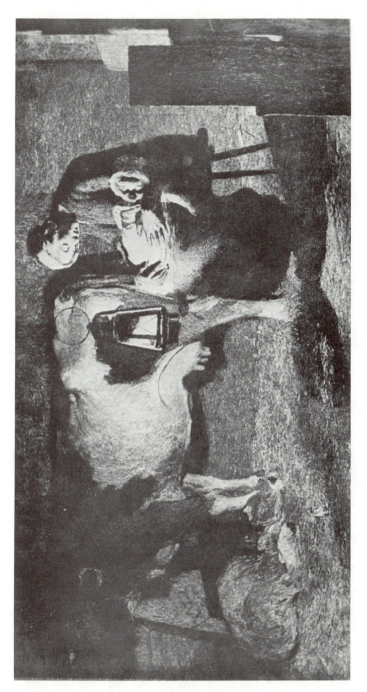

'The Two Mothers' by Giovanni Segantini

'The Hell of the Voluptuaries' by Giovanni Segantini

human mother appears, and her back takes up the severe horizontal line, letting it glide softly downwards. Just above, the picture is foreshortened by the frame, so that one can see distinctly (although one only feels it dimly) how the edge of the picture runs parallel to the cow's back. The subtle solemnity of the composition is transformed, almost unconsciously in the eye of the spectator, into emotional values. Thus with a gentle touch the artist guides our thoughts.'

In about 1890 Segantini's persistent endeavours were rewarded by his achieving perfection in the technique of colour disintegration. The beautiful picture, *The Ploughman* (called in its earlier form *The Unploughed Earth*) was the first mature fruit of this labour. By this time he had succeeded in representing the crystal clarity of the air and the scintillating colours of those heights better than anyone before or since. He put man, with his faithful companions the domestic animals, in wonderful plasticity into the foreground of the picture. All the details of the landscape are executed with typically loving care. The long range of the Alps in the background sparkles in an infinite variation of rock and snow; and over all is the shimmering blue dome of the bright clear sky.

Segantini achieved by his unaided efforts perfection in the technique of colour-analysis. The same problem occupied painters everywhere at that time, and many ways were tried of solving it. Segantini went on his way with calm self-confidence, independently of all these attempts, until he reached his goal.

The way was opened to him not merely by his superior artistic gifts. The search for light and colour was deeply imbedded in his instinctual life. His eye thirsted for light and colour, and following an inner urge he had to bend his utmost efforts to the perfect representation of both.

In his earliest works as a pupil at the Academy he had already set himself the problem of depicting light and had solved it independently. Later on, during his melancholy moods, he had gone over to dark tones. When, at a later date, he was drawn to the heights and wanted to dominate nature, his victorious mood found expression in his longing for the radiant sunlight revealed in its full glory on the mountain tops. We have already learnt from Segantini's own words what emotions the sight of all this splendour aroused in him. He looked upon nature with the eyes of a lover; it transported him into an ecstasy of bliss. We do not need any more proof of the fact that we are here faced with a far-reaching sublimation of that component of the sexual instinct which we call scopophilia. This impulse serves to stimulate the libido by contemplating the physical qualities of the sexual object, which we refer to in ordinary language as its 'charms'. The sublimation of the scopophilic impulse provides the main constituent for the establishment of the sexual inhibition which we call the feeling of shame. It also to a large extent lends itself to artistic and aesthetic sublimation.

Segantini's scopophilia, despite its prominent strength, was to a large degree deflected from the purely sexual sphere. We very rarely find in any of his pictures a nude figure. In a picture called *The Fount of Evil*, painted in his later period, however, a naked female form, reflected in water, is the allegorical representation of vanity. Here the artist, in his portrayal of nudity, pursues an ethical aim. He surrounds the pagan goddess of sensuality, the *Dea Pagana*, with a transparent veil. Characteristically neither of these works is among the artist's best. Quite a different intensity is to be found in the *Dea Christiana*, the kindly mother with the child. One can see that he has been able to imbue this picture with the full strength of his feelings. Crude sensuality is nowhere to be found in Segantini's works. Where he paints erotic scenes, he does so tenderly, subtly, and modestly.

His sublimated scopophilia turned towards nature; light and colour were to him sources of ecstatic joy. Segantini tells how in his childhood the sight of a house-painter handling his brushes and colours filled him with burning curiosity. Enthralled, the boy watched the worker's inartistic daubing. He saw in the splashes of paint shapes of phantastic animal and human figures; they appeared in a kaleidoscopic sequence. Further descriptions of his childhood show with what avidity he absorbed and retained optical impressions. The vigour of his visual presentation is remarkable; every scene of the autobiography has the feeling of a painting. Segantini was not merely a loving observer of nature; the form and colour which his eye absorbed were shaped by his artistic phantasy into a harmonious whole.

He himself never lost the feeling that his observations and his creative activity were used to give expression to his eroticism. Discussing one day why he never made a sketch before starting a painting, he wrote as follows: 'An artist who begins by making a sketch is like a young man who, because he feels delight at the sight of a beautiful woman, wants to possess her at once, to revel in caresses, cover mouth and eyes with his kisses, and to tremble in the ecstasy of an embrace. There he has his sketch ... I prefer, however, to let my love mature, to linger fondly over my ideas, and to treasure them in my heart. Although I am half mad with the desire to see these ideas take shape, I deny myself this satisfaction, content to harbour them safely within me. In the meantime I continue to contemplate them with my mind's eye, and to imagine them in changing light in different positions and in varying emotional context.'

It is, however, very characteristic that the painter who scorned to make preliminary sketches often returned again and again to the theme of a painting after its completion, giving it this variant or that, and trying to approach it from a new aspect. The train of ideas behind a work dominated him so completely that he was left with the sensation that he had not yet expressed every fine shade of his feelings.

4

With the whole force of his impulses Segantini had gained mastery over light and colour. Then sad moods began to intermingle with his triumphant joy, which were of a similar character to those he had experienced in Brianza. The inner reasons for this new change cannot be definitely ascertained. It is, however, permissible to make certain conjectures on the basis of general experience.

This vacillation between two extremes becomes comprehensible through our knowledge of the instinctual life of the neurotic. The opposing impulses are not harmoniously blended. If one of them dominates the conscious mind the other becomes repressed into the unconscious, there to remain active. In the guise of neurotic substitute-formations it gains admission to consciousness. If, for example, active masculinity has the upper hand and is about to become the dominant impulse with all the vigour characteristic of neurotic drives, the repressed feminine component is activated to the point where it breaks through into consciousness. The triumphant mood is then mixed with melancholic feelings.

There is a further factor at work in Segantini. By exerting all his energies he had perfected his artistic technique, and had wrested from nature the secrets of colour and light. Having gained the object for which he had striven, tension was suddenly relaxed. This achievement had been made possible by the sublimation of instincts which were suddenly deprived of their aim. These instincts seek a new aim and further outlet, success having made them more demanding. If such demands cannot be immediately fulfilled depression sets in and produces the feeling of being poorer than before, poorer in hopes, with the exultation of victory giving way to despair.

The Hour of Sadness is the title of the first picture which Segantini painted in this mood. It is in marked contrast to his preceding works. Again we encounter the evening twilight. 'A young peasant woman sits shivering on the stony ground, in front of a small smoking cauldron under which a red fire glimmers. It is evening. She is sunk in sad thoughts. Opposite her stands a brown and white cow stretching its neck and lowing.' (Servaes.)

The mood of the picture is one of lonely despondency. The artist's wonderful command of technique, however, brings the woman, the animal and the landscape into close communion. The consoling message to be drawn from the picture is that man is not deserted as long as he feels at one with nature. Such was the creed of the artist, who did not acknowledge the beneficence of a personal, paternal god.

Not long after the completion of this picture Segantini was drawn towards solitude. It now became apparent how largely all the artist's works sprang from the depths of his emotional life. He found in the little village of Tusagn, high above Savognin, the solitude which reflected his mood. There during the summer of the year 1893 he lived in a hut surrounded by rich Alpine vegetation. He could have revelled in light and colour, but instead he climbed for hours up to a high mountain pasture, where no lush grass or beautiful Alpine flowers grew. There he painted this wilderness relieved only by a few sheep grazing on it. 'A sad shepherd, little more than a boy, but feeble and tired like an old man, sits beside his sheep. His face is sun-tanned, his head is lowered, he is almost asleep; his hands lie slack and inactive on his lap. The ground rises ever darker and greyer behind him.' (Servaes.) The picture is called *Alpine Pasture*. Every line in it recalls the depression of the Brianza period. Segantini finds but one comfort in the wretched desolation of the Alpine pasture. Where nature gives only a few poor blades of grass to her creatures, motherhood reveals itself in all its greatness. In the foreground of the picture he puts a ewe suckling two lambs. The symbolic message is that for man and beast a mother's love is the surest refuge from desolation.

In the years 1890–1893 a series of works were produced which have been given the name of 'Nirvana pictures'. As so often before, Segantini painted a number of variations on the same theme. The first version, which has the title *The Hell of the*

Voluptuaries, now in the Walker Art Gallery at Liverpool, and the last, *The Wicked Mothers*, in the modern gallery at Vienna, are among Segantini's most important artistic works. These, and in particular *The Hell of the Voluptuaries*, met with great disapproval. They were not understood, and despite many attempts could not be completely explained and interpreted.

This happened at a time when Segantini's artistic ability had long since received the appreciation it deserved. A picture that required interpretation was something quite new from this artist. His former works, such as the pictures of mother love, spoke in clear and simple language to the heart of every man.

The problem of these pictures has as yet remained unsolved. Will psycho-analysis succeed in unravelling the mystery?

We know that Segantini derived his inspiration for *The Hell of the Voluptuaries* from Buddhist mythology. There he found the doctrine that women who have devoted their life to sensuality instead of dedicating it to the vocation of motherhood are condemned to drift restlessly over lonely snowfields after their death. He painted a wide expanse of snow in which one can scarcely find a point on which to rest the eye; in the background a line of dark mountains, in the furthest distance a glistening snow-capped range. Over the desolate plain drift rigid, ghostly, deathlike female forms.

The later example, *The Wicked Mothers*, contains in the foreground a drifting figure whose hair is caught in the branches of a low tree. 'The whole curve of the body is one of weeping lamentation; the outstretched arms convey a feeling of helpless despair; the streaming hair entangled in the tree suggests the suffering of a suicide; and the deathly pale face, the twisted mouth, the sunken eyes are eloquent of the torments of remorse. The sight of the head of the little abandoned child, vainly seeking sustenance at the naked breast of the mother, cold and dried up in lovelessness, is most moving.' (Servaes.) The child's figure has been added. Instead of several women only one drifts in the foreground, and in the far distance a stream of penitents is to be seen drifting over the snowfield.

As Servaes remarks, the loveless mother and the abandoned child in this picture stand in sharp contrast to the ewe and the lambs of the *Alpine Pasture*. Both these pictures were painted in Tusagn. As Segantini himself wrote later, in the picture *The Hell of the Voluptuaries* he wanted to punish the wicked mothers because the lives of such women were, in his opinion, a violation of the highest principle of nature. There is no doubt that this intention was in his mind as he worked. It can be shown, however, that the deepest and most essential motives behind this work eluded the artist's consciousness.

As Freud has proved, all products of human phantasy, both normal and pathological, show a latent content besides the visible or manifest content. The latter alone is known to consciousness, whereas the latent content eludes it. It is the latent content, however, which is most essential and significant in any phantasy-formation. Without it the manifest content remains in most cases incomprehensible. The latent sources of phantasy-formations can be reached only with the aid of psycho-analysis. It uncovers the repressed instinctual impulses, which are only admitted to consciousness under a disguise produced by far-reaching distortion.

Segantini's mystical phantasy-creations have as yet not been understood entirely because only their manifest content has been taken into account. It is the task of psycho-analysis to search for repressed wishes which have found expression in obscure symbols.

These wishful impulses must have been deeply repressed and particularly unacceptable to consciousness, otherwise Segantini could have represented them with his customary clarity and simplicity. He could have achieved his purpose of punishing the bad mothers directly and more effectively. Since they are incomprehensible, the pictures fail in their aim of speaking forcibly to such women.

As we have already learnt Segantini had repressed the sadistic component in his instinctual life with great intensity. The aggressive and cruel impulses against his mother had been the first to undergo a change into their opposite. In all his works he had appeared to be kindly, tender and sympathetic. Now he depicted cruel punishment in the hereafter, and it was for mothers that such punishment was reserved. Here we see the early hostile impulses, the child's death wishes against his own mother, returning from repression. It is true that *The Hell of the Voluptuaries* shows several drifting forms, and does not give the spectator the impression that the painter is drawing special attention to any particular one of them. The later version, however, is very different. In this he directs our eye to one penitent in her lonely despair, and to the deserted child. Had not Segantini himself been such a deserted child? His loneliness after his mother's death had aroused in him the first torments of anxiety. Behind his wish to punish bad mothers in general now appears the unconscious desire to punish his own mother and to take revenge upon her.

All the anxiety and depression which Segantini himself had experienced in his feeling of desolation he now projected on to the penitent mother. The Buddhist legend, prescribing torments of loneliness for wicked mothers, had aroused similar thoughts in his own mind. No other punishment could so forcibly bring home to such mothers what an abandoned child had to suffer.

The boy who clings to his mother with the whole passion of infantile eroticism, and who watches her every step with jealousy, feels abandoned by her if she turns away from him even for a moment. He is overwhelmed by feelings of anxiety, by jealousy of his rivals, and by hostile thoughts against his mother. However much love she may give him, she remains for him the wicked mother because she can never give him enough. As psycho-analysis shows, the unconscious of the adult neurotic wants to take revenge upon the mother for the fact that she once gave more love to his father than to himself. Certain symptoms of neurosis express the son's wish for vengeance on his mother for this crime. Segantini's picture *The Hell of the Voluptuaries* serves the purpose of taking such vengeance upon his mother.

It is not difficult to understand why the loveless mothers should be banished to wide wastes of snow to punish their coldness of heart. The reason why according to Buddhist ideas the wicked mothers drift across the snowfields remains to be elucidated. One obvious explanation would be that the drifting women are condemned to the torment of everlasting restlessness. It is just this constant, uniform movement over the desolate waste which heightens the impression of eternal punishment.

The myth might have expressed this idea in other ways, for example, by eternal wandering over desert sands. The exact analysis of a myth, like that of any other phantasy-formation, teaches us how strictly determined is every element in it.[1] Segantini, too, must have had a particular reason for taking over this imagery of the myth; his creative phantasy had usually no need to draw on outside sources in this way. We must therefore search for a deeper connection between the guilt of the mothers and the manner of their punishment.

The key to the solution of this problem is to be found in a work of the artist dating from the period of the Nirvana pictures. This is the *Dea Pagana* already mentioned. Segantini had represented the goddess of sensual love as floating through the air. Resting her head on her arm in voluptuous abandon, she appears to enjoy the sweet delight of gliding gently, whereas the

[1] Cf. my 'Dreams and Myths', mentioned above.

Madonna-like *Dea Christiana* is absorbed in still and blissful contemplation of her child.

We are confronted with the fact, strange at first sight, that the same movement symbolises in one picture the height of pleasure, and in another the depth of torment. To the psycho-analyst such paradoxes are familiar and comprehensible. He knows that in dreams, too, floating may sometimes be felt as most pleasurable, whilst at other times it is felt as anxiety.

Many people clearly remember having experienced the most primitive sensual feelings in their infancy when floating through the air. This happens in swinging, in jumping from a height, or in many other movements in children's play. These are expressions of infantile 'auto-eroticism'. In other words, physical stimulation produces pleasurable sensations without the participation of another person, as is involved in normal adult sexual activity. Many children are insatiable in such auto-erotic activity. The pleasure is often accompanied by anxious tension. We have learnt from Freud's work that such anxiety is due to the repression of instincts.

The dream gives a refuge to the repressed instinctual impulses. At a time when auto-eroticism has long since undergone far-reaching restrictions most, perhaps even all adults, have dreams in which they fly through the air, fall from a height, or experience some such movement. The emotional content of these dreams varies, according to the degree of repression, between pleasure and anxiety, or may be a mixture of both. Here we may see the direct transformation from highest pleasure to greatest torment.[1]

The symbolism which occurs in the dream occurs in all unconscious activities, and is therefore common to all phantasy-formations, to the works of an individual artist no less than to the myths of a people. The symbol of drifting, as used by Segantini, now becomes comprehensible. The *Dea Pagana* surrenders herself without restraint to the sweet delight of drifting. The wicked mothers, too, behave according to the prototype of this

---

[1] The reappearance of auto-erotic wishful stimuli in dreams may have a further meaning. They may often be replacements; that is to say, symbolical substitutes for such erotic wishes as find no fulfilment in the waking life of the adult. The dream, formed like all human phantasies from wishes, represents the fulfilment of these wishes; but the actual erotic desire, which must not be expressed, is replaced by an infantile, auto-erotic desire. The unconscious retains the memory of the original pleasurable activity as the prototype of all such gratification.

pagan goddess, instead of emulating the ideal of motherhood of the *Dea Christiana*. We know that Segantini directed such a reproach unconsciously against his own mother. He says, as it were, to her: 'You have given yourself to the father in sensual love, leaving nothing for me.' He gratifies his repressed desires for vengeance in the cruel phantasy which underlies the picture. The supreme sensual pleasure embodied in the act of drifting is transformed for the mothers, and particularly for his own mother, into the most terrible anxiety, the torments of which they must suffer after death in the hell of the voluptuaries. For them it is a painful punishment to be forced to continue drifting for all eternity. After all, the few seconds during which, in the dream, we feel ourselves falling, seem to us an eternity.

During the period when he painted these symbolical and mystical pictures a strong turning inward is discernible in Segantini. His flight into solitude illustrates his tendency to reject the outside world. His art developed visionary and phantastical features. The more a man turns away from reality, and replaces the real world by phantasy-fulfilment of his repressed wishes, the more incomprehensible he becomes. His work fails to evoke in us any sympathetic response. This is what happened to Segantini.

Communication by means of symbols is chosen by those who must not give free expression to their thoughts and yet are unwilling to suppress them completely. Symbolism is both revealing and concealing. Sometimes one aspect is uppermost, sometimes the other. The veiled language of the Nirvana pictures indicates that Segantini's deepest complexes demanded some kind of expression, and that the artist yielded to this urge, but that the power of repression was effective enough to conceal the deepest meaning of his pictures.

Segantini gave the first of these pictures—*The Hell of the Voluptuaries*—to the world without considering whether it would be understood or not. This very attitude makes it clear how much he was at this period withdrawn from reality and completely submerged in his complexes. Still more remarkable is the fact that in his representation of the drifting female forms, Segantini ignores reality and defies the laws of nature. He has, as Servaes put it, represented the voluptuaries lying on the air almost as if on invisible cushions, and has at the same time depicted them as too heavy and substantial to be taken for ghosts. Furthermore, whilst he had previously valued highly the advice and criticism of his friend Vittore Grubicy, he now reacted violently against the latter's unfavourable opinion, and never quite forgave him for it.

Restriction to one particular sphere of ideas, and withdrawal from reality, invariably result in an increased irritability. We can observe this phenomenon in the everyday life of normal people, and it is especially striking in neurotics. Segantini's irritability is revealed by a remarkable incident.

In 1891 he exhibited *The Hell of the Voluptuaries* in Berlin. The picture undoubtedly had outstanding artistic qualities in spite of the objections which could rightly be made against the manner of representation. The selection committee did not consider it worthy of the highest honour, but gave it an 'honourable mention', and this was felt by Segantini as an insult. At other times the master might have passed over this judgement with a smile or a shrug. This work, however, had a special significance for him, and whoever attacked it was bound to touch him in a particularly sensitive spot. Thus the full intensity of his feelings broke through without restraint in his reply to the judges.

He himself gives an account of this in a letter to Vittore Grubicy, which is so characteristic that it is worth reproducing here.[1]

Savognin, 5th *August* 1891

DEAR VITTORE,

I have received your postcard and thank you very much for it. I rejected the 'honourable mention' without a moment's hesitation. Immediately I heard the news, which was on the 29th, I sent the following telegram to Berlin:

'Berlin—To the officers and committee of the International Exhibition.

'In no exhibition in the world in which I have hitherto exhibited my pictures has any committee found it necessary to insult me except the Berlin committee. I have just one request to make and that is that you will publicly remove my name from your list of commendations. Giovanni Segantini.'

P.S. I sent a reply paid telegram, but the ——— did not even have the decency to reply. It is enough to drive anyone mad. Farewell.

Yours,

G.S.

As already mentioned, Segantini completed the last version of the Nirvana motif in 1893. Soon afterwards a process set in

[1] Cf. *Collection of Bianca Segantini*, p. 85.

which revealed a tendency similar to the change previously noted at the end of the Brianza period. A letter to Vittore Grubicy, dated 21st December, 1893, clearly shows the transformation from a mood of depression into one of joy in life and activity. The artist refers to an earlier letter and writes as follows: 'My letter, which you call melancholy, was conceived by me in one of those painful moments which are like barking your shin against something sharp, making you cry out. As I am in the habit of writing only what I feel, I put this outburst in my letter.' Then follows a reference to his plans for future work, after which he continues: 'Yes, real life is an unending dream, a dream of gradually attaining an ideal, which is so remote and so lofty as to approach the infinite.' [1]

The most outstanding characteristic of the artist's psychological make-up was undoubtedly his quite exceptional capacity for sublimation. He now took a great stride in this direction in order to overcome the repressed impulses, just as he had so successfully done seven years before. Even for him, however, there were limits in this respect which could not be exceeded with impunity. He was no longer able to banish these impulses entirely. In the year 1891 he produced *The Hell of the Voluptuaries* and from then onwards, they broke through again and again, and the succeeding years, up to his early death, were filled by an inner struggle which resulted in frequent changes of mood. In the prime of his life and at the height of his creative activity he was subject to neurotic alternations of mood which denoted a negative attitude to life. Although he overcame these moods time after time, each victory cost him immense sacrifices of psychic energy and often only by desperate means was he able to keep the advancing depression at bay.

From this time onwards Segantini retreated more than ever before into the realm of phantasy; he himself stated that life in the world of dreams appealed to him most strongly. Apart from the picture of *The Wicked Mothers*, he produced during the years 1891–1894 a number of imaginative works in other artistic media besides painting.

Here belongs, in the first place, the project for a musical drama, which Segantini mentions in a letter to his friend Vittore. It is of particular interest that this draft contains one paragraph revealing the same sadistic impulses which I have demonstrated in the Nirvana pictures. This is the description of

[1] 'Ja, das wahre Leben ist ein einziger Traum, der Traum, sich allmählich einem Ideal zu nähern, das möglichst fern, aber hoch ist, hoch bis zum Erlöschen der Materie.'

a fire. The artist has endowed it with such powerful emotions that we immediately suspect that he is speaking from the depths of the unconscious. The passage is as follows: 'A woman rushes in flight from a fire, half-naked, her hair falling round her shoulders, carrying in her arms two children, one of them terribly burnt. At the sight of the burnt child the woman begins to scream horribly and flings herself in front of a prie-dieu by the wayside, where she wails and prays, lifting up both children to the figure of the saint. She then puts them down again. The burnt child is dead. She stares at it vacantly, screams twice in agony, rises and shakes her fist threateningly towards the sky, and then falls backwards to the ground.'

There is no doubt that here Segantini is elaborating an early childhood memory charged with strong emotion. An elder brother of his had perished in a fire. I do not know whether Giovanni had witnessed this incident, but it is certain that he was a witness of his mother's grief for the dead child. One would not be far wrong in assuming that this impression at such an early age had aroused in the boy cruel feelings which gratified his sadistic component instinct. It should be remembered that Segantini's first artistic effort followed upon the death of a child and a mother's grief. Only now does it become fully comprehensible why this incident should have made such a powerful impression upon him; it had stirred up the repressed memory of a gratifying situation in his infancy. The artistic productions of the mature man were dominated by the same repressed childhood wishes. Under their influence he created the picture of *The Wicked Mothers*, and the outline of a musical drama.

Other products of his phantasy during this period serve to over-compensate his painfully repressed sadistic component instinct. Take, for instance, the *Dream of a Labourer*, a Utopian piece of phantasy. The dreamer first has visions which are a symbolical representation of the class-struggle. Then he falls from his vantage-point, but without touching the earth he remains floating in the air, glides for some distance and comes to a country whose inhabitants enjoy perfect social conditions. In this Utopia the poet lives to rejoice in the realisation of his socialistic ideals, thus turning the originally cruel egotistical disposition into its complete opposite. A remarkable feature of this dreamlike phantasy is the feeling of floating; here it is a thoroughly pleasurable sensation.

His phantastic description of an ideal, artistic community should also be mentioned here. All these productions show how much Segantini tended at that period to withdraw into dreams of distant and lofty ideals. His own personality, however, did not recede into the background in all his phantasies as it did in these Utopian dreams. On the contrary, I have already indicated that the repressed aggressive impulses or the wish for domination give rise to phantasy-formations which raise the individual far above his environment and may even make him the centre of the universe. Segantini harboured such phantasies of grandeur throughout his whole life. At this point, however, they clamoured more than ever for expression.

In his childhood-phantasies about his parentage he had endowed himself with a king as father, thereby exalting himself. Now he glorified his mother as a divine ideal. I have in the first place tried to explain such pictures as *The Fruit of Love* and *Dea Christiana* as manifestations of the mother-complex, as an expression of sublimated eroticism, and of over-compensated sadistic impulses which in early childhood had been directed against his mother. It must not be overlooked, however, that the apotheosis of the mother also serves to exalt the son. I have already drawn attention to the fact that in these pictures the child is identical to the artist himself. Segantini did not stop at representing himself as the Christ-child; soon after the *Dea Christiana* in 1895 he painted a self-portrait which bore all the characteristics of a picture of Christ. The dreamy eyes speak of suffering and melancholy; their glance is longingly directed towards distant ideals.[1] There is no inconsistency in the fact that Segantini, to whom religious dogma was so alien, and who denied the existence of a personal god, yet painted himself as Christ. What made him identify himself with Christ was his ethics, his deification of mother love, and his suffering. Here, as in so many other cases, we see how the feeling of greatness may

[1] These phantasies of grandeur express themselves in Segantini in numerous small traits which have for the most part been disregarded. Whilst, for instance, the early pictures of the artist are signed with his initials, a number of later pictures bear no such signature. The self-portrait mentioned above carries only the year. Obviously his self-confidence had so greatly increased that he no longer deemed it necessary to add any identifying mark to his picture. The spectator cannot help noticing that several of the mystical pictures contain a tree strangely curved in the shape of an S. I suspect that Segantini has used this particular shape, which is reminiscent of the first letter of his name, as a token of authenticity. By this means he put himself in the centre of the picture, thus stressing how much he felt at one with nature, which to him stood for his mother.

grow out of a melancholy so deep that it may approach a complete negation of life.

Yet Segantini did not turn into an idle dreamer. He sublimated a large part of his repressed impulses with the help of his work, as he had done before. There even came a time when he gave himself up to an excess of activity. When in 1894 he left Savognin and moved to Maloja in the Upper Engadine he entered the last phase of his life, in which, as Servaes puts it, he became a fanatical worker.

5

Eight years had passed since Segantini had gone up to Savognin. He went there as a seeker. Through being in constant communion with nature he had matured into a master. Now he was again drawn to the heights, just as at the time when he had shaken off the depression of the Brianza period. He was thirty-six years old when he moved into the Upper Engadine. He ventured into the very heart of the High Alps. Fully confident of his own ability he could now set himself the highest tasks. He grew to love passionately the valley in which he was to spend the last five years of his life. He revered the mountains of this region with religious fervour. On one occasion he wrote to a friend (cf. Servaes, p. 202): 'Some mornings, while I gaze for minutes on end at these mountains before taking up my brush, I feel the urge to prostrate myself before them as though they were altars set up beneath the sky.'

Segantini inevitably took root here immediately and thenceforth became completely at one with the country, the landscape, the mountains and the people who dwelt there. He gloried in the glittering splendour of the snowfields and glaciers, the bright blue of the sky and the brilliance of the Engadine sun. He gloried, too, in the profusion of flowers which the short summer brings forth in unique, colourful splendour. His eyes grew bright with the wondrous beauty of the Engadine, and his feelings and character were more in harmony with this country than with any other.[1] The valley possesses an ancient, inde-

[1] The following observations may help to explain the strange fact that among those who love the Alps there exists a particular variety of Engadine enthusiasts. This enthusiasm appears to coincide with certain character-traits which in Segantini were developed to an unusually high degree. If love of the Alps in general often serves as an outlet for sublimated drives, this particular form of Alpine-worship seems to arise from the gratification of a specific complex.

Editor's footnote: The author himself, like Segantini, was an Engadine enthusiast.

pendent culture. Through centuries of seclusion its inhabitants have preserved their own language, their own customs, and their own style of architecture. It needed hard work and unflagging energy to render this high valley fit for human habitation. To these people and their country Segantini felt very close.

The first work he produced in Maloja is still pervaded by his mood of painful melancholy. The mystical and visionary element is, however, absent. With moving sincerity the artist has portrayed an incident of everyday life as if he were echoing in this elegy the depression of the recent past. A family is bearing a son's dead body homewards. An infinite sadness lies over the picture. This is to be seen in all the figures, the father, with bowed head, holding the horse's reins, the two women seated on the bier, the horse wearily pulling its load along the mountain road, and the dog slinking dejectedly behind the little procession. This is *The Homecoming*, one of the artist's most moving works.

Here again we find the light of evening, as in all Segantini's pictures of death. Now, however, he sees it from a new aspect. The colouring of the clouds in the evening sky is of exceptional richness, and this acts as a soothing balm to the mood of sadness which dominates the procession.

Then followed a number of great masterpieces, as remarkable for the depth of their meaning as for their perfect technique. Some of them may be mentioned here: they show clearly the changing moods to which their creator was subject. There is, for instance, *Love at the Fountain of Life*. A young couple approach the Source of Life, over which an angel stands guard. This picture belongs to his symbolical works, but in contrast to earlier examples of this kind it is free from anxiety and sadness; it is done in light colours and radiates brightness.

Spring in the Alps, painted in 1897, shows a mood at once more tranquil and more joyous. Segantini himself considered this his best work. It is painted throughout in the brightest and most luminous tones. *Hay-making* is more severe in tone. In this we see women hard at work in the meadows, recalling Millet's *The Gleaners*. Dark storm clouds gather in the sky and chase each other like ghostly figures.

The Consolation of Faith takes up again the theme of death. It shows a mother and father standing at the grave of their child in a small churchyard deep in snow. In the attitudes of both figures Segantini has indicated with great delicacy how they find comfort in their faith.[1] Apart from its realistic content the

[1] Cf. Servaes' description, p. 210.

picture also contains a visionary element. 'On the cross at the head of a nearby grave appears a vision of St. Veronica's sudarium with the head of the Redeemer. When we look upwards over the rugged mountains into the clear blue of the sky, high above, we become aware—through the presence of a small inset picture—of a comforting heavenly apparition. Two angels with great wings tenderly carry the small naked corpse of the child upwards into the realms of eternal joy.' (Servaes.)

The tendency towards mysticism and towards the transcendental, which needs further discussion, had once more gained the upper hand.

The series of great works of the Maloja period ends with the triptych *Nature, Life, Death*, which has also been called *Growth, Life, and Decay*. This powerful creation reveals the artist's longing to reconcile the warring instincts within him, and to unify life and death into one harmony. In the language of art he proclaims the oneness of all existence, and so his last unfinished work becomes a profession of monistic faith.

The years Segantini spent in Maloja were filled with the most strenuous labour. His craving for work, which becomes comprehensible from what has already been said, grew ever stronger. 'My mind, reaching out greedily like an old miser, burning and trembling, and with staring eyes, spreads its wings towards the horizon of the spirit where all future works are born.' This is what he said in a letter to Vittore Grubicy shortly before he moved to Maloja.[1] In the years which followed he proved that these were no empty words. His enthusiasm for work was boundless and spurred him on to the utmost efforts. In the summer he would start at day-break, often walking long distances to the place where he had set up his easel, a place which he changed according to his needs. He would work untiringly until evening. In winter he was to be seen at work out in the open even in bitter frost. Before he had completed one picture he was full of plans and projects for the next.

His enthusiastic urge to create, together with his fervent love for nature and his tender adoration of beauty were the forces which sustained him in his black moods whenever they overtook him.

The end of this moving spiritual struggle was now close at hand.

Of the three parts of the triptych, the one about nature was almost completed. During 1899 Segantini worked on the other two sections with great eagerness. *Life* was for the greater part

[1] *Collection of Letters*, p. 192.

finished. *Death* he worked on during the last days he spent in Maloja. This picture was left unfinished when, on September 18th, he climbed the Schafberg accompanied by Baba and his youngest son Mario. Next day the centre-piece was taken up there, where he intended to continue his work on it.

His violent creative urge had driven him, in spite of the lateness of the season, up to the height of over 8,000 feet, where a simple little stone hut was to give him shelter. On a clear evening he arrived at this, his last station.

There he stood among the great figures of his kingdom. The peaks of the Bernina shone before him in the evening light, and inspired in him the words: 'I shall paint your mountains, people of the Engadine, so that the whole world will speak of their beauty.'

After one day's work on the picture of *Life*, the weather suddenly changed, and he was stricken with a fever. Its onset was very severe. The attic of the little hut, whose flimsy structure afforded the most inadequate protection against storm and cold, became a sickroom.

The account of the course of this illness must appear strange to us. During the night, despite his fever, Segantini rose several times and, scantily clad, went out into the snow-storm. On the following day he dragged himself out to the picture which had been set up near the hut and attempted to work. He was so weak that he fell asleep, and when roused he was taken back to the hut only with the greatest difficulty. Completely exhausted he then lay down, but refused to send for a doctor, although the nearest physician, Dr. Bernhard in Samaden, was a personal friend of his. Mario, who for other reasons had to go down to Samaden, was only permitted to mention to the doctor a slight indisposition of his father. Soon afterwards the doctor sent a message up to the Schafberg to say that he was willing to come immediately; but Segantini declined the offer. As he got worse Mario was eventually sent down to Pontresina. He telephoned the doctor, who came through a stormy night, but too late to save the patient.

The dying man, with his family gathered around him, seemed to be unaware of the danger which threatened him. On the contrary he was at times joking lightheartedly. Then the sky cleared once more. He insisted on having his bed taken to the little window. 'Voglio vedere le mie montagne': these were his last longing words. Then he lay there, his eyes fixed unwaveringly on the chain of mountains opposite, which he had intended to complete in his picture. But in this glance there lay no sad farewell; this was the voracious gaze of the painter and the lover. It took in the colour, the form, the light and the line because he wanted to make out of them something that was to be the height of artistic achievement.' (Servaes.)

Segantini's behaviour in the last days of his life throws a flood of light on the struggle of psychic forces within him. Fully conscious of his strength he climbs the Schafberg; in enthusiastic words he there proclaims the ultimate aim of all his striving. Straightaway he begins to work fervently and when, almost immediately, he is stricken by a severe fever, he endangers his life by going out into the stormy night, exhausts his strength when he most needs it to combat his illness, and obstinately refuses the help offered to him.

We must ask ourselves whether it was only his urge for activity and his joy in creation which made him seek the heights. Did he climb up there merely to live and to work, or, apart from his conscious motives, was he driven by an unconscious longing for death? We can answer this question only if we gain the fullest possible insight into the part played by thoughts of death in Segantini's psychic life.

Early in life he had come to know the effect of death in his own environment. He lost first his brother and then his mother. He heard that his mother's death was connected with his own birth. He had been told that when he was born he was so weak that it was considered unlikely that he would live. He recalled that he had twice escaped death by a miracle. Thus he must early have come to the realisation that death is at all times close to man and this must account for the sombre element in his philosophy of life.

These sad childhood experiences, however, are not sufficient to account for the enormous power which thoughts of death had over Segantini. We must rather return to the inner motives which we have already discussed. The sadistic impulses, the feelings of hatred, and the death wishes had to be withdrawn from those objects on to which they had mainly been directed. They were partly transformed into thoughts of his own death, and partly sublimated by means of reaction-formation into their opposite.

The whole significance which the sublimation of death-phantasies possessed for Segantini becomes clear from the fact that his first attempt at drawing and his last unfinished painting both have death as their subject.

Soon after leaving the Brera Academy, he obtained admission to the School of Anatomy and there made his first studies of nature—studies of dead bodies. Just as, many years previously, he had steadfastly remained at the side of a child's dead body, so now, too, he was attracted by the sight of death. This was how one of the earliest pictures, *Il Prode,* (*The Dead Hero*) was created. As he worked, a strange incident occurred which left a deep impression upon him. He had propped the corpse which served him as his model upright against the wall. Whilst he was absorbed in his work the body which, exposed to the rays of the sun, lost its rigidity, overbalanced and fell forward. The young Segantini took this incident as a bad omen, and for a long time was unable to free himself from the fear of death.

This tendency to be superstitious, which was very marked in the artist, again reminds us of the psychic peculiarities of obsessional neurotics. The doubts of such patients are particularly concerned with the duration of their life and with their fate after death. In this connection, they are always ready to believe in omens. Segantini's behaviour was exactly the same. We shall soon discover more about this. *Il Prode* was followed by other pictures of death. From this time, for instance, date *For Our Dead, The Empty Cradle* and *The Orphans*. Then came the pictures of the Brianza period, with their mood of weariness of life. In Savognin the thoughts of death found their expression in the Nirvana pictures. Finally in Maloja came *The Homecoming, The Consolation of Faith* and last of all the *Death* section of the great triptych. These, however, are but a few examples from a great number of pictures concerned with death.

Premonitions of death never left him. He certainly warded them off, but they came back, returning from the depths of the unconscious. Among Segantini's notes [1] there is a story under the heading *An Ugly Dream*, which shows with great vividness this struggle of opposing forces. I reproduce here the first half of the dream:

'I sat in sadness in a mysterious place which was both a room and a church. A strange, idiotic looking figure, hideous in appearance and repellent in shape, stood facing me. It had white, glassy eyes, and the tone of its flesh was yellow; it seemed half-cretin and half-skeleton. I rose and chased it away with imperious look, and it withdrew, after glancing at me sideways. I pursued it with my eyes until it disappeared into a dark hiding-place. I thought to myself, this apparition of a corpse must be a bad omen for me. When I turned to sit down this wretched shape again appeared before me, and my whole body began to

[1] *Collection of Bianca Segantini, p. 52.*

shake. I rose up in fury, cursing and threatening it. It meekly disappeared again. I then said to myself: "perhaps I did wrong to chase it away in such a manner; it will take its revenge." '

All the essential elements are condensed into this dream-fragment: the terror of death, the attempt at warding off, the re-currence of the thoughts which have barely been expelled, the outburst of suppressed feeling, the renewed victory over the thoughts of death, and finally the resigned acceptance—they will take their revenge, and in the end I shall be vanquished.

Segantini regarded such dreams, as well as certain other occurrences, as omens of disaster. The more often he was frightened by portents of death, the more he needed to counter-balance them. This explains why he lent his ear to all kinds of prophecies. He clung particularly to a prophecy made to him that he would reach Titian's age. It is reported that he put his confidence in this prediction at the very time when melancholy thoughts assailed him with particular force.

He went even further. He took the road which is known to us from the analysis of obsessional neuroses. The most effective defence against thoughts of death, whether directed against oneself or against others, is the denial of death. That there is no death has been the wishful phantasy of mankind in all ages. Those, however, who cling most strenuously to the idea of a life after death are the ones whose lives have been most dis-turbed by death-phantasies, namely the obsessional neurotics. We find in them a particular form of religious faith, in which the belief in immortality plays a large part. If there is an after life, then the reproaches with which such persons torment themselves are groundless; those whose death they fear they have caused are not really dead; they live on in another place.

Once before we have seen Segantini deny the fact of death in a strange manner. He painted over the portrait of the dying consumptive, transforming it into a picture of the fullness of life. In later years his needs drove him to further lengths. He de-veloped a leaning towards the transcendental, and devoted himself particularly to spiritualism. At the same time some of his works acquired that mystical element which we have previously discussed.

As in the 'ugly dream', so in reality the thoughts of death gained more and more power over him. With an enormous expense of energy he overcame them; but whilst he turned consciously to new plans and new ideas, whilst he spoke in enthusiastic words of his programme of work, in his uncon-scious the call of death became ever more insistent.

Segantini himself relates an incident, probably occurring about a year before his death, as proof of the existence of a link with the dead. On a winter's day, whilst out walking, he had lost his way, had sat down exhausted in the snow, and had fallen asleep. He would certainly have died from the cold but for the fact that at the critical moment he heard a voice, which he recognised as the voice of his mother, calling him. To this incident he himself attributed his belief in a hereafter.

The study of the unconscious has taught us that many of the trivial incidents of life have a meaning deeper than that usually attributed to them,[1] though not in the sense of an omen for the future. They prove to be determined by unconscious influences emanating from repressed complexes. We may draw particular attention to the frequent little slips which we call clumsiness, picking up the wrong thing, or mislaying things. Such incidents have the appearance of being accidental and purposeless, whilst in reality they happen according to definite rules and serve the fulfilment of a definite purpose, albeit an unconscious one.

Of special interest to us are the frequent cases of suicide, or attempted suicide, arising from unconscious motives. Persons suffering from depressive moods may often fail to take the most elementary precautions. They may carelessly run in front of a motor-car, or by mistake take poison instead of a medicine, or may do themselves injuries which could easily have been avoided. All such actions may take place without conscious intention, and arise entirely from unconscious impulses. Into the category of unconsciously motivated suicide fall, for instance, many of the accidents so frequent in mountains.

It is remarkable that Segantini, who knew the mountains so well, who had painted them, walked in them, hunted in them, and had wandered over them at all seasons, should not only lose his way but should be foolish enough to sit in the snow to rest in mid-winter. His losing his way and falling asleep in the snow must arouse in us the suspicion that we are faced here with an unconscious attempt at suicide. This suspicion is borne out by the fact that sombre thoughts often broke through from Segantini's unconscious during this period, and that his longing for death was particularly marked. It was, however, no more than an attempt. The opposing will to live, which made itself felt in the form of a voice, interrupted the beginning of his sleep. The voice of his mother, coming from within, but projected by him outside himself, called the sleeper back to life. It

[1] Freud: *Psychopathology of Everyday Life.*

is precisely this which has such deep significance; motherhood was to him the guiding principle of all life.

Is it possible to draw conclusions from this incident which are relevant to Segantini's death not long afterwards?

Let us see what happened shortly before his ascent of the Schafberg. The artist's wife tells us the following story.[1]

'On the last Sunday which he spent in Maloja, he lay down on some chairs in his studio for a rest. I stayed outside talking to the children. When I entered I thought he was asleep and said: "Oh, sorry to wake you. You needed sleep so badly." He replied at once: "No, my dear, it's lucky you did come in. Just imagine, I was dreaming,—and believe me, I was dreaming with open eyes, of that I am positive—that it was my body they were carrying on their bier from that hut", and he pointed towards the picture with the title "Death". "One of the women standing nearby was you, and I could see that you were crying." Of course I assured him that he had been asleep and that it had been a dream, but he was still firmly convinced that he had been awake and had seen it all with open eyes. All he had told me he repeated shortly afterwards to Baba. Well, what he then saw came to pass twelve days later. His picture of death was the picture of his own end; they carried him in his coffin from that very hut. The scene was just as he had painted it in the picture, the woman in the picture crying near the bier was myself. It should be remembered that at the time of this vision he was in good health, so much so that on that same Sunday he continued with his writing. The following day he worked from four o'clock in the morning until nine, and then brought the picture, locked in a case, from the place where he was painting, back to the house; that very evening he managed to make the strenuous three hours ascent from Pontresina to the top of the Schafberg. He was so superstitious that he would certainly not have left Maloja if he had not felt himself to be in perfect health.'

In this waking-dream I do not see a premonition in the usual sense, but an expression of his longing for death, which forced its way into consciousness. A comparison with the 'ugly dream' quoted above shows one remarkable difference: where formerly there was a strong, even passionate rejection of death, there is now only frozen horror at its proximity.

Segantini's wife vividly relates how on the day after the waking-dream he achieved a superhuman amount of work. When he reached the top of the mountain he uttered those

[1] Servaes, p. 264.

proud words which seemed to arise from a feeling of boundless strength. We understand, however, that this urge to live could only withstand the onslaught of death-thoughts by the fullest sublimation of all the available instinctual forces.

It is said that right up to the last those around him were only occasionally aware of the sombre moods which Segantini had to combat. It might, therefore, appear as an exaggeration if I attribute so much significance to this inner struggle.

The struggle against repressed instinctual forces is, however, a silent one, of which a man as sensitive as Segantini shows as little as possible to the outside world. Until shortly before his death the forces ranged on the side of life were victorious. Only when the longing for death had gained the upper hand did the signs of the struggle become noticeable to those around him.

Thus it was with Segantini when he climbed the Schafberg. Then came the illness which was to prove fatal. Perhaps if his illness had not overcome him he might, on those heights, in sight of all that splendour, have drawn new courage to live, new energy to fulfil the promise he had made to the people of the Engadine. When this illness overtook him, who had never known what it was to be ill, the unconscious forces seized their chance. His behaviour, which has already been described, may at first sight give the impression that, relying on his good health, he had paid no attention to his physical indisposition; and, indeed, that is how Segantini himself explained his behaviour. Can we call it resisting, however, to open the gates to the enemy trying to breach the stronghold? As we so often find, the conscious mind seeks to ascribe to conscious motives, and to find a logical explanation for, actions which in fact arise from unconscious impulses—impulses which are not only alien to the conscious mind but which run entirely counter to it.

Segantini succumbed to the treacherous illness, but not to that alone. He might possibly have overcome it, but the sinister forces in his unconscious ranged themselves on the side of the disease, furthering the work of destruction, and bringing about his death.

Meanwhile, in his conscious mind, he clung with passionate love to all that life held for him. As death drew near, he cast his eyes with longing towards his mountains, to the beauty his art had sought to make yet more glorious. We are reminded of Moses who, at the end of his life, climbed a mountain from which he was vouchsafed a glimpse of the promised land, albeit this ascent was his last journey.

*   *   *

I

Spenti son gli occhi umili e degni ove s'accolse l'infinita
bellezza, partita e l'anima ove l'ombra e la luce la vita
e la morte furon come una sola
preghiera, e la melodia del ruscello e il mugghio de l'armento e il tuono
de la tempesta e il grido de l'auila e il gemito de l'uomo
furon come un sola parola.

These beautiful lines on the death of Segantini were written by Gabriele d'Annunzio to commemorate the all-embracing love of the master, reminiscent of that of Francis of Assisi.

We know, however, that the man who aspired to encompass with his infinite love every living thing, hid within himself the will to destroy his own life.

Psycho-analytical observation, which gives us an insight into the struggle between conscious and unconscious forces, enables us to understand and to sympathise with this inner duality. It reveals to us the whole tragedy in the life of one who died so young, and who whilst working tirelessly walked ever in the shadow of death.

EPILOGUE

In the foregoing pages we have frequently mentioned the psychological depressions to which Segantini was subject at various times of his life. The increased scientific experience of recent years now enables us to penetrate more deeply into the origin and causes of such depressive states. Certainly each individual case needs detailed psycho-analytical investigation of the unconscious if we wish to reach satisfactory conclusions. We must use the greatest caution and reserve in applying the general findings of the psychological analysis of such states to the illness of a man we were unable to study in this manner during his lifetime.

Psychological investigation teaches us that depressive states described by medical science under the name of melancholic disturbances arise from specific causes. It is not our intention to try to fit Segantini's illness into a definite clinical category. We shall only make a very tentative suggestion as to how far certain results of recent investigations could throw more light upon the psychic state of the artist.

Melancholic states follow with great regularity upon some event to which the psychic constitution of the individual is unequal. A loss may shake a person's mental constitution to its very depths and appear to that person to be completely unbearable and insuperable, so that he believes that never throughout his whole life will he be able to replace the loss or to find a compensation for it. In every case the loss is that of the person at the centre of the sufferer's emotional life, and upon whom he had concentrated all his love. The loss may not necessarily be caused by death; it may just as easily be brought about by the feeling that the previous emotional relationship to such a person has been completely destroyed. The most frequent example of such a loss is a serious, irreparable disappointment suffered at the hands of a particularly beloved person. It is the feeling of complete desolation which then produces the psychological depression.

An actual event of this kind is, however, in itself insufficient to bring about so grave a disturbance of the psychological balance as is involved in a melancholic depression or in similar states. The strength of the emotion which is linked with the incident is largely derived from earlier impressions of a similar kind, which at the time had resulted in the same kind of upheaval. In the psycho-analysis of such cases we get back, with the aid of gradually awakening memories, to incidents of early childhood, which had imposed tests of the utmost severity upon the inadequate psychic powers of resistance of the individual. Our experience is that in the case of the man it is always the mother who is the cause of such disappointment in the earliest phase of childhood.

In the case of Segantini we are certainly not in a position to go into all the ramifications of that process which formed a pattern for his later life. As we have already demonstrated, the artist must have carried over from his childhood into later years an emotional conflict which was reactivated from time to time by psychic causes.

The recent progress of psycho-analysis enables us to gain yet further insight. We have not only discovered that various psychic states in the mature person are patterned on the form and content of early experiences, but that in fact man is compelled to repeat his early experiences.

We have come to the conclusion that in Segantini's life a happy early childhood was followed by a time of desolation and an urge for revenge which was restrained only with difficulty. We find a similar alternation of varying psychic states in his later life. We remember the happy days in Savognin, filled with joyful activity, which were followed by such a sombre mood. The artist's self-imposed solitude is a repetition of that state of desolation which we have described, and which we must interpret as an overpowering urge to enshroud himself in sadness. It was from that period that the pictures date which, according to Segantini's own words, were devised to punish the wicked mothers. It is as if his unconscious had compelled the artist to repeat over and over again the happiness, the disappointment, the lingering hostility and its subsequent subduing all according to the pattern of his childhood.

If by means of psycho-analysis we penetrate deeper into the psychic life of persons who are subject to psychological depressions, they often reveal to us trains of thought very similar to those we have met with in Segantini. Recently a patient reported to me a dream which reminded me in a surprising way of Segantini's paintings of *The Wicked Mothers*. The dreamer was unaware either of the pictures or of the Indian sources used by Segantini. In the dream he saw a female figure floating through the air. As he beheld it, it became more and more like his mother. The figure came alluringly towards him, only to recede again. This process was repeated several times.

The psychological disturbance which had brought this patient to psycho-analysis was very closely connected with his relationship to his mother, which in his childhood had caused his love to undergo a series of severe disappointments. Originally she had been loving and tender, but had one day withdrawn all signs of tenderness towards the little boy, because he had reacted to them in a manner which was openly erotic. The reason given by his mother to justify the change in her attitude had evoked in the boy the most violent emotions. His mother had declared that she felt disgusted by such displays of affection. Both before and after this time, however, the little boy had occasion to observe intimacies between his parents and, as he believed, to see that his mother actively participated in such intimacies and even encouraged his father to them.

The mother in the dream who approaches the dreamer, only to recede immediately, now becomes readily comprehensible. Her floating attitude indicates sensual pleasure; this symbolism is familiar to us not only from many dreams but also from other realms of human phantasy. It should be added that certain details of the dream indicate a wish to take revenge on his mother. The similarity of the dream to Segantini's picture of *The Wicked Mothers* thus becomes unmistakably clear.

In cases of illness which follow the clinical pattern of melancholia we find, in the deepest layer of the mind, covered by such phantasies of revenge, the longing for the mother in her original role. In certain psychological manifestations this longing for the earliest satisfaction at the mother's breast becomes apparent.

One example may suffice to demonstrate this. The patient, whose dream I have reported, once found himself in a state of depression from which he felt he would never escape. At that time he was meeting a woman who in his psychic life represented his mother, in both her good and bad aspects. From her side there was no obstacle to a sexual relationship. She even gave him clear signs of her own inclinations. With him, however, it was otherwise. With his head on her breast he went to sleep. When he awakened he felt liberated from his state of depression. Whilst hitherto he had been despondent and weary of life, he now regained, at least temporarily, some contact with life.

How similar to this is Segantini's behaviour shortly before his death! On a winter's day he lies down in the snow, overcome with fatigue. After a time he is awakened by the voice of his mother, long since dead. He regains his hold on life and can, for the moment at least, shake off his mood of sadness.

The first and most lasting psychological contact of one human being with another, according to all the findings of psychoanalysis, derives from the earliest pleasurable impressions which are associated with suckling. The strength of this relationship to the feeding mother becomes apparent in human psychic life in many ways. We have already seen that earth, nature, and the Alps all represent the mother in Segantini's life. The ardour with which he absorbed the sight of nature was the strongest driving-force in his life for many years, even to his last words in which he once more gave expression to his longing for the mountains.

It thus becomes even clearer than before that the longing for his mother, originally gratified, but later disappointed, lay at the root of Segantini's alternating moods; by this longing he lived and through it he died.

III

AMENHOTEP IV: A PSYCHO-ANALYTICAL CONTRIBUTION TOWARDS THE UNDERSTANDING OF HIS PERSONALITY AND OF THE MONOTHEISTIC CULT OF ATON

(1912)

In the year 1880, near the Egyptian village of Tell el-Amarna, a great number of tablets with Asiatic texts were found. These tablets were discovered to be important historical documents, containing the strangest revelations, especially about King Amenhotep IV and his reign. The hieroglyphic texts preserved from that period, together with the 'Amarna tablets', make it possible for the historian to form a clear picture of the king's personality. We possess a number of reference books and treatises on Egyptian history which tell us an abundance of interesting things about that epoch.[1] They provide the material basis for the present investigation. I refer in particular to the works of Breasted, whose *History of Egypt* appeared recently in an excellent German edition, as well as to Weigall's outstanding monograph on the life of Amenhotep IV.

Egyptologists have taken particular interest in the 'heretical king', who assumed the name of Ikhnaton, a name to be explained later, and have shown a measure of enthusiasm which to the uninitiated must appear strange and even unintelligible. Three millenia and several centuries separate us from the Amarna period. When an authority of Breasted's calibre characterises the king as the most noteworthy figure of early oriental history, and is even inclined to give him a special place in world history, we are naturally eager to learn of the qualities or deeds which have earned Amenhotep IV such a position of honour.

[1] Breasted: *Ancient Records of Egypt*, 2. Chicago, 1906.—Breasted: *History of Egypt*. Chicago, 1905.—Weigall: *The Life and Times of Akhnaton, Pharaoh of Egypt*. Edinburgh and London, 1910.—Niebuhr: 'Die Amarna-Zeit.' In: *Der alte Orient*. Jahrgang 1, Heft 2. Leipzig, 1899.—Sethe: Urkunden der 18. Dynastie. Vol. 4 of *Urkunden des aegyptischen Altertums*. Leipzig, 1906.—Flinders Petrie: *A History of Egypt*, 2. London, 1896.

Amenhotep IV, who belonged to the eighteenth dynasty, lived in the fourteenth century B.C. He was neither a conqueror nor a statesman, as some of his ancestors had been. On the contrary, during his short reign the young king looked on passively while the world empire which they had built up fell into ruin. His greatness lay in another realm: the spiritual realm. One is amazed at what one learns from a few brief details about the fullness of this short life.

At the age of ten Amenhotep IV ascended the throne; at the age of twenty-eight he died. In the few intervening years he brought about great revolutionary changes in religion, ethics, philosophy, and art. All we know of this spiritual revolution leads us to the conclusion that the king was far in advance of his time. He appears as the bearer of ideas some of which were taken up after an interval of more than a thousand years. Whilst his forbears were mighty in action, this last direct descendant of the eighteenth dynasty was every inch a dreamer, thinker, idealist, philosopher and aesthete. He is the first great man in the realm of ideas in recorded history.

Those who are accustomed to study the mind in the light of Freudian theory must feel the life of Amenhotep IV almost as a challenge for psycho-analytical investigation. It shows us with singular clarity how a man of that remote cultural era was dominated by the same complexes and motivated by the same psychic mechanisms as the study of neuroses by Freud and his school has revealed in contemporary man.

*   *   *

It was during the eighteenth dynasty that Egypt first became a world empire. Thutmose III, a direct ancestor of Amenhotep IV, was its founder. During his long reign he extended his realm as far as the Euphrates. It required a considerable number of annually repeated campaigns to consolidate the Egyptian rule. From all these enterprises the energetic Thutmose emerged victorious. His successor, Amenhotep II, was fully occupied with the final subjugation of the Asiatic peoples. He surpassed all his predecessors in martial spirit, ferocity and cruelty. His physical strength was famous: no other man, it was said, was capable of drawing the king's bow. His son, Thutmose IV, who reigned only a short time, had little physical strength. He maintained Egypt's political power at its height, not so much through military exploits as through his marriage with the Asiatic Princess Gilukhipa, the daughter of King Artatama of Mitanni (Mesopotamia). When he died his son was still a minor, and his mother acted as regent until he was able to ascend the throne as Amenhotep III. This regency prepared the way for the advent of Asiatic influences at the Egyptian court. During the reign of Amenhotep III the zenith of Egyptian power had already been passed. He lacked martial spirit even more than his father. He was, however, an enthusiastic hunter who left to posterity a record of his prowess in the chase, in the same way as his ancestors had left a record of their deeds in war. At court he maintained a splendour hitherto unknown. The arts flourished during a long period of peace. This king, too, married a foreign woman, by the name of Tiy, which again opened the way for foreign influences. This had the most momentous consequences. Tiy was the daughter of a priest who apparently emigrated from Asia, and who was closely connected with the court. As she bore no male heirs, the king took a second consort who, again, was not an Egyptian, but an Asiatic. This was Tadukhipa, Princess of Mitanni, daughter of the king Dushratta who was then reigning in that country. In marrying her, Amenhotep III chose a cousin of his mother's family. Later, however, his first consort Tiy gave birth to the long hoped-for son, the future King Amenhotep IV.

In the years which followed, the reins of government passed more and more from the hands of the king to those of the queen. The country's foreign policy remained essentially unaltered, but in the sphere of religion the change soon became noticeable. The queen and her followers attempted to displace the traditional cult of Amon in favour of that of the god Aton, which up to that time had been less popular.

Until then Amon had been undisputed as the chief god of Egypt.[1] Thebes, the residence of the Pharaohs, was the stronghold of his cult and the Amon priests of Thebes possessed an extraordinary influence both with the court and with the people. The chief god of Lower Egypt, Ra or Re, had previously held the same dominant role, until inner political changes had shifted the centre of political and religious life to the newer capital of Thebes. The cult of Ra, however, was by no means completely superseded. We even find an attempt, characteristic of Egyptian religious thought, to unite the two rival deities into a single god 'Amon-Ra'. There were many such composite deities. The priesthood of a less revered god liked to add Ra or Amon to the name of such a god in order to increase his authority. Historians have drawn attention to the remarkable fact mentioned above, that the father of Queen Tiy

[1] For this reason the Greeks identified him with their god Zeus.

was priest of just such a composite deity, namely that of Min-Ra. Min corresponded roughly to the Pan of the Greeks. Min-Ra then signified a combination of the god of fertility and the life-giving sun-god. The cult of such a deity, Adonis, had its home in the neighbouring country of Syria. The Asiatic influence was on the increase at that time. As the queen's father was a priest who had probably come from Asia, the assumption may be made that Asiatic influences made themselves felt in the cult of Min-Ra. In the inscriptions of the later years of the reign of Amenhotep III, the name of the god Aton repeatedly occurs. He had been worshipped in the remote past alongside Ra as sun-god in the Lower Egyptian kingdom of the Pharaohs. The phonetic similarity between the two names, Aton and Adonis, is striking. Adonis was the god of the setting sun. The possibility cannot be ruled out that the Adonis-cult had originated in Asia and under the ancient name of Aton had spread from there. The best known historians mention such a theory.

As I have already mentioned, after the death of Amenhotep III the cult of Aton spread more widely. The beginning of the reign of the boy king Amenhotep IV coincided with this transitional period (1375–1358 B.C.).

The young king was of delicate and weakly physique; he never attained full health, and died at the early age of twenty-eight. It is also said that he suffered from 'fits', though I have been unable to find anywhere further details on this point. He was also said to have had visionary states. It has been assumed, with as little justification in his case as with other great historical figures, that he was an epileptic. Epilepsy always brings with it a progressive mental deterioration in the sufferer. If a man has excelled through his special intellectual powers, and remained to the end in the full possession of such powers, this alone is sufficient to rule out completely any suspicion of epilepsy. Amenhotep IV, as all the available evidence shows, was an idealist and a dreamer who stood perplexed and inactive when confronted with the pressing demands of life. He did not possess the impulsiveness of an epileptic. The far-reaching repression in his instinctual life and the marked reaction-formations in his character tend rather to remind us of the characteristics of neurotics. If we remember that according to established experience imaginative persons such as poets and artists always show some neurotic traits we shall place Amenhotep IV in this category.

If the young king was more or less subject to neurotic states, he certainly also possessed an exceptionally precocious and many-sided intelligence, and an emotional life of unusual richness. We recognise in him a type of personality still to be seen at the present day. Nowadays, too, we can often observe a family in which the general level of vigour and physical efficiency of its members declines, but in which the declining stock manages to produce one or two individuals who in respect of their intellectual qualities represent an advance, but in whom a neurotic disposition prevents a harmonious physical and mental development.

A glance at many family histories reveals to us how a personality may emerge who strikes out along new paths. The offspring of such a personality may often usher in the decline of the family. He frequently lacks his father's strong constitution. Even if he inherits it, however, as he grows up in the shadow of an overpowering father he is prevented from developing freely. He continues his father's work without surpassing his successes. His craving for power shows itself more in his increased demands upon life and in his inclination towards self-indulgence and luxury. The next generation shows a still further decline in energy and vitality, displaying a tendency towards intellectual over-refinement and sentimentality. Unequal to the demands of reality, its members drift towards neurosis.

This pattern of development largely corresponds to the history of the eighteenth Egyptian dynasty, from its earlier and more powerful representatives, through Amenhotep III to his son, the dreamer and philosopher, whose personality is now to be considered in the light of psycho-analytical knowledge.

In applying the psycho-analytical method to a neurotic we do not content ourselves merely with knowing the incidents of his life and the pathological picture he presents. We penetrate into his unconscious, uncovering its relations to the manifestations of his neurosis. Working in co-operation with the patient we reconstruct the history of his libido, that is to say, its state during his childhood, the effects of sexual repression, and the return of repressed wishful impulses into consciousness. Each case which we investigate in this manner demonstrates anew the importance which must be attached to the child's relationship to his parents.

We have learned that the unconscious of the normal person contains the same instinctual forces as that of the neurotic; that in him, too, the unconscious attitude towards his parents forms the central complex. The fact that the boy's libido is primarily directed towards his mother, and his first hostile, jealous impulses towards his father, can be observed over and over again in every human being. The only difference is that the normal person is able to sublimate these instinctual forces, which must be repressed for social reasons, and in order to establish a balance between drive and repression, whilst the neurotic swings constantly from one extreme to the other.

To take Amenhotep IV as the subject of a psycho-analytical investigation would be a completely fantastic and futile enterprise, without the clear information concerning his 'parent-complex' which the young king's history contains. The facts, however, which will shortly be discussed, are striking in their far-reaching analogy with the experiences of psycho-analysis.

In the marriage of his parents, King Amenhotep III and Queen Tiy, the queen undoubtedly had the upper hand. A woman of great intelligence and mental agility, she took the reins of government more and more into her own hands. In energy, initiative, and practical wisdom she far surpassed her consort, who during the last years of his life appears to have shown little interest in the business of government. Her influence is most clearly discernible in every department of her son's life. Right from infancy he must have been particularly close to her. His libido must have been fixated on to his mother to an unusual degree, whilst his markedly negative attitude towards his father is equally evident.

We can attribute the young king's lasting fixation on to his mother to another cause apart from her intellectual superiority, and that is her beauty. We are in a position to form a vivid picture of the appearance of this remarkable woman. A small portrait bust,[1] in private ownership, of which there is a copy in the Berlin Museum, shows in her features a rare combination of beauty, intelligence and energy. Her vitality is so fascinating that even today she cannot fail to make an impression upon the beholder. By looking at a mere reproduction the expert can comprehend why the refined, sensitive son was fixated to this mother to an unusual degree.

Such a strong and lasting attachment of the libido to the mother leads in later life to certain effects upon the eroticism of the maturing or adult son. It makes it more difficult for him, as I have demonstrated in an earlier paper,[2] to detach his libido

[1] The reproduction is taken from the German edition of Breasted's *History of Egypt*.

[2] 'The Significance of Intermarriage between Close Relatives in the Psychology of the Neuroses.' See this vol., Part I, p. 21. I have there considered particularly the frequent marriages between cousins. I therefore wish to underline the fact that the second marriage of Amenhotep III was to a cousin on his mother's side.

at the time of puberty from his mother and to transfer it to new love-objects. Not infrequently such detachment fails entirely. In most cases it succeeds but partially, and a tendency becomes apparent to form a monogamous attachment to one person, who becomes a substitute for the mother. The transference of the libido, once established, is usually final and irrevocable.

This monogamous trait is to be found in the young king to a marked degree. The incidents of his love life are simple to relate. Soon after his father's death he was married, before he was ten years old. He was given as a consort an Asiatic princess who was also still a child. It is noteworthy that this was the third time an Asiatic was chosen to become the future queen. I say the future queen, since for the time being the government remained in the hands of the queen-mother Tiy, and her advisers. When she grew up the young queen gave birth to a number of daughters, but failed to provide the longed-for male heir to the throne. Amenhotep IV did not, as his father had done, take a second consort, but remained with his beloved Nofretete. This fact is all the more striking if one bears in mind that the earlier kings had, according to Oriental custom, kept a harem. As Weigall has rightly emphasised, Amenhotep IV was the first of the Pharaohs to live in a strictly monogamous marriage. He never took more than one wife—the wife who had been married to him when he was still a child. He relinquished therefore, throughout his life, the right to make his own object-choice. He became attached to his wife with an intensity equal to that of his attachment to his mother. Even after he had attained his majority he liked to show himself in public in the company of these two women, both of whom exercised a considerable influence upon the government.[1]

[1] Another fact which might appear insignificant may be mentioned here. Among the love-objects of infancy to which the neurotically disposed may cling with tenacity, the wet-nurse often takes a special place. It is very common for the wet-nurse to remain close to the child after weaning. The child's pleasurable memories of sucking at the wet-nurse's breast are kept alive by her special devotion to him. In the psycho-analysis of neurotics I have often been able to demonstrate the after-effects of this attachment to the nurse. The significance which the nurse has in the dreams of adults has recently been shown in detail by Stekel (*Die Sprache des Traumes*, Bergmann, Wiesbaden, 1911). We know that at the court of Amenhotep IV the wet-nurse and her husband played a considerable role. A relief, for instance, shows the king and queen throwing gifts from a balcony to the priest Eye and his wife, the wet-nurse. It may be not

Immediately after the death of Amenhotep III, the widowed queen made it clear how strongly she inclined towards the cult of Aton, and how important it was for her to use her young son as the instrument of her plans for reform. At the outset of his reign Amenhotep IV was given a very significant title. To his name, Amenhotep, which means something like 'he who is loved by Amon', was added 'High Priest of Ra-Horakhti, who at the place where the sun goes down is hailed by the name of "The Fire of Aton" '. In this way the mother, as it were, prescribed the path which, according to her will, her son was to follow.

Aton was now officially established as the rival of Amon. There was as yet no indication, however, that a few years later he was to be exalted to the position of the one and only god, as happened when the king came of age. No one as yet foresaw the new philosophy, whose focal point Aton was to be. Tiy was wise and prudent enough to avoid too sudden a transition to the new cult; and also to avoid antagonising the devotees of the old cult. Moreover, it would at that time have been a hopeless undertaking to join issue at once with the priesthood of Amon. The first measures of her regency, however, clearly revealed where her true aim lay.

The first building which was erected during the nominal rule of Amenhotep IV was the temple of Ra-Horakhti-Aton at Karnak. A sculpture in this building shows the king, in perfect accord with his name, worshipping the god Amon. The same sculpture, however, contains the symbol of Aton, the sun's orb in the heavens, with its rays culminating in hands which embrace the king. We may discern here a diplomatic tribute to the Amon priesthood in the fact that the king is here placed in juxtaposition to both deities. Thebes, however, the capital and centre of the Amon cult, was given a new name, the 'City of the Splendour of Aton'.

When he was about fifteen years old Amenhotep IV himself took over the government. He had by now completed the process of physical maturation. It soon became apparent that the young man possessed a strong personality, and it must also have become apparent in course of time that Amenhotep would go his own way. Yet the mother's influence was unmistakable to the end of her life. The son continued with all his youthful enthusiasm the work she had begun. The attachment to his mother only appears in its full strength when his efforts to detach himself from his father are appreciated.

without significance that she was called by the same name, Tiy, as the king's mother.

The whole behaviour of the young king in the years that followed is evidence of his rebellion against his father, who had been dead for some considerable time. Unfortunately we are completely uninformed about the relationship he had as a boy to his father, but his attitude in puberty and in subsequent years is perfectly consistent with that which we can nowadays observe in many people. Their attitude towards their father unconsciously remains as dependent as it was in childhood. When they are grown up they try to free themselves from this inner dependence. This presents the external appearance of a struggle against the father in person. In reality it is the attachment to the father which dominates their unconscious and against which they rebel: it is the father's *imago* whose ascendancy they want to shake off. Only thus can one account for the fact that the neurotic carries on a struggle which, superficially at least, appears to be directed against someone already dead.

In the young king there existed, therefore, a conflict between two forces, the conservative and the revolutionary. We learn from experience that in such circumstances a psychic compromise-formation is usual.

After all that has so far been related about this youth, one would be inclined to expect that his rebellion against the father-complex would not take a stormy and violent form. Indeed, it will be shown how this rebellion against the paternal power and authority was sublimated into idealistic aspirations. At the same time these aspirations were directed in the most decisive manner against the tradition which his father had handed down. If, in spite of this, the violent revolutionary tendencies later succeeded in breaking through in certain respects, we may infer from this that the struggle taking place within Amenhotep was of great intensity. The revolutionary tendency was, as previously mentioned, offset by a conservative one. We can observe in Amenhotep IV a process familiar to us in neurotics. They rebel against the father's authority where religion, politics, or other matters are concerned, only to put some other authority in its place. This indicates to those versed in such matters that in fact they have never lost the need for such paternal authority.

It would be difficult to find more poignant examples of such compromise-formations than are contained in the history of Amenhotep IV. Soon after he takes over the government he finally breaks with the religious tradition, with Amon, the god of his father, and goes over to Aton, whom he endows with a power and authority such as no god before him had ever possessed. He thereby revives the ancient sun-cult of Lower

Egypt in a new form. By going back to the cult of Ra-Horakhti-Aton he acts according to the pattern of the oldest kings who derived their descent directly from Ra. To prove even more clearly how close he feels to them and how far from his father, he always wears the crown of Lower Egypt, that is, of the far more ancient realm, to which he had from the first felt more strongly drawn. There are further noteworthy symptoms to be added.

The first changes in the style of art date from about this time. They are particularly characteristic. Connoisseurs of Egyptian art will notice certain peculiarities in the pictures of the king by which they can be distinguished at a glance from works of the previous period. These are the elongated head and neck, the protruding abdomen, and the exaggerated length of the hips and thighs. Historians have tried to explain these deviations in various ways. It has frequently been assumed, for instance, that the king had some physical deformity similar to those portrayed in the pictures and sculptures of him. This theory, however, had to be abandoned when the mummy of the king was discovered. Deformities such as appear in the pictorial representations of Amenhotep IV were not found in the bones of the mummy. Weigall has proved, in a most ingenious and convincing manner, that the strange art-forms of that period are traceable to archaic patterns—indeed to patterns dating from the time of the most ancient kings of Lower Egypt. Weigall reproduces, in most instructive juxtaposition, plates of the very earliest Egyptian art, and of the epoch which concerns us here. The similarity between the style of this later period and that of the archaic period is perfectly evident.[1] By the revival of the most archaic style the young king establishes a particularly close relationship between himself and the earliest kings.

The meaning of the first changes in religion and art which Amenhotep IV carried through is clear. The king does not wish to be the son and successor of his father, but the son of the god Ra. He does not wish to worship the god of his real father, but an imaginary father Ra (Aton).

We are thereby reminded of well-known manifestations which have been explained by the psycho-analytical investigation of neuroses. They are the so-called phantasies of high parentage, also to be found in normal persons.

The father is originally, for the child, the prototype of all power and greatness. If the boy feels hostile impulses against his father he often degrades him, in his phantasy, by making himself

[1] Contemporary art offers, in the Pre-Raphaelites, an analogous example of this reversion to primitive models.

the son of an imaginary king, for instance, and by attributing to his father the role of a foster-father. To be a prince is one of the commonest phantasies of boyhood. In cases of mental illness such rejection of the father gives rise to delusions concerning the high parentage of the patient. The same train of ideas is also familiar to us from myths and fairy-tales where the hero is often brought up as the son of lowly parents, later to acquire the sovereign rank which is his birth-right. These are the myths which express, in a variety of disguises, the age-old conflict between father and son.[1]

Amenhotep IV conforms to this pattern. He despises his descent from his true father and replaces him by a higher one. As, however, he was in reality the son of a king, he could not raise himself above his father by the usual phantasies of royal parentage: he had to go even higher—to the gods. It must be remembered that at that time the king of Egypt was ruler of a world empire. His power was surpassed by no mortal man. For his phantasy only one possibility remained: that was, to link his own existence with a supernatural being. The father's role could not be attributed to Amon, for he was the god worshipped by Amenhotep III. The influence of his mother led him to turn to Aton, or Ra, who had in fact been considered in ancient times the forbear of the first kings.

Thus the rule of Amenhotep IV was not ushered in by martial deeds or foreign exploits, but by innovations in the realm of ideas. At first they were not true innovations, but rather a return to the oldest, pre-historic ideas. As the king grew to manhood he added new ideas and ideas of his own to the old foundation which he had used as a basis. That this revolution in art was inspired by the king's personal initiative is confirmed by the valuable evidence contained in epitaphs found in the tombs of artists who had carried out the king's building projects. It was the general custom in Egypt that an epitaph should, as it were, relate in the first person the life-story of the deceased. As is well known, we owe no small part of our knowledge of Egyptian history to these inscriptions, a great number of which have been preserved. The royal architect Bek, who built the new capital, shortly to be mentioned, relates in his epitaph that he had been personally instructed by his majesty. One might see in this a piece of courtly flattery addressed to the king; but this would be a mistake. Even with-

[1] Cf. here my 'Dreams and Myths', and also Rank's 'Der Mythus von der Geburt des Helden'. ('The Myth of the Birth of the Hero: a Psychological Interpretation of Mythology'.)

out such evidence we can recognise the king's ideas in the plastic arts of that period; the painting and sculpture of that time are an embodiment of those ideals to whose cultivation the youthful enthusiast had whole-heartedly devoted himself. Mention will later be made of the constant emphasis on truth in his ethical teachings, and of the corresponding realism, which to us appears quite modern, in the art of his time.

Where his ancestors had aimed at an extension and con-solidation of their political power, he strove for a continuous widening of his intellectual horizon. He turned his interest to foreign art and to foreign religions and myths, and he seems to have succeeded in interesting the leading circles in his capital in his own ideas.

Two years after he came to the throne, when he was only seventeen, he took a step of the most far-reaching consequence; he founded a new capital which he named 'Akhetaton', Horizon of Aton. He built this city about two hundred and eighty miles to the north of the older capital, Thebes. He thereby publicly dissociated himself from the old city of Amon and moved nearer to the Nile delta, that is to say, to the oldest part of the empire. The new city of Aton lay on the site of the present day Tell el-Amarna. It was here that the tablets mentioned above were discovered. Soon palaces and temples of great splendour arose. In both Nubia and Syria new cities were founded, their names expressing the fact that they were dedi-cated to the god Aton. Two years later, at the age of nineteen, Amenhotep IV finally left Thebes and moved his residence to Akhetaton. At the same time he changed his name and thence-forward called himself Ikhnaton, 'he who is agreeable to Aton.' [1]

Meanwhile grave conflicts with the Amon priesthood, who were opposed to these innovations, developed. Ikhnaton never-theless carried out his intentions with unswerving determination. He dissolved and dispossessed all religious bodies hostile to Aton, and by waging a campaign against the worship of all other gods, raised Aton to be the only god in the land. He declared war above all upon Amon. He sought to obliterate all traces of the god after whom his father and himself had been named. Never again was that hated name to be uttered. He therefore caused the name of Amon, as well as that of his father, Amen-hotep, to be removed from all inscriptions and memorials. In this strange act of purification the ancient, long-suppressed or sublimated hostility of the son breaks through in an aggressive

[1] The king's daughters were given at birth such names as 'Merit-Aton' (Beloved of Aton), or 'Beket-Aton' (Servant of Aton).

manner. This action of the king seems like the realisation of an ancient oriental curse directed against a malignant foe, expressing the wish that his memory be extinguished. Ikhnaton strove to erase the memory of Amon, and with it that of his own father. Later, when his mother Tiy died, he took the final step towards that end. Tiy's embalmed body was not interred beside that of her consort, but in a new mausoleum near the city of Aton, in which Ikhnaton himself one day wished to rest. In the epitaph she is described as the consort of 'Nebmaara'. Nebmaara was a personal name of Amenhotep III, but one which he did not use officially when king. It is even more noteworthy that the word 'mother' is not written in hieroglyphics with the customary sign of the vulture, but in letters. The sign of the vulture signifies not only 'mother', but also the goddess Mut who was Amon's consort. The sign would therefore have contained a distinct, albeit indirect, reference to Amon, and for this reason had to be avoided. Ikhnaton wanted to lie in death next to his mother, whom he had separated from her consort. His rivalry with his father for the possession of his mother was to extend beyond the grave. So he realised with the dead what he had been unable to achieve with the living. In this respect he particularly reminds us of the behaviour of neurotics.

The manner in which the king henceforth seized every opportunity to describe himself as the son of Aton was as conspicuous as his avoidance of his father's name. The inscriptions of Akhetaton show this clearly. There is one, for instance, which says with reference to a region dedicated to the god, 'The region from . . . to . . . shall belong to my father Aton.'

The building of the new residence and of its sanctuaries went hand in hand with the further development of the new religion and its cult.

Aton is the father of Ikhnaton, but not in the same sense as Ra was once believed to be the father of the first kings. The new god is an idealised father, and he is not only the king's father in the strictest sense of the word, but the father of all creatures and the founder of the universe. He is not, as were Ra and Amon, a god among or above other gods, but the one and only god, not a local but a universal god, to whom all creatures are equally near.

It must be particularly emphasised that Ikhnaton did not worship the sun as a god, but that he personified in Aton the warmth of the sun as the life-giving power. Breasted rightly stresses this in the following words: 'While he made no attempt to conceal the identity of his new deity with the old sun-god, Re, it was not merely sun-worship; the word Aton was employed in place of the old word for "god" (nuter), and the god is clearly distinguished from the material sun. To the old sun-god's name is appended the explanatory phrase, under his name: "Heat which is in the Sun (Aton)", and he is likewise called "Lord of the Sun (Aton)".'

Flinders Petrie sees in Ikhnaton a prophet of monotheism, but one may well go considerably further. Ikhnaton's teachings not only contain essential elements of the Jewish monotheism of the Old Testament, but are in many ways in advance of it. The same holds true if Ikhnaton's ideas are compared with those of Christianity, thirteen centuries nearer our time. There is much in them that reminds us of modern concepts which have evolved under the influence of natural science.

The prayers and hymns which survive from that time, the most important of which we shall shortly reproduce, clearly demonstrate Ikhnaton's conception of the essential nature of the one true god. Aton is the loving, infinitely good being, pervading space and time. Such goodness and tenderness had been completely alien to the earlier Egyptian gods, just as it had been alien to the human beings who worshipped them. Aton knows nothing of the hatred, the jealousy, and the punishment of the God of the Old Testament. He is the lord of peace, not of war. He is free from all human passions. Ikhnaton does not imagine him as corporeal, like the old gods, but as spiritual and impersonal. He therefore forbids all pictorial representation of this god, thus making himself in this respect a forerunner of Moses the lawgiver. Aton is the life-giving force to which all living things owe their existence.

Weigall points out that Ikhnaton's conception of god has more in common with the Christian than with the Mosaic conception. The following remark of his is especially relevant: 'The faith of the patriarchs is the lineal ancestor of the Christian faith, but the creed of Akhnaton is its isolated prototype.' (p. 117.)

The whole world of ideas and the whole religious system of Ikhnaton show a unique tendency towards spiritualisation. Idolatry was discarded and along with it all the old trappings and appendages of religion. The ceremonial of the Aton cult was extremely simple, and everything was directed towards the greatest possible spiritual intensity. There were no obscuring mysteries. The meaning of the new creed was presented in a comprehensible and arresting form in the hymns composed by the king. Furthermore, there was nothing suggestive of a withdrawal from the world or of asceticism. The gods of death and the underworld were also discarded, and even Osiris lost his significance. The torments of hell, which had formed an essential part of the old creed, were no longer mentioned. Only one single wish was ascribed to the dead: the desire to see again the light of the sun, that is, the splendour of Aton. Thenceforth the one plea in prayers carved on tombstones was that the soul might see the light.

The great hymn mentioned above illustrates better than any description the religious ideas of Ikhnaton. For this reason it is here reproduced in full.[1]

UNIVERSAL SPLENDOUR AND POWER OF ATON

Thou dawnest beautifully in the horizon of the sky,
O living Aton who wast the Beginning of life!
When thou didst rise in the eastern horizon,
Thou didst fill every land with thy beauty.
Thou art beautiful, great, glittering, high over every land,
Thy rays, they encompass the lands, even to the end of all that thou hast
　　made.
Thou art Re, and thou penetratest to the very end of them;[2]
Thou bindest them for thy beloved son (the Pharaoh).

[1] Editor's footnote: The translation in the German text was taken from the German edition of Breasted's *History of Egypt*. I have instead used the more recent version given in *The Dawn of Conscience*, Scribner, New York, 1934, of which the author writes in a footnote: 'Some changes in the above translation, as compared with that in the author's *History*, are due to a few new readings in Davies's carefully copied text (*Rock Tombs of El Amarna*, Vol. VI. pl. XXVII, London), as well as to further study of the document also. A translation by Sethe has added some interesting new interpretations of which I have adopted several (see H. Schaefer, *Amarna in Religion und Kunst*, pp. 63–70, Leipzig, 1931). The divisions into strophes are not in the original, but are indicated here for the sake of clearness. Titles of the strophes have been inserted to aid the modern reader.'

The following explanatory note is given in Breasted's *The Dawn of Conscience:* 'Words enclosed in half-brackets ⌈thus⌉ are of uncertain meaning in the original. Words enclosed in brackets are restorations, supposed to have been either originally in the source and now lost, or justifiably to be understood as the meaning of the original. Words enclosed in parentheses are explanations by the author and are not in the original.'

[2] Footnote from Breasted's *Dawn of Conscience*. 'There is a pun here on the word Re, which is the same as the word used for "end".'

Though thou art far away, thy rays are upon earth;
Though thou art in the faces of men, thy footsteps are unseen.

NIGHT AND MAN

When thou settest in the western horizon of the sky,
The earth is in darkness like death.
They sleep in their chambers,
Their heads are wrapped up,
Their nostrils are stopped,
And none seeth the other,
While all their things are stolen,
Which are under their heads,
And they know it not.

NIGHT AND ANIMALS

Every lion cometh forth from his den,
All serpents, they sting.
Darkness broods,
The world is in silence,
He that made them resteth in his horizon.

DAY AND MAN

Bright is the earth when thou risest in the horizon;
When thou shinest as Aton by day
Thou drivest away the darkness.
When thou sendest forth thy rays,
The Two Lands (Egypt) are in daily festivity.
Men waken and stand upon their feet
When thou hast raised them up.
Their limbs bathed, they take their clothing,
Their arms uplifted in adoration to thy dawning.
Then in all the world they do their work.

DAY AND THE ANIMALS AND PLANTS

All cattle rest upon their pasturage,
The trees and the plants flourish,
The birds flutter in their marshes,
Their wings uplifted in adoration to thee.
All the antelopes dance upon their feet,
All creatures that fly or alight,
They live when thou hast shone upon them.

DAY AND THE WATERS

The barques sail up-stream and down-stream alike.
Every highway is open because thou dawnest.
The fish in the river leap up before thee.
Thy rays are in the midst of the great green sea.

CREATION OF MAN

Creator of the germ in woman,
Who makest seed into men,
Making alive the son in the body of his mother,
Soothing him that he may not weep,
Nurse even in the womb,
Giver of breath to sustain alive every one that he maketh!
When he descendeth from the body (of his mother) on the day of his birth,
Thou openest his mouth altogether,
Thou suppliest his necessities.

CREATION OF ANIMALS

When the fledgling in the egg chirps in the shell,
Thou givest him breath in the midst of it to preserve him alive.
Thou hast made for him his term in the egg, for breaking it.
He cometh forth from the egg to chirp at his term;

*   *   *

He goeth about upon his two feet
When he cometh forth therefrom.

UNIVERSAL CREATION

How manifold are thy works!
They are hidden before men
O sole God, beside whom there is no other.
Thou didst create the earth according to thy heart.[1]
While thou wast alone:
Even men, all herds of cattle and the antelopes;
All that are upon the earth,
That go about upon their feet;
They that are on high,
That fly with their wings.

[1] Footnote from Breasted's *Dawn of Conscience*. 'The word "heart" may mean either "pleasure" or "understanding" here.'

The highland countries, Syria and Kush,
And the land of Egypt;
Thou settest every man into his place,
Thou suppliest their necessities,
Every one has his food,
And his days are reckoned.
The tongues are divers in speech,
Their forms likewise and their skins are distinguished,
For thou makest different the strangers.

WATERING THE EARTH IN EGYPT AND ABROAD

Thou makest the Nile in the Nether World,
Thou bringest it as thou desirest,
To preserve alive the people of Egypt [1]
For thou has made them for thyself,
Thou lord of them all, who weariest thyself for them;
Thou lord of every land, who risest for them,
Thou Sun of day, great in glory,
All the distant highland countries,
Thou makest also their life,
Thou didst set a Nile in the sky.
When it falleth for them,
It maketh waves upon the mountains,
Like the great green sea,
Watering their fields in their towns.

How benevolent are thy designs, O lord of eternity!
There is a Nile in the sky for the strangers
And for the antelopes of all the highlands that go about upon their feet.
But the Nile, it cometh from the Nether World for Egypt.

THE SEASONS

Thy rays nourish [2] *every garden;*
When thou risest they live,
They grow by thee.
Thou makest seasons
In order to make develop all that thou hast made.

[1] Footnote from Breasted's *Dawn of Conscience*. 'The word is one used only of the people of Egypt.'
[2] Footnote from Breasted's *Dawn of Conscience*. 'The word used implies the nourishment of a mother at the breast.'

Winter to bring them coolness,
And heat that they may taste thee.

UNIVERSAL DOMINION

Thou didst make the distant sky in order to rise therein,
In order to behold all that thou hast made,
While thou wast yet alone
Shining in thy form as living Aton,
Dawning, glittering, going afar and returning.
Thou makest millions of forms
Through thyself alone;
Cities, villages, and fields, highways and rivers.
All eyes see thee before them,
For thou art Aton of the day over the earth.
When thou hast gone away,
And all men, whose faces thou hast fashioned
In order that thou mightest no longer see thyself alone,
[Have fallen asleep, so that not] one [seeth] that which thou hast made,
Yet art thou still in my heart.

REVELATION TO THE KING

*   *   *

There is no other that knoweth thee
Save thy son Ikhnaton.
Thou hast made him wise
In thy designs and in thy might.

UNIVERSAL MAINTENANCE

The world subsists in thy hand,
Even as thou hast made them.
When thou hast risen they live,
When thou settest they die;
For thou art length of life of thyself,
Men live through thee
The eyes of men see beauty
Until thou settest.
All labour is put away
When thou settest in the west.
When thou risest again
[Thou] makest ⌐every hand⌐ to flourish for the king

And ⌜prosperity⌝ is in every foot,
Since thou didst establish the world,
And raise them up for thy son,
Who came forth from thy flesh,
The king of Upper and Lower Egypt,
Living in Truth, Lord of the Two Lands,
Nefer-khepru-Re, Wan-Re (Ikhnaton),
Son of Re, living in Truth, lord of diadems,
Ikhnaton, whose life is long;
(And for) the chief royal wife, his beloved,
Mistress of the Two Lands, Nefer-nefru-Aton, Nofretete,
Living and flourishing for ever and ever.'[1]

The language of the poem is so clear that it needs no comment. We shall merely point out some particularly characteristic passages. The introductory verse describes the love of Aton, which encompasses all lands and all creatures. This is probably the first time in the spiritual life of mankind that love is extolled as the power which conquers the world. We shall return to this when discussing Ikhnaton's ethics.

The description of divine kindness, in which all beings share without distinction, strongly reminds us of the Hebrew Psalms. Breasted and other authors draw special attention to the surprising similarity between certain parts of the Aton-hymn and the 104th Psalm. Verses 20–24 and 27–30, in particular, reveal this likeness.

Thou makest darkness, and it is night: wherein all the beasts of the forest do creep forth.

The young lions roar after their prey, and seek their meat from God.

The sun ariseth, they gather themselves together, and lay them down in their dens.

Man goeth forth unto his work and to his labour until the evening.

O Lord, how manifold are thy works! in wisdom hast thou made them all: the earth is full of thy riches.

These wait all upon thee; that thou mayest give them their meat in due season.

That thou givest them they gather: thou openest thine hand, they are filled with good.

[1] 'The Universal Splendour and Power of Aton' from *The Dawn of Conscience* by James Henry Breasted. Published by Charles Scribner's Sons, New York and used with their permission.

Thou hidest thy face, they are troubled: thou takest away their breath,
*   they die, and return to their dust.*
Thou sendest forth thy spirit, they are created: and thou renewest the
*   face of the earth.*

One may assume that the 104th Psalm was composed under
the direct influence of Ikhnaton's poem.[1]

In his discussion of the Aton-hymn Flinders Petrie emphasises
that it is completely free from any hint of polytheism, or of
anthropomorphism in its concept of the one true god. This,
though not entirely true without qualification, is certainly
truer than in any other monotheistic conception. One must
take into consideration that the Aton cult, in its deepest sense,
is the worship of a natural force, in itself an impersonal entity.

As previously mentioned, Aton was not pictorially represented. He was symbolised by a sun-disc, with every one of its
beams ending in a hand. In such pictures, however, these hands
surround the king himself, with his consort or with his children.

If the king saw in Aton his father, then, strictly speaking, he
derived his descent from an impersonal power. We are thereby
reminded of the conceiving of Christ by the Holy Ghost.
Ikhnaton, however, is not conceived by Aton of a mortal
woman; at least there are no references to such an idea. Aton
is both father and mother to him.

Ikhnaton's religion cannot be considered on its own. It only
becomes fully comprehensible when taken in conjunction with
his ethics, which were really the focal point of all his interest, his
religious feeling, and his conduct of life.

Like Christ many centuries later, Ikhnaton rejects in his
ethics all show of hatred and all acts of violence. He desires, as
the hymn of Aton proclaims, to rule through love. He is
opposed to every form of bloodshed. Everywhere he erases
pictures of human sacrifices. All warlike aims are alien to him.
Worshipping Aton as the lord of peace, he eschews war in his
own kingdom. It is particularly interesting to compare Ikhnaton in this respect with his predecessors, particularly with the

[1] Weigall suspects that the 19th Psalm, too, owes its peculiar
character to this influence. In Verses 5–6 it is said of the sun, whose
gender is masculine in Hebrew: 'Which is as a bridegroom coming
out of his chamber, and rejoiceth as a strong man to run a race. His
going forth is from the end of the heaven, and his circuit unto the
ends of it: and there is nothing hid from the heat thereof.' Surely
we have here the remnants of a hymn to the sun-god, though it
remains a moot question whether this is of Egyptian origin.

bellicose and cruel Amenhotep II. It was said of him that he had the Syrian princes whom he took prisoner in his campaigns hanged from the yard-arm and then sailed his ship in triumph up the Nile. Ikhnaton's father, less warlike than his ancestors, had to some extent given vent to his aggressive desires in his passion for hunting. The son suppressed almost every expression of aggressive or of cruel impulses. His ethics were based in the first place on his unusually far-reaching sublimation of the sadistic instinctual components. The most serious consequences both for him and his realm were to follow from the rigid adherence to these ethical principles.

Ikhnaton tried to put his ideals into practice, especially after his mother's death, without regard for the obstacles he was bound to encounter. He wanted to bring the blessing of peace to his kingdom, which at that time meant the whole world. He completely ignored the fact that the time was not yet ripe for such idealistic aspirations; he also entirely overlooked the part played by hatred and greed in the life of the individual and of the people. He ruled over a powerful realm, which was bound to fall apart unless held together by a strong hand. Yet he attempted, after the manner he attributed to Aton, to enfold the whole world in the bonds of his love.

Ikhnaton not only scorned to extend or maintain his realm by force, but he also refused to exercise his kingly power in times of peace. He strove to approach his people as an ordinary man, and this meant a breach with all the traditions of the court. From time immemorial the pharaohs had enjoyed an almost divine worship throughout the land. Ikhnaton displayed a simple and unaffected demeanour, free from the imperious attitude of a ruler. He is shown in all pictorial representations as being simple and kind and without any of the heroic gestures to be found in old pictures of the pharaohs. In a number of pictures he is shown displaying himself with his family to the people. He proclaims to the people over and over again that he is not an unapproachable and severe ruler such as they had been used to, that he took no pleasure in exercising power and the prerogatives of kingship, but knew only aesthetic pleasures. He preferred to call himself 'the king who lives for the truth'.

It is this striving for truth which requires particular attention. It was centuries after Ikhnaton's death before even the most civilised nations came to condemn dishonesty. Ikhnaton, however, exalted truth above a mere ethical principle and made it an essential principle of art.

As Breasted put it: 'The artists of his court were taught to make the chisel and the brush tell the story of what they actually saw. The result was a simple and beautiful realism that saw more clearly than ever any art had seen before. They caught the instantaneous postures of animal life; the coursing hound, the fleeing game, the wild bull leaping in the swamp; for all these belonged to the "truth", in which Ikhnaton lived.'

Ikhnaton's sexual ethics need particular mention, although these have already to some extent been discussed. His rigid monogamy has previously been mentioned. All the available sources testify to the intensity of Ikhnaton's love for his consort. He did not take a second wife when the male heir to the throne failed to appear. Instead he took every opportunity to show himself to the people surrounded by his family. Nofretete bore him four daughters, all of whom he loved dearly. Ikhnaton gave expression to the happiness of his family life by particularly emphasising in all his public orations and inscriptions his reverence for the queen. He gave her many titles, such as 'mistress of his happiness'. In this way he tried to foster a new conception of marriage, and a different attitude on the part of the husband to his wife. It has already been pointed out that in Ikhnaton's reign women gained an influence at court never known before.

The tenderness of the relationship between the king and queen is most beautifully revealed in a relief which is in the Berlin Museum. It portrays the king in youthful, almost feminine lines, leaning on his staff, and facing him the queen holds a bouquet for him to smell. Nowhere previously throughout the whole of Egyptian art can one find anything either in execution or conception comparable to this.[1]

A carving in a tomb of one of his daughters who died young also reveals the king's tender feelings for his family. Never before had the mourning of a family for a dead child been expressed in such a way.

What a depth of feeling is to be found in the Aton-hymn! We have only to remember the description of the chickens creeping out of the egg-shells.

Closely related to his avoidance of all that is crude and brutal, is Ikhnaton's revulsion against all ugliness and his need for beauty. The Aton-hymn begins by extolling the beauty of Aton. It was not only the plastic arts which were Ikhnaton's particular concern. He laid out splendid gardens and revelled in the beauty of the flowers and the animals which they contained. He was also especially interested in music. His desire for

[1] Cf. the reproduction in Breasted's *History of Egypt*.

refined pleasures and his need for sublimation thus took many forms.

Ikhnaton's religion, philosophy, and ethics together form a composite system which is impressive even at the present day not only for the greatness of its conception, but also for the harmony of its structure. The ambition of the king to carry through far-reaching reforms which radically affected the lives of his people demanded the utmost energy. It also called for a practical approach which would enable him to assess the strength of the forces impeding him. The youth who had inherited a world empire planned nothing less than the introduction of a world religion and of one universal god. In the course of laying the foundations of god's kingdom, however, he lost his own.

It is clear that Ikhnaton could only strengthen Aton's dominion if he preserved his own authority as king. The more he effaced, in accordance with his ideals, the distinction between himself and the people, the more he made enemies of the priests of the old god. Similarly, the more uncompromising the reforms he tried to introduce, the more his influence on the people was bound to wane. Himself apart, only a handful of the élite were ready to receive his religion, which took no account of the needs of the majority. Weigall draws a comparison between the introduction of the Aton cult and that of Christianity. He comes to the conclusion that Christianity was only able to spread so rapidly and so widely because it gave scope to the needs of the people for physically tangible and anthropomorphic objects of worship. It comprised, apart from the one god, the figure of Christ, which was much nearer to man, the devil, angels, saints, and ghosts. The belief in a single divine being, invisible to man, would certainly not have conquered the minds of the people. This fact, rightly recognised by Weigall, also explains why the monotheism of Moses, which chronologically came soon after the Aton cult, appealed so little to the people.

We learn a great deal from historical sources about the internal changes which took place in Ikhnaton's reign, but very little about foreign political events. Nothing was done, and precisely for this reason marauding tribes began to overrun the frontiers. At the same time some of the Syrian vassal princes rebelled, turning on those who remained loyal. The latter appealed to Egypt for help, but all these appeals fell on deaf ears. Then in the sixteenth year of his reign the Hittites invaded Syria. At that time the king already suffered from the illness which was to cause his death two years later. Disinclined for any forcible intervention, he abandoned the gravely threatened Asiatic provinces to their fate. It was at this time that there began the strange correspondence which, as a result of the discovery of the tablets of El-Amarna, has been handed down to us almost intact. This correspondence consisted of a number of cuneiform tablets sent from Asia during the immediately succeeding years. They record the complaints, of ever-increasing urgency, made by the Asiatic vassals who were unable to defend themselves against their disaffected princes and the invading barbarians. A characteristic passage from one of these appeals for help, quoted by Breasted from Knudtzon's 'Amarna Letters', is reproduced here. The elders of the threatened town of Tunip beg for help against the disloyal prince Aziru in the following words: 'When Aziru invades Simyra, he will do unto us that which pleases him in the territory of our lord, the king, and despite all that our lord stays aloof from us. And now your city of Tunip is weeping and its tears are being shed, and there is no help for us. For twenty years we have sent messengers to our lord the king of Egypt, but no answer has reached us, not a single word.'

The disturbances in the provinces increased more and more, and one after the other the most important towns and strategic points of Egyptian power were lost; among them the towns and regions of Askalon, Tyre, Sidon, Simyra, Byblos, Ashdod, Jerusalem, Kadesh, and Tunip, the valleys of the Jordan and Orontes, and many others. Ikhnaton remained unmoved by all this; he continued to live in the world of his own ideas and let the whole of his empire beyond the boundaries of Egypt, which his ancestors had built up with such great sacrifices, fall in ruins.

How indifferent the dreamer on the throne remained in the face of all the perils threatening his empire is shown even in the last months of his life. Instead of defending himself against the external danger menacing him, he was intent only upon the removal of all traces of the former polytheism. The last important measure of his reign of which we have knowledge was the erasure of the names of the old gods wherever they still remained. Even the word 'gods' was eliminated. Such action was extremely ill-advised at this time. As the king's authority was declining, no overt pretext for rebellion should have been given to the people, or rather to the priests who influenced them. Ikhnaton took this very unwise step, and it seems that only his death shortly after saved him from living to see the forcible overthrow of his rule.

Immediately after Ikhnaton's death the counter-reformation of the Amon priests began. Externally, too, they soon regained their power. Ikhnaton's son-in-law, Sakere, was not the man to protect the work of his predecessor. He was not destined to reign for long. Ikhnaton was branded a heretic, and his work was obliterated just as thoroughly as he himself had obliterated tradition. His name underwent the same fate as he himself had prepared for his father's name and that of the god Amon. It was chiselled out, and even the vaults were entered in order to erase, the hated name so reminiscent of Aton. In addition to this, the mummy of Queen Tiny, which rested near the remains of Ikhnaton, was removed and buried at the side of Amenhotep III. As Ikhnaton himself once discarded his own name of Amenhotep, so one of his successors, who followed quickly one upon the other, was forced to change his name from Tutenk-haton to Tutenkhamon.

Ikhnaton was a revolutionary, but not in the usual sense of the word. He had sublimated his aggressive instinctual impulses to an extraordinary extent, and had transformed them into an overflowing love for all beings, so that he did not use violence even against the enemies of his empire. His strongest hostility was directed against his father who, however, was not hurt by it in reality, as he was no longer alive. We are here reminded in a striking way of the behaviour of certain neurotics who, too weak to struggle actively against the living, direct their hatred and their wish for revenge against the dead, although for the most part merely in phantasies, or in the form of neurotic symptoms.

As already mentioned, Ikhnaton, in spite of all his rebellion against his father's power, could not do without an authority to take its place. So he created a new religion according to his own personal needs, with a paternal god at its centre. He ascribed to him unlimited power, that omnipotence which every child originally ascribes to his father. He made him the one and only god, in transparent imitation of the uniqueness of the father. He thereby became the precursor of Moses and his monotheism, in which the one and only god unmistakably bears the features of the patriarch, the sole ruler of the family. Furthermore, he attributed to the new god the boundless love and kindness which were his own characteristics. He thus created a god in his own image so that he might, as men have so often done, derive his descent from him. In Aton Ikhnaton himself is re-flected with all his qualities. If he calls Aton, who was in fact a child of his phantasy and spirit of his own spirit, his father, then we see in this nothing but Ikhnaton's desire to be descended from a father who had the same personal qualities as himself.

In our times, too, as we know from neurotics, many persons construct a private religion, and some also their own private cult. They are, as psycho-analysis is often able to demonstrate, persons who in the depth of their unconscious rebel against their father, but transfer their need for dependence on to a divine being, to whom even the father is subordinate. Frequently they feel the call to spread the ideas which are rooted in their father-complex, and thus they become founders of religions or of sects.

In other cases the son seeks to supplant his real father by an ideal father created in his phantasy. This ideal father possesses, as we might expect, all those qualities and characteristics in which the son believes that he excels his father. At the centre of these phantasy-productions lies the wish to have begotten one-self, that is to say, to be one's own father. Aton, indeed, who for us is no more than a reflection of Ikhnaton, invested with paternal omnipotence and raised to the status of a god, is said in the hymn reproduced above to have begotten himself.

If Ikhnaton's attitude to his father explains why he became the founder of a monotheistic cult and of a religion of love, it still remains to be explained why it was just Aton, and not some other god, whom he made the centre of this new cult. Various reasons have already been put forward, such as the infiltration of the ancient Adonis-worship, the queen-mother's preference for Aton, and her influence on her young son. Such external reasons alone, however, do not explain the fervour shown, for instance, in the great hymn, nor the fact that all Ikhnaton's thoughts, his greatest efforts, indeed his whole life, were devoted to the service of Aton. I shall now attempt to give the inner reasons for the king's attitude, based partly on psycho-analytical experiences and partly on the facts of folk-psychology.

Recent investigations [1] have directed our attention to the significance of the sun as a father-symbol. Evidence for this is to be found not only in the psychology of neuroses and other mental disorders, but also in the phantasies of the most diverse peoples. The sun is, indeed, particularly suitable as a symbol of an only god because, in contrast to the other planets, it makes its way alone across the heavens.

As previously shown, Ikhnaton worships not the actual planet itself, but the heat of the sun. In the phantasy-life of

[1] I refer here particularly to Freud's *Psycho-analytic Notes Upon an Autobiographical Account of a Case of Paranoia*, and also to the Post-script to this Paper.

peoples, the warmth of the sun has the significance of a creative, life-giving force. This also holds good for Ikhnaton's conception. With him, however, as a sign of his unusually strong inclination to sublimate, we find that the warmth of the sun has a second significance; it becomes the symbol of the all-embracing love of Aton. The first verses of the hymn put this beyond doubt. The rays of the sun, which embrace the whole world, are identified with Aton's love by which he conquers every land. This symbolism is well known to us from the dreams of both normal and neurotic persons. Furthermore, in the pathology of neurosis abnormal feelings of heat and cold are very common. They are closely related to the eroticism of such patients, to which only a passing reference can here be made.

It may be permissible to take a further step, although this certainly leads into the realm of pure hypothesis. Attention has already been drawn to the relationship between Aton and the Syrian god Adonis. Adonis was worshipped in the shape of a beautiful youth who met an untimely death.[1] If one remembers that the young king worshipped in the god he created merely his own image, then one might assume that in his phantasy he at first identified himself with Adonis. Delicate and sickly from childhood onwards, and with the prospect of an early death always before his eyes, he might well have compared himself with Adonis. His aim, after all, was not to perform manly deeds, but to attain to a life of beauty.

Ikhnaton agrees with his god Aton in one particular characteristic: he too is aloof. Although he gathered around him a small retinue of admirers he was never in close contact with his people, in spite of all his attempts to approach them. An exaggerated sexual repression disturbs a person's emotional relationship to other people and robs him of the sense of reality. This leads to the auto-erotic restriction so often met with in neurotics, and especially in the most gifted ones; their own wishful-phantasies become the exclusive centre of their interest. Thus the neurotic no longer lives in the world of real events, but in another world created by his phantasy. He becomes indifferent to real happenings, as if they did not exist for him at all. Ikhnaton's behaviour is in perfect conformity with this. Living entirely in his own world of dreams and ideals, in which there is only love and beauty, he is blind to the hatred and enmity, the injustice and misery, to which men are subject in reality. In nature, too, as the hymn clearly shows, he ignores the domination of the strong and the affliction of the weak; he sees all creatures full of

[1] Cf. the similar figure of Baldur in the Germanic myths.

x

joyful thanks, leaping and dancing, and to his ears ever re-joicing in the glory of their creator.

Thus he turned a deaf ear to the cries for help from his Asiatic subjects; so, too, he was blind to the atrocities which took place in his provinces. His eyes saw only beauty and harmony whilst his empire fell in ruins. 'In Akhetaton, the new and brilliant capital, the magnificent temple of Aton echoed with songs of praise sung to the new god of the empire—but this empire no longer existed.' (Breasted.)

Greek mythology tells of the youth Phaeton, the son of Helios, who had the temerity to seek to drive the chariot of the sun across the heavens in place of his father. He was unable to hold the horses and, falling from the chariot, lost his life. The story of the fate of this son of Helios seems like a parable of the story of Ikhnaton who, with daring flights of phantasy, set out on a similar journey. In striving to reach the height of the sun he dropped the reins which his forefathers had held with a strong hand, and so shared the fate of many an idealist: living in their world of dreams, they perish in reality.

Head of Queen Tiy

THE HISTORY OF AN IMPOSTOR IN THE LIGHT OF PSYCHO-ANALYTICAL KNOWLEDGE
(1925)

THE clinical observations on which the following psychological study of a criminal is based, do not arise from psycho-analytical practice in the strict sense of the word. They concern the life-history of a man, on whom I had to make a psychiatric report as an army medical officer in 1918, and whom I saw again five years later in peculiar circumstances. The limited period of investigation ordered by the court, as well as the working conditions in a psychiatric ward, made a proper psycho-analysis impossible.

The life of this man, whom I shall henceforth call N, shows some quite unusual psychological features. A change in the pattern of his social behaviour which occurred recently is in striking contrast to general psychiatric experience. It is just these unusual features, running counter to our experience, however, which can be satisfactorily explained if we draw upon the familiar and empirically firmly established results of psycho-analysis. On the other hand the facts of the case of N seem especially well suited to indicate one of the future spheres of applied psycho-analysis, namely criminology. I therefore trust that the unusual facts of the case will, in the eyes of the reader, justify its publication in this Psycho-Analytical Journal.[1]

* * *

N was twenty-two years old when he was conscripted into the army. He had already served a number of prison sentences imposed by the civil courts of various countries. At the end of his last term of imprisonment he was transferred directly to the army unit in which he received his military training. His officers were fully informed of his previous record. Nevertheless what had happened so often in N's previous life was repeated once again. In a very short time he had become generally popular, enjoyed the special confidence of his comrades, and was a particular favourite with his company commander. No sooner had he gained the trust of his fellows, however, than he began

[1] *Imago*, **Xi**, **4**, 1925.

to abuse it. Just when his deceptions were about to come to light, he was posted, along with a number of his comrades, to the Balkan front.

As nothing of N's past was known in the field regiment it was even easier for him to gain the confidence of the authorities by his astute behaviour. Being a draughtsman by profession, he was soon employed as such. His demeanour made him appear particularly suitable to deal with money matters, and he was therefore entrusted with cash and sent to the towns behind the line to make purchases for his company. In the town X he struck up an acquaintance with some soldiers who lived there in a lavish style. His earlier tendencies, which will later be discussed, immediately reasserted themselves. He, too, behaved like a man of means and within four days he had spent 150 marks [1] of the money entrusted to him. On a second similar mission he learned that his defalcations had already been discovered. He therefore deserted from his regiment, and went to a larger town. Here he got hold of some stripes for his uniform and posed as a corporal. He had also purloined a number of railway vouchers from his unit and had stamped them, so that he could use them to travel to any destination at will. In this way he got back to Germany, but the strict military control there and his running across former acquaintances, particularly in Berlin, made it impossible for him to stay there for long. N therefore went to Budapest, after having added the insignia of a sergeant-major to his uniform. From there he went on to Bucharest, always using forged papers. Here the military control was so strict that N returned to Budapest. He managed to obtain introductions to well-to-do families; in the most winning way he undertook to procure foodstuffs; he was advanced considerable sums of money by these persons, but used the money for his own purposes and failed to produce the promised provisions. When Budapest became too dangerous for him, he went to Vienna where, however, he was soon arrested and taken back to his base. It should be mentioned here that N knew how to gain the confidence of people of any age, status, or sex, only to betray such confidence immediately. On the other hand he never showed much aptitude for eluding the arm of the law. Only when he was in prison did his astuteness reassert itself. Then he would contrive to make his guards careless, thereby enabling him to escape without using the slightest violence.

When N had been in custody awaiting trial for two and a half

[1] Editor's note: Approximately £8 in 1915.

months his influence on the prison guards who were normally conscientious and shrewd had grown so strong that the doors of the prison seemed, as it were, to spring open on their own accord before him. While speaking to N one of the guards was called away, and carelessly left his keys in the prisoner's cell. N took them, unlocked the doors, and was free. He walked to a small railway station, where he boarded a train which he left on arrival at the nearest big town. Everywhere he succeeded in deceiving the railway officials. For three weeks he worked in a department store. Then the danger of discovery forced him to leave the town. With forged papers he succeeded in making his way across Germany. In one large town he again posed as a man of means, describing himself as a historian of art. He obtained money by false pretences from his newly acquired benefactors and proceeded to spend it lavishly. After a spell of this kind of 'civilian life' he had to change the scene of his activities. He stayed for a short while in Berlin, and then returned once more to Budapest, where he donned an officer's uniform for the first time. He returned to Germany as a second lieutenant and lived for months in grand style in a number of spas, but only in the most fashionable ones. Everywhere he went the young officer gained an entrée into society. His poised and amiable demeanour invariably made him, within the shortest possible time, the centre of a large circle. If in any seaside resort the danger of discovery of his countless frauds became too great he would disappear and go to some large spa in the Bavarian Alps, only to reappear at the seaside after some time. Meanwhile he promoted himself to the rank of first lieutenant, that is to say, the highest rank attainable at his age. Nobody suspected the truth about the decorated young officer who could recount his experiences in so interesting and modest a way. Finally, however, he was arrested and once more taken to his base.

The proceedings against him had assumed enormous proportions. He had, after all, been guilty of desertion, had falsely assumed military rank and had committed an extraordinary number of thefts, forgeries and frauds.

The presiding officer at the court martial showed great understanding of, and interest in, N's psychological peculiarities, and as he suspected some kind of psychological compulsion as the driving force in N's behaviour, a psychiatric investigation of the accused was ordered.

I first saw N whilst he was on remand, but realised immediately that his case was so complicated that it would be necessary to admit him into my hospital for a more extensive investigation.

There were, however, no adequate arrangements at the hospital for detaining a prisoner remanded in custody, particularly such a resourceful one. When I explained this to the court, it was ordered that N should be put in a room on the top storey. Special measures were taken to prevent his escape. Three particularly reliable and intelligent sergeants were detailed for guard duty outside N's room. To avoid their being influenced by N the guards had strict instructions not to enter his room or to hold any conversation with him.

Consequently N was transferred by his three guards to the military hospital, and this move was accomplished without difficulty. Ten minutes after his admission I went to make sure that he was being accommodated and guarded as the court had ordered. To my amazement I found no guard outside his room; only three empty chairs. On entering the room an astonishing sight met my eyes. N was sitting at a table drawing; one of his guards was posing for him, and the other two were looking on. It turned out that on the way to the hospital N had won over his guards by telling them of his artistic ability and promising to sketch them. N's stay of several weeks in the hospital passed off, however, without any attempt to escape or other incident.

In order to form an opinion about N's psychological condition I needed above all to learn the story of his childhood. As he seemed to be a genius at phantastic story-telling, his own reports had to be taken with reserve and checked by inquiries in reliable quarters. I may add at once, however, that N's statements about his past were entirely consistent with the official information. I never found, in his many conversations with me, that he suppressed anything, or made any false additions, or changed anything in his favour. On the contrary, he spoke with the greatest frankness about all his misdeeds, as he later did during the court proceedings. Only when it came to revealing anything about his inner life did he show any reticence.

I soon learnt that N's delinquencies went back to the very early years of his life, and the files of the reformatory to which N had been sent for several years as being in need of care and protection fully confirmed these statements.

N was the youngest of a large number of children in the family of a low grade civil servant. As to heredity, there was no history of mental disease in the family. The boy, however, from a very early age and in complete contrast to his older siblings, showed an uncontrollable desire for aggrandisement. In his fifth year, when he spent the mornings at a nursery-school, he turned away from the poorly dressed children, and played only with those from well-to-do families. He had barely started school when he noticed with envy that some boys had posses· sions superior to his own, such as, for instance, a lacquered pencil-box or a pencil of a special colour. One day the six-year-old boy went into a stationer's shop near the school and pretended to be the son of a general living in the neighbourhood. He was at once given the coveted objects on credit. Now he could proudly keep up with the sons of well-to-do families. His first deception was of course soon discovered and punished, but his wish to rival his more fortunate comrades remained uncontrollable and found expression in further delinquent actions. One of his schoolfellows possessed a great army of tin soldiers, whilst N only had a few. The longing not to be left behind by his classmate did not let him rest. Finally he stole from his mother a sum of six or seven shillings with which he immediately bought tin soldiers, and showed his friend that he had as many and as fine soldiers as he.

N's ability became evident when he started school. It appeared, however, that his achievements were proportionate to his abilities only when he felt himself noticed or favoured in some way by his teacher. He repeatedly planned adventures which involved running away. On one occasion he obtained money from his teacher by false pretences; on others he borrowed books from his classmates and sold them. The experiment of sending him to a secondary school failed owing to his lack of perseverance. The phantastic trait in N's make-up always asserted itself. One of his teachers said of him that he seemed to suffer from megalomania. So his schooling was interrupted and N was apprenticed to a business.

So far N's delinquent actions had mostly taken place within the circle of his family and school. As an apprentice he soon began to steal money from the petty cash, and was discharged after a few months. He disliked his second job and left it on his own accord after a few days. He was then sent to work as a gardener, but soon ran away again, after which he got into bad company, loafed about, and was finally sent to a reformatory.

In the reformatory there occurred a series of events whose pattern was to be so often repeated later. The headmaster, recognising N's artistic gifts and also his desire for social betterment, tried to use both in order to guide his life into lawful channels. As a favourite pupil N felt comparatively happy and for some time there seem to have been no complaints against him. Through the mediation of the headmaster N, though still a pupil at the reformatory, was permitted to attend the school of commercial art in another town. Here he missed the head-master's fatherly support and after a short time became involved in a court case and had to leave the school. On returning to the reformatory he behaved in a way similar to that of many young people in the same position. Some slight, real or imagined, gave him an excuse to run away, and during the short time he was at large he committed many delinquent actions.

At the age of nineteen N appeared in Berlin, found a job, but did hardly any work, posed as a man of substance and fraudulently incurred debts. He contrived to gain entry into those social circles on which his heart had always been set. The boy from the reformatory became a welcome guest in the most exclusive students' clubs. In his dress, his manner of living and his demeanour he had completely assimilated himself to the upper ten. The means to do this, however, came from illicit sources, and finally N had to save himself from threatened arrest by running away. Then began an adventurous journey through Southern Germany, the Tyrol and Switzerland. Wherever he went he infringed the law by eating and drinking in restaurants without paying, and by other fraudulent acts, and was prosecuted in a number of courts. In Switzerland he served a month's prison sentence after which he had to leave the country. In Germany he was punished for a number of previous offences. He went from court to court and from prison to prison. During his last prison sentence he very quickly ingratiated himself with the prison governor and was put in charge of the library. When, in 1915, he had served all his sentences he entered military service, as previously mentioned.

I shall defer until later in this paper any psychological assessment of N's case, and will confine myself here to a summary of the contents of my psychiatric report. There were no signs whatever of a mental disorder in the usual sense of the term. Nor could there be any question of mental deficiency. On the contrary, I was dealing with a man whose intelligence was above the average, and who, in addition, showed considerable artistic gifts. The deviation from the normal lay exclusively in N's social behaviour. I suspected a deep-seated disturbance of the emotional life, from which his anti-social impulses originated. Such impulses had only remained in abeyance for short periods of time, and under the most favourable conditions. They had soon succeeded in breaking through again with compelling force.

In such cases clinical terminology speaks of moral deficiency. The criminal law of our time, however,[1] does not recognise the influence of such aberrations of the emotional life upon a person's legal responsibility. The military court, which had shown a humane understanding of the accused which was wholly praiseworthy, was bound to treat N as responsible in law for his actions, and sentenced him to a long term of imprisonment.

I would emphasise that in my psychiatric report I described N's condition as chronic and, according to general psychiatric experience, unalterable.

The war came to an end a few months after N's conviction in August 1918, and I heard nothing of him for the next four or five years. Then one day I was asked by a civil court, in somewhat unusual circumstances, for a fresh psychiatric report on N. By the spring of 1919 he had committed several further offences exactly similar to his previous ones. In the criminal proceedings which, for various reasons, did not take place until several years later, N said that he had committed these latter crimes under the influence of the same pathological compulsion as had induced the earlier offences. He further said that shortly after that date, however, the criminal propensities which had existed since his childhood had disappeared and that throughout the last four years he had been settled and industrious and had committed no further offences.

If these statements of N's were correct, I had made a serious mistake in my assessment of his condition, and especially in the prognosis. First of all it was necessary to obtain reliable information about his behaviour since his conviction five years earlier. From what N himself told me when he came to me for a second investigation, and from information I obtained from official sources, the following picture emerged.

At the end of the war N was released under the general amnesty. He soon committed further offences on the same pattern as the earlier ones. Anyone as astute as N could easily turn to his own advantage the general upheaval which was then taking place. Although he had just undergone a period of detention awaiting trial, followed by a prison sentence, once again he straightaway won the confidence of people in authority, only to betray it immediately. Thus no sooner had he regained his freedom than he committed a series of fresh offences. At that

[1] Editor's note: Although this refers to the German law of the early nineteen-twenties, it is equally true of the law of England at the present day.

time the so-called Free Corps and other military organisations were formed. Within the space of a few months N joined several of them. He was universally popular and such was the confidence he inspired that he was entrusted with money; this he misappropriated, had to abscond, only to begin the same conduct somewhere else. In one organisation his statement that he had been an officer during the war was believed, with the result that he really did serve as an officer.

The opportunity for such play-acting, however, soon came to an end, and N returned to civilian life. Between March and June 1919 he committed a number of thefts, defrauded restaurant proprietors as he had previously done, and several prosecutions were instituted against him.

Then came the great transformation. It was definitely established that after June 1919 N committed no further offence. No police or other authority instituted any proceedings against him. Two trustworthy witnesses testified that since that time he had been steady and industrious. His work was praised; businessmen of standing who went into partnership with him gave evidence of his conscientiousness, and his complete reliability, especially where money-matters were concerned, was proved over several years. Both witnesses were fully informed about N's past, and had therefore kept a careful eye upon him, but had never found any reason for complaint. N was married and led the life of a typical middle-class family-man. In the social life of the large town where he lived he was popular and respected without, however, dazzling people in the manner so familiar to us from his previous life.

The fact of this complete transformation in N's social behaviour was beyond dispute. If these reports of him were accepted as true, however, such a change would be contrary to all psychiatric experience. If a person displays dis-social behaviour so early in life and if he has not found his niche in social life by the time he is twenty-six, but has been a confirmed impostor, all our experience impels us to believe that there is no hope of a spontaneous improvement. Moreover, we know of no influences which could effect so unprecedented a change. The circumstances of any such change would be so unusual that in practice they could not be foreseen.

The solution of the enigma is to be found in the realm of psychology. We shall therefore have to turn now to certain facts in N's life and to his emotional reaction to his experiences. It may be mentioned here that at the time when he was under observation in 1918 N had been disinclined to discuss such questions with me. As we shall soon see, his attitude at that time towards any representation of paternal authority was defiant and rebellious. Further, I was at that time his military superior. In 1923, however, he gave the impression of a man who was comfortably settled in his surroundings. He felt himself to be on the same social level as myself and could therefore confide in me without his previous distrust. Thus it was only our second and far shorter meeting that revealed many important and fundamental explanations for N's previous social behaviour, and threw light on his recent transformation.

As may be remembered, N was the youngest of several children in a family in very poor circumstances. It must be added that many years separated him from his siblings who, at the time of his birth, were already adolescent or fully adult. As a very small boy, and later, he heard his mother say again and again how unwelcome to her he, the latecomer, had been. Whilst the older siblings were already out at work, N was one more mouth to feed and he learned, from their heartless remarks, that he was regarded by them as a burden on the family budget. At any rate he felt himself unloved by both his parents and by all his siblings; he even felt them to be hostile. This is in complete contrast to the frequent spoiling of late or last-born children. His subsequent social behaviour represents, in the last resort, his psychological reaction to these impressions of his earlier childhood.

We need here only recall the well-established psychoanalytical finding, according to which a child experiences his first feelings of love in relation to the persons of his earliest environment and in this way himself learns how to love. In circumstances such as have just been described no proper object-relationship can develop. The child's first attempts to invest with his libido the human objects nearest to him will be doomed to fail and a regressive narcissistic charge of the ego will occur. At the same time there will be a marked tendency to hate the objects in the child's environment.

Seen from this point of view N's behaviour during the nursery and school period becomes comprehensible. He spurns his parents just as they spurned him. He longs for rich parents, who would not look upon him as an economic liability. From an early age he shows himself to every person who might stand for his father, mother, brother or sister at his most engaging. Every teacher, every classmate must like him—and this is an unending source of gratification for his narcissism. The identification of the people around him at any given time with his parents and siblings goes still further: he has to disappoint those who have come to love him, in order to take revenge upon them. That all without exception become his dupes gives further intensive gratification to his narcissism. One could sum this up by saying that N who felt himself unloved in his childhood, had an inner urge to show himself 'lovable' to everybody, that is to say worthy of their love, only to prove to himself and to them soon afterwards how unworthy he was of such feeling. We are here reminded of the bi-phasic actions of obsessional neurotics.

N's burning desire to be the centre of a large circle of friends is particularly noteworthy. He himself explained to me that it was his greatest pleasure to feel that 'everything revolved around him'. Such a state of affairs was in fact in complete contrast to that of his early childhood. Invariably, however, N himself did everything possible to bring these happy conditions to a speedy end. An overpowering repetition-compulsion forced him to make himself an outcast over and over again, just when he had become everybody's favourite, until one day the great change occurred, which has not yet been accounted for.

In June 1919 N was travelling restlessly from place to place, always on the move and maintaining himself by swindling restaurants, and by other frauds. He then had a stroke of good fortune, whose special significance must be perfectly clear to those who are psycho-analytically trained.

At that time N made the acquaintance of a woman, who took an interest in him from their very first meeting. She was a good deal older than he and was a partner in an industrial undertaking. As soon as she heard that N was out of a job and in needy circumstances she promised him that she would look after him. In the business in which she was a partner he found occupation which gave scope for his artistic gifts, mixed with highly respected persons, and was well paid. Between himself and his benefactress a closer relationship developed. She was a widow, and mother of several adolescent children. They married, and at the same time N took over a responsible post in the business. This further consolidated his social position. In this ideal state of middle-class security there was only one thing which troubled him: the criminal proceedings which were still outstanding against him.

When I saw N again in 1923 this state of outward happiness and, we may add, of inner peace, had remained stable for several years. Previously N had been compelled by unconscious drives to ruin every favourable situation. Why did not such a breakdown now take place, and why could N enjoy this fortunate turn of events in full harmony with another person?

We can briefly formulate the answer to this question in psychoanalytical terms. All earlier states of temporary prosperity in N's life represented merely momentary gratifications of his narcissism. Such states, however, contained within themselves the elements of their own rapid downfall. The ambivalence of N's inner drives was far too strong to permit him to achieve any sort of psychological equilibrium. We may add our suspicion that N's temporary successes were associated with strong unconscious guilt-feelings, which had to bring about a rapid end to his happiness as an act of self-punishment.

We have already attempted to explain the fixation of the libido in a state of narcissism as a regressive process, resulting from deeply disappointing impressions from early childhood. Thus as a small boy N had been unable to derive from his Oedipal relationship to his parents even a minimal amount of that pleasure which children normally obtain albeit in varying degrees. Of maternal tenderness there was none. Nor was he able to exalt his father into an ideal figure. On the contrary, we saw how from an early age the wish for another father dominated him. Nor could he identify himself with his siblings in the Oedipal struggle against the father, for in his case they combined with the parents in an unbroken union of hostility against him. Thus the normal development of the Oedipus complex did not take place. Accordingly those processes of sublimation which evidence a successful overcoming of the Oedipus complex, and which are the prerequisite of a satisfactory integration of the individual into the social organism, could not take place.[1]

The change which took place in N's life in the year 1919 meant no more and no less than the complete reversal of the conditions of his earliest childhood environment. A woman older than himself is attracted to him at first sight, and showers

[1] Incidentally, we should not forget that the Oedipal relationship which we rightly look upon as a source of serious and lasting conflict in the psychic life of the child and of the adult originally constitutes a source of pleasure, both in reality and in phantasy. If, however, the child is allowed a certain limited amount of pleasure, he gradually learns to renounce the greatest and most important of such wishes, namely those which are socially unacceptable. This seems to be, for the child, an indispensable aid to the successful overcoming of ambivalence towards the parents. If the child is entirely denied all such pleasure, then a favourable sublimation of the Oedipus complex fails to take place, and all libido flows back into the ego.

him with proofs of maternal care. To these, proofs of love are presently added. No one stands in the way of this love between mother and son, for the woman's husband has been long since dead. There are, however, some sons who had a right to the mother's love long before N. Nevertheless she prefers him to her other sons, although he came into her life so late, marries him, and thereby offers to him rather than to her own sons the place of her deceased husband.

Through this woman, therefore, N experienced not only a sudden transformation into favourable social and financial circumstances, but also a complete fulfilment of all his childhood wishes deriving from the Oedipus complex. When I pointed out to him the obvious fact that his wife stood for his mother, N replied: 'You are quite right. Very soon after the beginning of our acquaintance I began to call my wife "Mummy", and even today I cannot bring myself to call her anything else.' As he said this he showed a very strong emotional reaction of sympathy and gratitude. This indicated that in N there was now more than a mere gratification of his narcissistic desire for proofs of love. I gained the impression that N had achieved with a substitute figure what he could never achieve in his childhood, namely the transference of his libido on to his mother. I do not of course mean that a complete object-love, a successful overcoming of his narcissism, had been achieved, but that he had progressed, though to what extent could not be precisely determined, from the narcissistic fixation of his libido, in the direction of object-love. A more exact statement could only be made after a full psycho-analysis.

Furthermore, it must be emphasised that all the wishfulfilments mentioned above are unaccompanied by guilt-feelings. There is no father to get rid of; he died long ago. No attack upon the mother is necessary; she extends to him as her son feelings of maternal tenderness as well as of sexual love, and all this of her own volition. There are no siblings to contend against; his special position in the new family is fully recognised. Thus N enjoys for the first time in his life a situation of complete and, we must add, guilt-free pleasure.

The full gratification by a mother-substitute not only of his longing for maternal tenderness, but also of his erotic desires, has brought a belated fulfilment of his Oedipus wishes, which had remained unsatisfied in his childhood. At the same time it drew N's libido away from its narcissistic fixation. Thus for the first time he succeeded, to a certain extent, in transferring his libido on to an object.

The complete fulfilment, in a psychological sense, of an infantile wish-situation, which we have witnessed in this case, can be described as an exceptional event. No one could count upon such a happening as occurred, as though by a miracle, in this particular case. The gloomy prognosis of the psychiatric report retains its general validity, although it turned out to be wrong on this occasion. From another point of view, however, it remains justifiable.

On his last visit to me N himself stressed how well he had done in every respect, but he was intelligent enough not to be without some misgivings. He admitted both to himself and to me that he felt the continuance of his present condition to be dependent upon his relationship to his wife, and that if this were ever shaken his old tendencies would break through again, for deep down he felt that the old impulsive restlessness was still there.[1]

It would be easy in the case just described to speak of 'healing through love', if only we could be sure that a true healing, a lasting change for the better, had taken place. Be that as it may, the transformation in the social behaviour of a person with such a past record remains a strange phenomenon, which can only be understood in the light of the psycho-analytical theory of the libido, but which also deserves our full attention for practical reasons.

This case impressively shows how important it is not to overestimate the part played by heredity—or 'degeneration' as it is called—in the formation of dis-social and criminal drives. The characteristics which academic opinion still one-sidedly regards as inborn and therefore unalterable must to a great extent be recognised as acquired in early infancy, that is to say, as being due to the effects of the earliest psycho-sexual impressions. This does not only mean that we may correct an erroneous opinion; it also gives us new techniques, new potentialities, and new points of approach for the treatment of delinquents, especially in their youth. I am happy to be in full agreement on this point with so eminent an expert in this field as Aichhorn.

Aichhorn's [2] papers help us to see how essential in a

---

[1] Here the result of the second psychiatric report, which was made in 1923, may be mentioned. The last criminal offences were committed just before the great change came about and so must be regarded, along with the earlier offences, as manifestations of an irresistible urge originating from unconscious sources.

[2] 'Verwahrloste Jugend. Die Psychoanalyse in der Fürsorgeerziehung.' *Internationale Psychoanalytische Bibliothek*, **19**, 1925. (*Wayward Youth.*)

reformatory school is the pupil's positive transference to the teacher. He has rightly made the establishment and maintenance of such a transference the keystone of corrective education.

If we remember the astounding effects of the first successful transference in the case of N, when he was already grown up, we can imagine what results might be achieved in young persons by a successfully established transference directed along the right lines. N was certainly fortunate in finding, as an inmate in a reformatory school, a humane and understanding master. In spite of his deep concern with N's fate, however, this man did not succeed in establishing a lasting transference. The absence of a firm attachment of his feelings caused N to relapse again and again and prevented the achievement of a lasting instinctual sublimation. Such a sublimation only came about when N's libido was permanently transferred on to one person.

We who practise psycho-analysis have often complained that our therapeutic work is always concerned with a relatively small number of people, that it penetrates deeply into each individual case, but not sufficiently widely into society as a whole. If Aichhorn's view is correct that in general the establishment of transference forms an adequate basis for the influencing of dis-social youths, whilst only those cases which are complicated by neurotic disturbances require proper psycho-analytical treatment, then we have here a sphere in which the results of psycho-analytical research and practice gained from the treatment of neurotics could have a far-reaching application. Aichhorn's thesis opens up a promising educational approach for which Freud's psychology has provided the basis. The warm-hearted enthusiasm with which he sets out to build up his educational work deserves our admiration.

Let us take one last look at the life of our impostor. In the psycho-analysis of neurotics we often come across the results of early pampering, which intensifies the child's demands for love to an extent which can never be adequately satisfied. Among delinquents we are more likely to come across a different fate of the libido in early childhood. It is the absence of love, comparable to psychological under-nourishment, which provides the pre-condition for the establishment of dis-social traits. An excess of hatred and fury is generated which, first directed against a small circle of persons, is later directed against society as a whole. Where such pre-conditions exist there will be no spontaneous character-development favourable to social adjustment. The narcissistic regression of the libido, which we had to assume in N's case, will show a corresponding inhibition of character-formation, a fixation at a lower level.

It is inevitable that the results of psycho-analysis will gradually receive the attention they deserve from criminologists. Reik, in his book, *Geständniszwang und Strafbedürfnis*, has recently made extensive investigations into the feeling of guilt, and has thereby opened up an important connection between criminology and the psycho-analytical investigation of neuroses. The science of criminology and of the psychology of the criminal can benefit from psycho-analytical teachings in two ways. Psycho-analysis provides criminologists with new psychological points of view for the understanding of the persons they are concerned with. Furthermore, the treatment of juvenile delinquents with the help of psycho-analysis or in the light of psycho-analytical knowledge seems to be a promising way of preventing crime.

It is hoped that this communication will have contributed something towards bridging the gap between psycho-analysis and criminology.

V

PSYCHO-ANALYTICAL NOTES ON COUÉ'S SYSTEM OF SELF-MASTERY[1]

(1925)

DURING the last few years we have witnessed the enthusiastic reception of a new system, according to which anyone can free himself by his own efforts from ill-health or moral defects, or from the effects of an adverse fate. Such a promise would probably have found a great number of enthusiastic adherents at any time. The devastating psychological after-effects of the Great War increased people's inclination to welcome with faith and gratitude a new message of salvation. The enormous number of those who suffered in one way or another helped to fill the assembly-halls in which they could hear this 'self-mastery' expounded. The method was so simple that every person, no matter what his mental capacity, could apply it immediately after the first instruction. One read and heard of astonishing results; in particular there were sensational reports of cures of organic diseases by this new form of auto-suggestion.

On the other hand critical voices were raised, but these failed to shake the faith of Coué's disciples. The opposition for the most part came, as was to be expected, from the ranks of academic medicine. Three main objections were advanced against Coué and his followers.

In the first place it was emphasised that a cure of organic disease by means of self-mastery is impossible. The reports of successes were said to be the outcome of insufficient observation and criticism. Secondly, mass treatment without any individual care and even without prior investigation was condemned. It was pointed out that it was a gross abuse to treat a mental disorder, a pulmonary tuberculosis, an eye-disease, and a cancer indiscriminately and collectively. People who were led to hope that they might be cured in this way were running the risk of missing the right time for a vital operation. Finally, the actual

<hr>

[1] Editor's note: Published posthumously from a manuscript found among Dr. Abraham's papers. The article is not quite complete, since the author planned, particularly in the last part, to make additions and extensions which he was unable to carry out.

formula which constituted the main means of auto-suggestion, and which had to be uttered and repeated in a certain way, was violently attacked. It was not difficult to ridicule it by comparing it with magical incantations and other products of outworn superstition. We psycho-analysts will hardly be inclined to give unqualified approval to either side.

We cannot very well support the Coué enthusiasts. From our daily dealings with neurotics, who undoubtedly make up the majority of Coué's followers, we have always had the impression that the curing of nervous disorders is a very difficult task. Whether or not it is successful depends upon the strength of psychic resistances, and we will find it hard to imagine that such resistances, which cause us so much difficulty, will melt away before a suggestive formula. If the formula says that every day and in every way the patient will get better and better, it is no different from the usual allo-suggestion promising the neurotic victory over his symptoms. We know, however, that the result of such suggestion is merely to increase the process of repression in the patient. We therefore believe that auto-suggestion is simply a palliative of uncertain effect and duration. Nevertheless we must admit that even a temporary alleviation of troublesome symptoms must be welcome and valuable to the patient. If in addition it can be brought about in so simple and rapid a way, he can hardly be expected to do otherwise than clutch at it eagerly. Other objections which psycho-analysis can bring against such a method will become clear in the following analytical investigation.

We certainly have no reason to support the opponents, and especially the medical critics, of Coué. Their superior, sceptical attitude and their preconceived objections have, after all, often enough been directed against us. From our work with neuroses we have reached a conviction which has remained alien to them. I refer to the conviction of the great influence which unconscious psychological factors exert upon the origin, course and cure of organic diseases. We never lose sight of this fact, even though we do not go all the way with Groddeck. In this connection one particular instance is especially instructive. The improvement of a tubercular illness by Coué's method has been represented as 'unbelievable', and this was probably a euphemism of the critics, who would certainly have preferred to stigmatise such reports as fraudulent. Let us assume that a patient with this disease has strong psychological reasons to resist his cure. His unconscious may exploit the organic disease to alienate him from life and gradually to bring about his death.

If now, by means of auto-suggestion or otherwise, this process is arrested, the possibility may arise, which had not previously existed, of marshalling all the psychological and physical forces to effect an improvement. If, therefore, Coué's method should in such a case call a halt to the earlier workings of the death instinct, a cure of an organic disease might well be achieved. We shall thus approach the objections of academic medicine with due scepticism.

The first of the three objections voiced by medical critics need concern us here no longer. We analysts are far more interested in the two other objections. To be more precise, we must go into the question of the dynamics of Coué's method. We shall be better able to specify the particular direction of our interest, if we take the two other critical objections as our starting-point.

The second of the objections made from the medical point of view is directed against the treatment of patients in large gatherings irrespective of their numbers and without regard for the differences in their illnesses and afflictions. How far this objection is justified in the interests of those seeking help need not concern us here, for this is not a psycho-analytical problem, but a matter for social medicine. Psycho-analysis may feel entitled to investigate Coué's system of mass-treatment from a completely different point of view. There is no doubt that the successes of this method or, if one refuses to admit that it has successes, the fascination it exercises, are a phenomenon of group psychology. The insight which Freud has given us in his paper on 'Group Psychology and the Analysis of the Ego' [1] justifies our expectation that psycho-analysis may elucidate how the Coué method may influence an indefinite number of people. If we consider in particular the curative effects, it is the task of psycho-analysis to investigate the therapeutic factors underlying this famous technique. Let us take the first step in this direction, which needs no special preparation, because it links our investigation immediately with Freud's findings. Coué (or Baudouin or whoever represents him) is a leader, around whom a group of people gathers. It is then our task to make a psychological investigation into the effects of the particular interaction between such a leader and the masses under his influence.

The third objection to the system is that it cloaks suggestion or auto-suggestion in the trappings of a kind of magic formula of universal application. We will not indulge in scientific

[1] Standard edn., **18.**

arrogance by merely ridiculing it, but will examine whether our psychological insight may help us to understand the efficacy of such a uniform technique.

In other words, we try to analyse the dynamics of Coué's method by subjecting it to our scientific investigation. We are undoubtedly justified in so doing, since we are just as ready to examine our own working methods analytically. Some time ago, Dr. Horney spoke in the Berlin Psycho-analytical Association about the analysis of the analyst. This paper and the discussion which followed sought to establish the hidden motives underlying the conscious, rational basis of our procedure.

The ground for this investigation of the Coué method has been prepared in psycho-analytical literature mainly by three authors. It was Ferenczi [1] who made the first psycho-analytical advance into the dark realm of hypnosis and suggestion. He laid particular stress on the emotional tie between the subject of hypnosis and the hypnotist, and saw in it a manifestation of the Oedipus complex. There is no need to go more closely here into Ferenczi's discoveries, as we are only indirectly concerned with individual hypnosis and its effects. Moreover, the contents of his paper can be looked upon as the common property of psycho-analytical research, and therefore familiar to every analyst.

Freud's *Group Psychology* widened our horizon considerably. It threw light upon the relationship between leader and follower, not merely in the case of groups, in the usual meaning of the term, but also in the 'group of two', that is to say, the emotional (libidinal) relationship between hypnotist and hypnotised. Furthermore, it gave us a basic explanation as to what takes place in the ego of the person who is hypnotised. The assumption of the ego-ideal, or super-ego, has become indispensable to us for the complete explanation of many psychological manifestations. We shall shortly return to those particular results of Freud's investigations which are of special importance for our purpose.

In the third place, we should mention a work which touches directly upon our subject. Using this material as his starting-point, Ernest Jones has investigated the most important problems of auto-suggestion.[2] As his work contains several references to the publications of Coué and Baudouin we shall repeatedly refer to his conclusions.

Let us begin by recalling some fundamental statements in

[1] *Introjection and Transference*, 1908.

[2] 'The Nature of Auto-suggestion.' *The British Journal of Medical Psychology*, **3**, Part III, 1923.

Freud's *Group Psychology*. Suggestibility is the expression of libidinal attachment to a person who to the unconscious stands for father or mother. The individuals in a group follow and obey the leader by reason of such an attachment. Each person lets the leader take the place of his ego-ideal. In a certain sense the members of a group have a uniform super-ego. They are bound to each other by mutual identification. The power of suggestion exercised by the leader is strengthened by this mutual identification. As a member of a group every person is more susceptible to suggestion. His emotions are intensified and freed from certain restraints; his intellectual powers, and particularly his critical faculty, are lessened. He feels in himself the strength of the whole group, and tends to over-estimate his own strength by indulging in phantasies of omnipotence.

We will start from the assumption that the followers of a prophet or healer form a group, whether they merely assemble together without knowing one another individually, or whether they constitute an organised band of followers. The case now under consideration, however, shows some special features. In other groups the relationship of the individual to the leader is subject to definite rules. This is not so in our case. There are some adherents who have perhaps only read a pamphlet by the leader. Yet they are attached to him and his doctrine in the same way as others who regularly attend his meetings. How can such an indirect contact with the leader result in so powerful an attachment? In other words, how can such a variety of circumstances produce in all adherents the same relationship to the leader which, in agreement with Freud, we consider an important criterion of group-formation.

I do not think we can remain long in doubt about the answer to this question. Within the group the fiction is maintained that all its members are equally dear to the leader, so that he appears as a just father. In the case of Coué this is, in fact, true in a very special sense. He gives to all, regardless of who they are and what their particular trouble is, the same invariable formula: 'Every day, and in every way, I am becoming better and better'. He really gives to all as much, or, one might say, as little. He is not only a father who is just to all his 'children', but also, as among primitive peoples, a father with a powerful 'mana', who by means of a formula can banish all evil; he is a typical exponent of the omnipotence of thought, and a master of word-magic. This bearer of 'mana' does something completely unexpected, which makes him different from other fathers.

The commander of an army, the leader of a religious community or of a political party, has to preserve his authority. Certain favourites are placed between himself and the group, and he delegates part of his power to them; they are, however, no less bound in obedience to him than the least member of the group. The hypnotist in his 'group of two' must be just as careful to maintain his authority. The relationship always somehow remains that of one who commands towards one who obeys, one who is strong to one who is weak. How different is our case! Coué permits everyone, without distinction, to have an equal share in his 'mana'. He gives his magic formula to all, and instructs them in its use. Expressed in psycho-analytical terms, he permits everyone to behave as though they were Coué himself. He is a father who allows all his sons to identify themselves entirely with him, not merely in phantasy but also in practice, by actually asking them to take over his 'mana' and to use it.

Those who attend their first Coué meeting, ready to become merged in the mass of followers and to put the leader in the place of the super-ego, receive a gift which will particularly satisfy their unconscious; this is fundamentally the fulfilment of infantile wishes belonging to the Oedipus complex. They are authorised to identify themselves with the father.

We shall be best able to realise what this means if we remind ourselves of Freud's views on the relationship of the primal father to his sons. His theories on group-psychology are intimately bound up with the theory of the primal horde. What Coué does may be applied to relationships within the primal horde somewhat as follows. One day the father permits his sons, while he is still alive, to participate in his powers and privileges. This means not only his power over life and death and his material possessions, but, according to Freud's convincing exposition, also his sexual privileges. The sharing by the sons in the power and privileges of the father stands also for the lifting of the existing sexual barriers, that is to say, the prohibition against incest hitherto imposed upon them.

What Coué grants to his followers, so far as his conscious mind and theirs is concerned, is very far removed from such liberty. We, however, whose special task is to take account of the unconscious, must keep our eyes open. We may at first sight be misled into thinking that the adherents of Coué are in no way libidinally attached to him and his doctrine. We may certainly expect to find the same attachment as that which Freud holds to be responsible for group-formations in general. Yet we must admit that the outward impression is quite different. The contact between Coué and the individual follower is wholly impersonal, in direct contrast to that between the hypnotist and his subject. It is in this respect that it seems to us possible to throw further light on the fascination Coué's method wields. Our first step was to assume that every follower is gratified by the part of the leader's 'mana' which falls to him. All the sons praise the kind and just father. We must now add that they would not be able to enjoy this gift if they were aware of the libidinal nature of their attachment. We may now say that Coué's method ensures that they remain completely unconscious of all these facts, far more so than in hypnosis. I here follow Ernest Jones' stimulating work. The method of auto-suggestion makes the patient far less aware of the transference than does the method of allo-suggestion. It is true that in hypnosis the patient need not be conscious of the erotic character of the transference on to the hypnotist, though he often is. Even if all physical contact is avoided, an erotic rapport is easily established. It manifests itself in physical sensations as well as in day-dreams and in the dreams of sleep. We know that the hypnotic situation is felt by the patient's phantasy as a 'going to sleep with the hypnotist', that is to say, as a direct erotic act. Those, however, who undergo instruction for self-administered suggestion completely avoid an awareness of such psychic processes. Added to this is the fact that hundreds are receiving the instruction at the same time. How then could any phantasy of a personal, erotic relationship arise? Jones rightly adds that in such a case the physician shares the advantage of his patients in avoiding unpleasure. He points out that many well-known practitioners of hypnosis have gone over to waking suggestion because they felt uneasy about the transference-phenomena in hypnosis.

It has already been mentioned that every individual sufferer has, so to speak, been given by Coué a share in his omnipotence. His ego feels elated now that is is able to put an end to all his previous troubles. With neurotic patients in particular the focussing of attention upon the power of the ego has the effect of diverting attention from the sexual forces hidden in the neurosis. One might say that in this respect Coué's method is a flight from the more obviously erotic character of the hypnosis, like Adler's attempt to modify Freud's libido-theory and to make it ego-syntonic by over-emphasising the ego's desire for power.

This psychological process becomes even more striking if we follow Jones one step further. The physician showing the masses the way to auto-suggestion enjoys the hypnotist's feeling of omnipotence in a particularly marked form. He is aware of his influence over an unlimited number of people, whilst the hypnotist can only exert his power over a relatively small number. We might add that in the hypnotist this feeling of power operates intensively with single individuals, whereas with Coué it operates extensively by influencing large numbers.

We revert once more to the feeling of power with which Coué endows the sufferer. Only then shall we fully comprehend how this narcissistic gratification helps the patient to banish from consciousness those forbidden object-relations which had sought expression in neurotic symptoms. Two points seem to deserve further attention.

We know how frequently illness tends to bring about the narcissistic regression of a person's libido. An inevitable consequence of this process is an over-estimation of one's own suffering. The sufferer, however, who sees his salvation in Coué's method, gains the impression that his misfortune is no greater than that of other people, for it can, after all, be got rid of in the same way, by the very same auto-suggestion. The emphasis is thus transferred from the exceptional severity of the suffering to the miraculous powers of auto-suggestion. This is expressed in the description of the method as 'self-mastery'. In saying this I must not be taken to be implying anything about the actual efficacy of the method; here, as elsewhere in this investigation, it is the manifest and latent tendencies contained in the method which are under discussion. We shall maintain throughout the scepticism we have already expressed as to the actual successes of the method. The effects just described are nothing more than a consolation, which may be felt in one case and not in another, or which may be enduring in some cases and shortlived in others.

The second point which is worth while discussing here is again concerned with the particular category of neurotic illness. We know that many of our patients lay special emphasis in their complaints upon their feelings of inferiority, making these the ornate facade of their neurotic structure. In agreement with Janet, Adler attributes the highest importance for the psychology of neuroses to inferiority feelings. He calls the factors operating to counteract these inferiority feelings the 'masculine protest'; the combined driving forces of the neurosis find their ego-syntonic expression in the masculine protest. Coué's method shows an unmistakable tendency to do away with every kind of inferiority, whether real or imaginary, by an optimistic denial. Thus Adler's 'masculine protest' has become crystallised, as it were, in Coué's auto-suggestive formula into a stereotyped sequence of words.

Let us now recall the starting point of our investigation: the misgivings of medical critics and the questions raised by them. How, they asked, could one hope to achieve therapeutic results in people of normal intelligence, in full possession of their critical faculties, by putting into their hands, irrespective of the nature of their suffering, and in common with an indefinite number of others in need of help, a stereotyped formula of auto-suggestion, and then leaving them to their own devices? It is now easy to see that to pose the problem in this way is unsound because it is unpsychological.

The effect of Coué's method depends upon the very fact that a person in need of help is transformed from an individual into a component part of a group. He thereby becomes credulous and suggestible, that is to say, he loses his critical faculty and allows himself to be psychologically regimented. Hence we can understand why Coué's meetings are packed not only by people of poor intelligence, but even more by intellectuals. Among the latter are a great many who have to transform a large part of their libido into intellectual or artistic effort. This involves a fight against severe resistances. They find a temporary release from this servitude by becoming for once merely one of a crowd. We can therefore give the medical critics the following reply: Coué's method does not achieve its results in spite of working with such simple means; rather the essential condition for its fascinating effects and its practical results, so far as such are achieved, lies precisely in making the individual a member of a group; this inevitably involves a lowering of his intellectual level. The effect of the method is made clear by the special way in which it deals with the Oedipus complex. It actually exhorts the individual to identify himself with the father and to appropriate his 'mana', without bringing to consciousness the libidinal character of this process.

If we regard the transformation of the individual into a particle of a mass as the precondition for the efficacy of Coué's method, we conform closely to Freud's exposition, in which he clearly postulates: 'Group-formation temporarily abolishes neurosis' (*Group Psychology*). We can reinforce this by examples from our wartime experiences. Contrary to the expectations held by many, a considerable number of neurotics became symptom-free when they joined the army, and especially if they went into a fighting unit. The strangest and most grotesque instance which I came across may be recorded here. A young man suffered from the gravest manifestations of doubting and brooding mania. In his occupation as a business man the simplest transactions, such as the buying or selling of goods, became the source of endless doubts and self-torments. These were attached to every decision he had to make. From the moment he went into the army all this misery came to an end. Having become a small cog in the vast machine of the army he had no more decisions to make; henceforth he belonged to the mass of those who had merely to obey. For years he took part in the heaviest fighting on the French front, was exposed to the severest fire, and was often confined for days on end in a dug-out. During the last months of the war he was a prisoner-of-war in English hands. He was psychologically fully able to cope with all these situations. When the war ended he returned home and resumed his former occupation. Immediately all his old symptoms returned. When the patient consulted me again he said: 'You will see, doctor, that in a short time all the benefit I gained from the last four and a half years will be lost.' He had ceased to be just one of a crowd and went to pieces as soon as he once more became an individual with responsibilities of his own. In complete accordance with Freud's thesis he had experienced a temporary recession of his neurosis, but when he ceased to be merely an atom in a mass he became subject once more to his old neurotic symptoms.

So far we have tried to understand Coué's influence over his followers. We now come to a second problem, the question of how the auto-suggestive effects are produced. We have already seen that every sufferer is expressly authorised to identify himself with the master, and that in every one there is a readiness to do this since strong unconscious causes favour such a response. Yet this does not explain everything. There still remains the problem why a great number of people are so ready to dispense with something which otherwise appears important and which from a rational point of view entails a recognisable gain of pleasure. This is the renunciation of the individual relationship to the physician, whose medical care and personal sympathy generally seem indispensable to the patient. Here we encounter the strange phenomenon of untold numbers of people giving up all this, and withdrawing into privacy to recite the auto-suggestive formula the prescribed number of times. It must thus become clear that we have not yet understood every aspect of the sufferer's attitude in a mass-treatment. Our attention will naturally be focussed in a particular direction. If the super-ego of every patient is identified with the leader, then the super-ego receives that part of the libido which was in fact turned towards the leader. In other words, we are faced with a narcissistic process, and it is here that we touch again upon Jones' work on the problem of auto-suggestion.

If we now scrutinise the behaviour of the neurotic, which is our particular concern, we learn from our experience that in every case we are faced with disturbances of his libidinal relationship to the external world, that is, disturbances in his object-relationship. Psycho-analysis reveals in such persons fixations to the objects of childhood which, however, are precluded by the incest barrier from being love-objects. Towards the permitted objects the libido is inhibited. The sexuality of the neurotic therefore finds its expression mostly in phantasies, in day-dreams, and in neurotic symptoms which we have come to recognise as derivatives of such phantasies. The estrangement from the outer world varies widely in degree in the different neurotic illnesses, but we can always find a retrogressive tendency which separates the libido from the objects, and tries to take it back to the infantile narcissistic fixation to the ego. It is just this regressive tendency which is encouraged by the auto-suggestive method. Hypnosis results in an infantile attachment to the hypnotist, who takes over the role of father or mother. Coué's auto-suggestive method allows the patient a far-reaching regression into infantilism, by promoting, in the manner already shown, the identification of the ego with the father, corresponding to that of an early phase of childhood. The place of an infantile form of object-relationship is taken by a narcissistic fixation to the ego.

This attitude of the libido permits the revival of primitive concepts such as that of the omnipotence of thought. In hypnosis this omnipotence is ascribed to the representative of the father, just as happens in a certain phase of childhood. When, through the development of his libido, the increase of his intellectual powers, and through his experiences, the child has become more critical towards himself, he abandons the idea of his own omnipotence and displaces it on to his parents. This is still an incomplete renunciation, as the attributing of omnipotence to the parents permits the child to hope that one day he may gain what he now lacks. In hypnosis the individual behaves like a child in this phase. The prescribed auto-suggestion, however, brings with it a reversion to the concept of one's own omnipotence. We can make a more definite statement if we recall Ferenczi's investigations on 'The Developmental Stages of the Sense of Reality'.[1] As the author shows, the narcissistic attitude of the child towards the outside world and his belief

[1] Ferenczi, 1913, *Contributions to Psycho-Analysis*.

in the omnipotence of his wishes find expression in his behaviour. With all the means of expression at his disposal he
tries to command his surroundings; he uses words, gestures,
and in particular the primitive language of the organs, which
in his view are all endowed with magical powers. Coué not only
permits but commands his followers to proclaim their feeling of
power in a formula of undoubtedly magical character. It is no
valid objection to say that children apply such magical methods
in their relationship to objects, whilst Coué's followers use their
formula in relation to their own person. The super-ego,
identifying itself with Coué,? behaves towards the rest of the
ego as if it were another person. In addition, as in all spell-
casting, we are here concerned with the exercising and overcoming of powers which are felt by the ego to be alien, hostile
invaders.

As the experience of recent years has shown, countless
numbers of people eagerly seize the opportunity to regress to a
more primitive stage of development when exhorted to do so in
so authoritative a manner. Here, too, there is a guilt-free enjoyment of freedom in the infantile sense. Added to this is the fact
that the other followers, who have joined with the single individual to form a group, do likewise. The responsibility for actions
carried out by a group to a uniform pattern is shared among the
whole group; this exonerates the individual to some extent at least
from a feeling of guilt which he would be unable to endure alone.
Freud first demonstrated this in relation to the totem-feast, that
is to say, in the communal killing and eating of the primal
father by the rebellious sons. Where all the individual members
of a group participate together in an act on the authority of an
ideal father, on whom the whole responsibility is placed, the
guilt-feeling of each individual must finally disappear, especially
if the purpose of his action—to become healthy—does not
incur moral censorship, that is, the condemnation of the conscience.

It should here be mentioned that quite a large number of
people feel themselves debarred from joining the Coué movement for conscientious reasons. To devout believers the Coué
method appears to be a rebellious casting-off of their submissive
attitude towards God. From the religious point of view the
assumption of omnipotence in the sense discussed above
amounts to blasphemy. It is therefore only consistent that
Christian Science, which uses prayer for therapeutic purposes,
condemns Couéism as unchristian.

Without considering this attitude further let us return to the psychological problems. We have learned that every member of a group puts the leader in the place of his super-ego. We have also seen how, in our particular case, the individual, by reason of a special sanction, identifies himself with the leader. The efficacy of the whole process is psychologically easily comprehensible. Here we will follow again the investigations of Freud and Jones. The tension between the super-ego, with its demands, and the ego, which has to obey, is to some extent removed. The fact that the individual regains some measure of his infantile feeling of omnipotence brings about a partial mitigation of the severity of the ego-ideal, as described by Freud in his 'Group Psychology'. The extent of this mitigation needs further discussion. Freud's investigations refer in particular to the psychology of mania. In melancholia, following an object-loss, introjection of the lost object into the ego takes place. The censoring function of the super-ego appears to turn against the ego, whilst in reality all its severity is directed against the lost and introjected object. In mania, on the other hand, the functioning of the super-ego is temporarily suspended so that the ego enjoys a longed-for freedom and its self-esteem is increased. To a limited degree this is what happens under the influence of the Coué method, so that it produces a raising of the morale and with it an improvement in health and an increase in the capacity for work and enjoyment. On the other hand, one can discern essential differences, both quantitative and qualitative, between this feeling and the heady feeling of being liberated characteristic of the maniac patient. In our case the element of rebelliousness is absent, for here everything takes place under parental authorisation. Moreover, in contrast to the manifold excesses of mania, all that is involved is the recitation of a harmless formula, whose effects, even in the most favourable cases, only influence a limited sphere of life. The formula pretends, as we have seen, that sexuality does not belong to the realm of human wishes. Thus the follower of self-mastery, too, celebrates a feast of liberation. We shall see later that this liberation has a slightly different meaning in the two cases.

These considerations extend somewhat beyond those of Ernest Jones. We still agree with his view, however, that auto-suggestion is based upon a reconciliation between ego and super-ego. The renunciation of pleasure from the sources of object-love which auto-suggestion entails, is compensated for by a narcissistic auto-erotic gain in pleasure. We have merely tried to make this process psychologically more comprehensible.

We now believe that we have gained a certain amount of insight into the nature and mechanism of auto-suggestion, but we are still faced with an unsolved problem, and this time we are not in the fortunate position of being able to fall back upon established observations. As we stated at the beginning of this essay, the third point of criticism usually is the indiscriminate, universal application of a stereotyped formula, and it is this, in particular, which has laid the method open to cheap ridicule. If at the beginning we could not share such a facile attitude, we shall be even less prepared to do so now, for in the meantime we have become convinced that the inventor of this method has recognised with acute psychological intuition what kind of psychological results the mass of sufferers expect at the deepest level of their unconscious. Everyone of them renounces certain sources of pleasure which are too closely associated with guilt-feelings, but gladly accepts permission to indulge in certain infantile wish-fulfilments, especially as his self-confidence is at the same time increased. For this he pays the price of allowing himself to be transformed from a relatively self-reliant individual into an insignificant particle of a mass. If Coué could invent on the basis of his intuition a method relatively so pleasurable and entailing so little unpleasure, then the auto-suggestive instrument which he gives to everyone will, after all, not be so poor nor so ill-chosen. It also speaks, I think, for a correct intuitive understanding that Coué, who addresses himself to the masses, takes a path completely contrary to that, for instance, of Dubois with his technique of persuasion. To adopt a logical or rational approach, whether it be to the masses or to the unconscious, which means the same thing, would be seriously to disregard man's psychic constitution. The method of Dubois, of which little has recently been heard, is fundamentally based upon a similar narcissistic attitude on the part of the physician. In one case the power of the conscious functions of reason and logic are overestimated; in the other the infantile omnipotence of thought is re-established. The strength of Coué's method is that he seeks other paths to the unconscious than those of logic and reason, and chooses a vehicle which corresponds more closely to the functioning of the unconscious. We shall learn later where he probably gained such insight. This is not to say that the psychological basis of Coué's system is complete and unassailable. We shall have further opportunity to demonstrate that he has an intuitive understanding of the art of healing, but not of psychological research.

As is well known, his formula runs in English as follows:

'Every day, and in every way, I am becoming better and better.' It has been phrased in such general terms so that every individual may apply it in his own way to his own sufferings. The words 'in every way' have been devised to free the sufferer from the obligation to think of his various complaints whilst reciting the formula, which has to be repeated twenty times, three times a day. Coué advises that the patient should try to imagine himself near Coué when reciting the formula. The fact that the sufferer identifies himself with the leader here again becomes obvious. The mode and tempo of reciting the formula are not to be slow and solemn, but rapid. An emphatic, deliberate intonation is not essential; what is needed is a monotonous rattling-off of the simple text. A piece of string with twenty knots is indispensable. During the auto-suggestive exercise the patient's fingers take hold of the knots one after the other until the prescribed number has been completed.

We shall limit ourselves to this one formula although it is not the only one. There is another short one for special cases, such as occasional complaints of all kinds, particularly pain. Here the sufferer is enjoined to repeat as rapidly as possible, without counting, the words: 'It will be over soon, it will be over soon.' He continues this until—after a few minutes they say—it takes effect.

The main formula is in complete conformity with the magical word-sequences which we find in use among both primitive and civilised peoples. With us, too, the incantation of magic spells over wounds and diseases is by no means a thing of the past. Auto-suggestion practised three times per day reminds us of the ritual observances of many peoples; it is also reminiscent of medical prescriptions. It is quite obvious that the piece of string is a modern version of the rosary of the Catholic church. We know that such devices result in prayer becoming merely an automatic formula. Similar rituals can be found in the most diverse peoples. We have only to think of the prayer-mills of the Tibetans. Why Coué has chosen the number twenty I am unable to explain. I doubt if he himself could explain it either. We frequently find such numerical rules with obsessional neurotics who, however, cannot spontaneously give a reason for choosing the obsessional number. For this psycho-analytical investigation is necessary. We will deal later with the assumption that the whole system is the work of a man with a latent obsessional neurosis. Here we shall merely mention that not only do obsessional patients tend to repeat many things a certain number of times, but that they also frequently make up formulae which are of the nature of a self-protection against an obsession. Coué's prescription to recite the formula in rapid repetition is reminiscent of the 'verbigeration' of mental patients.

This automatic reeling-off of a ready-made formula is often criticised, and how anyone should, at the present day, base a therapeutic method upon such feeble intellectual foundations, is found incomprehensible. Our view is, in fact, diametrically opposed to this.

The general effect of Coué's method becomes explicable to us from the fact that the individual is transformed into a particle of a mass. He loses his critical faculty; the mental superstructure is more or less dissolved, and unconscious psychic processes of an impulsive character gain the upper hand. The tendency to adopt the auto-suggestive formula as one's own presupposes a decrease of the critical faculty and a corresponding increase of credulity. It is the disappearance of the power of criticism which opens up the way to the unconscious. I need only mention here that in psycho-analytical treatment we begin by explaining to the patient that in free association, which is designed to give us an entry to the unconscious, he should forgo his critical thinking.

The formula is undoubtedly intended to influence the patient's unconscious. Coué specifically says so, although his ideas of the unconscious are open to many objections. According to our theories, the unconscious has found in illness, and particularly in neurosis, a means of expression for certain repressed tendencies. It has, therefore, an interest in the continuation of the illness, the dissolution of which would mean a loss for the unconscious. We analysts are very familiar with the resistance against this change. If, then, by way of suggestion the unconscious is, let us say, to be won over, then success will depend upon a suitable choice of technique. In the case of allo-suggestion the most important factor is a libidinal fixation, that is to say, the transference on to the hypnotist. Added to this is a particular technique designed to produce a suggestive effect. In the case of auto-suggestion there is, as we have seen, a need for a good relationship between super-ego and ego, and also a special method of suggestion.

If we want to understand why Coué's formula, or any other magical formula, is in this respect applicable and, within certain limits, successful, we shall do well to consider it in the light of a statement of Freud's, and of certain parallel manifestations from neighbouring fields.

In his critical summary of Le Bon's *The Crowd: A Study of the Popular Mind* Freud says: [1] 'Anyone who wishes to produce an

[1] *Group Psychology.*

effect upon it (the group) needs no logical consistency in his arguments; he must paint in the most lurid colours, he must exaggerate, and he must repeat the same thing over and over again.' We may add that the repetition of the same thing, especially when expressed in a formula, is particularly effective in opening the way into the unconscious. It is, as it were, a language to which the unconscious responds. We best understand the language we ourselves speak, and we may immediately add that repetition is a frequent and familiar means of expression of unconscious impulses. We shall not go here into what Freud has termed the 'repetition compulsion'. From this powerful compulsion, which forces the individual to repeat the same act at certain intervals of time, we are led by gradual stages to the manifestations which interest us here.

Folk-psychology offers us some remarkable examples upon which we may draw for comparison. Long ago I read a description by the African explorer, Stanley, of how during his expedition he had to fight against hostile natives. He divided his men into several groups, giving each one a leader. When they went into battle, every group produced a kind of battle-song or war-cry. The group, for instance, which was led by a man called Uledi, sang in endless repetition, 'Uledi-ledi-ledi. . . .' The meaning of this usage is clear. It stresses the fixation of every man to the leader, and at the same time binds the comrades-in-arms together.

In a certain type of mental disorder, which is associated with a far-reaching regression of the libido to its earliest stages of development, namely catatonia, and in other forms of psychosis, we encounter the symptom of verbigeration. One or more words are repeatedly uttered in an impulsive way. Psychoanalysis recognises in these word-sequences a substitute, often but little distorted, for actions inspired by the unconscious. Earlier murderous impulses, for instance, may be transformed into a stereotyped, rattled-off formula containing suggestions of death. Sexual drives find extenuated expression in a stereotyped repetition of obscene words. The same persons also frequently show stereotyped movements, in which a purposive movement, originally highly charged with emotion, has become fixed into a rigid and bizarre one. Such movements are often to be observed among chronic mental patients. For those readers who have no psychiatric experience of their own I shall now give a few examples.

In my schooldays I used to see in the streets of my home town a man who behaved in an odd way, in whom any psychiatrist could easily have recognised the residual state of catatonic hebephrenia. As he limped through the streets he was invariably followed by a crowd of schoolchildren. He would break into a run, talking aloud to himself, always repeating the same words in the same tones: 'Ten thousand coffins, ten thousand coffins. . . .' Another phrase was: 'Death is near, time is up, time is up, death is near,' which he would repeat endlessly. These words of the poor madman served as a last, petrified expression of his hostile impulses. We recognise in them a kind of magic spell against his persecutors. It should be mentioned that according to the findings of psycho-analysis such formulae, even under the cover of aggressive impulses, always serve to express sexual aims, as is shown not only by their wording and content, but particularly by their rhythm. This is clearly evident in the stereotyped movements, where the erotic meaning is quite unmistakable.

The construction of word-formulae also occurs very often in obsessional neuroses, although they are, externally at least, different from the formulae of catatonics. They are used quite consciously to repel the patient's own impulses. They frequently take very eccentric forms which are, however, easily seen to have a meaning. One of my patients used to drive away certain impulses with the formula: 'It's nothing to do with me; I'll kick you; get away.' It should be mentioned that these formulae which are brought into service against the frightening obsession always become themselves obsessional. What is of particular interest to us is the ambivalence of instinctual drives, which is clearly seen even in the most minute psychic productions of obsessional patients. In everything an obsessional does or says, drive and inhibition, the wish for pleasure and the need for punishment, appear simultaneously. One of my patients gave me a very instructive example from his childhood. His behaviour at that time, even when he seemed to be full of guilt-feelings and repentance, was a mixture of hostile and tormenting drives. These feelings were secretly closely linked with masturbation, whilst externally they appeared to be connected with other small misdeeds in the nursery. Any trivial wrong-doing was invariably followed by the same reaction. The boy would cling to his mother and say in endless repetition: 'Forgive me, mother, forgive me, mother!' This behaviour did in fact express his contrition, but it also expressed far more strongly two other tendencies. In the first place, he continued in this way to torment his mother, whilst asking her forgiveness. Furthermore, it was apparent then, as also in later years, that instead of trying to reform himself, he always preferred to repeat his faults and to obtain forgiveness for them. This was also a disturbing factor during his psycho-analytical treatment. We found, moreover, that the rapid rattling-off of the formula of atonement had been devised in imitation of the rhythm of his masturbation. Thus the forbidden sexual wish contrived to break through in this concealed form. I am giving an extensive report of this case because the patient had later, some time before he came to psycho-analytical treatment, tried the Coué formula. There one could atone for everything by mumbling thrice daily twenty sentences, without having to subject oneself to any other effort of the will.

We are beginning to see that for some people Coué's system provides a ready and cheap form of self-punishment which is far easier than avoiding a repetition of previous mistakes. In fact the system meets them half-way. The idea of punishment is universally associated with numerical images. One receives twenty-five strokes with the cane, six months imprisonment, a fine of ten pounds. If we again recall the relationship of this system to the counting of the beads of the rosary, we may point out that devout Roman Catholics are often ordered by their priest to say a certain number of rosaries by way of atonement for their sins. Like the rosary Coué's method is suited to give expression to the common human feelings of guilt and the need for punishment. The association between sin and illness is long-standing and deep-rooted. The widespread human 'failing' of masturbation carries with it guilt-feelings, and at the same time frequently produces a fear of illness. This fear is the manifestation of the expectation of punishment—punishment for all the 'wicked', forbidden wishes of childhood, which find their collective and active expression in masturbation.

We can now state precisely how Coué's method works upon the individual, where it is successful. The patient, by adopting a behaviour reminiscent of that of obsessional neurotics, exchanges his previous illness for a mild form of obsessional neurosis, without realising it. The feeling of omnipotence which is associated with self-mastery is sufficiently pleasurable to blind him to the drawbacks of the method. It used to be said that hypnosis induces an artificial hysteria. Radó [1] has recently expressed a similar opinion with regard to the cathartic method. The therapeutic effect of the Coué method is thus bound up with increased regression. This view is fully consistent with what we have said about the regressive manifestations leading to

[1] 'Das ökonomische Prinzip der Technik: I. Hypnose und Kathar-sis.' *International Journal*, **12**, 1926.

narcissism. We may add that the ideas of personal omnipotence are most strongly marked in obsessional neuroses. The first case history in which Freud described this manifestation was one of obsessional neurosis. We are also familiar with the way in which the obsessional neurotic fights his illness, partly, as previously mentioned, with the help of formulae.

As something very similar takes place in the process of 'self-mastery', there is much to support our view that its inventor is subject to an obsessional neurosis, which although probably no longer in the phase of symptom-formation, nevertheless seems to impel him to test the omnipotence of thought on the masses seeking his help. A striking feature of the system is the avoidance of all knowledge of the origin of the illness. We are here at once reminded of the prohibitions against enquiry and knowledge which we encounter in the analyses of obsessional patients.

The economic significance of the Coué formula in consciousness and in the unconscious of the patient proves to be as over-determined as the significance of a compulsive symptom for the neurotic. There is first of all the manifest significance of the formula as a consolation and self-encouragement, which is strongly reinforced by repetition. The reiteration of a formula received from the leader enables the disciple to identify himself with his master in a particularly noticeable way. Furthermore, the formula serves as self-punishment. If the individual suffered from an illness which, to the unconscious, signified punishment, that form of atonement is replaced by another, far more agreeable to the ego. Finally, this formula stands for the return of the repressed, of the forbidden wish, the indulgence of which was met by punishment. Rhythm and tempo participate especially in this unconscious representation of the prohibited activity, which now takes place with the complete approval of the father.

In the deepest layer of the unconscious the use of the formula thus stands for a hidden substitute for masturbation sanctioned by the father. The prescribed piece of string is also significant. It would be possible, for instance, to count on one's fingers; but Coué insists on the use of string. Its handling can be seen as the reappearance of the forbidden manipulations in the shape of an action which appears at first sight to serve the purpose of repression. Thus forbidden sexual wishes, punishment, the striving for reformation, and consolation all unite in this one formula.

In the course of our investigation we have discovered the psychological reasons why countless people all over the world have so readily adopted Coué's method and why all these people have willingly and uncritically turned themselves into mere talking-machines, reproducing the healing formula in the prescribed manner. We incidentally succeeded in uncovering the psychological relationship of self-mastery to other methods of psycho-therapy. We may assume that there are different levels in therapeutic methods corresponding to the different levels at which the conditions most frequently treated by psycho-therapy, namely the neuroses, are met with.

By calling Coué's method a therapeutic procedure on the obsessional level we do not only mean that it makes use of the same archaic modes of thinking, familiar to us from the psychology of obsessional neuroses. We also mean that Coué's method is, psychologically speaking, the direct antithesis of psychoanalysis. It is true that in Coué's writings the unconscious is taken into account, but the psychological basis is extremely weak and full of inner contradictions. The full contrast of the two methods becomes apparent if we compare their respective attitudes towards one decisive question, namely the patient's knowledge of the origin and structure of his illness. To the psycho-analyst, the making conscious of the repressed, which forms a large part of his method, is an indispensable means for the attaining of the therapeutic aim. It is quite otherwise with Coué. Let us hear what he has to say:

'It is better not to know from where an ill comes, and yet to drive it away, than to know and be unable to get rid of it.' [1]

In contrast to this, the method of psycho-analysis most strongly compels people to recognise the reality-principle. At the same time, as the treatment progresses, unconscious processes become conscious and consciousness is thereby enriched. Psycho-analysis demands of the individual the subjugation of psychic resistances and, according to Freud, is to be carried through 'in abstinence'. Coué's doctrine, although it stresses the unconscious origin of symptoms, rejects all closer knowledge of such origin: it thus largely surrenders to the pleasure-principle, and must be characterised as regressive, just as psycho-analysis can claim to be called progressive. The approximation of Coué's method to the therapeutic procedures of primitive peoples is unmistakable. With him as with them magical thinking is paramount, and spares the patient a laborious adjustment to reality.

As already mentioned, Jones has penetratingly observed that such a method appears to achieve cheap successes, but only at

[1] Coué: *Self-Mastery by Conscious Auto-Suggestion:* George Allen and Unwin, London, 1922.

the cost of inhibiting development in some important sphere. This amounts to the same conclusion as our own, which is that in the case of successful self-mastery the patient exchanges his previous illness for an obsessional psychological state.

One of Coué's critics, Décsi, makes the objection that whereas before the treatment the patient suffered from an auto-suggested illness, he now enjoys an auto-suggested health. The author is obviously referring to the same psychic process as that described by us as an obsessional feeling of omnipotence.

The successes obtained by this method are illusory. It is not easy to test their permanence, because those patients who relapse as well as those who have been unsuccessful from the start do not advertise the fact. From those few patients treated by the Coué method whom I have met, I have gained the impression that the suggestive effect is most superficial and ephemeral. This is easily comprehensible. Whether or not the therapeutic effects of hypnosis are long lasting depends upon whether there is an enduring transference of the libido on to the hypnotist. Here, too, experience shows that we are dealing with unstable psychic conditions, and how much more unstable must be the successes of auto-suggestion. The patient is, after all, not completely removed from reality. The incidents of life can so easily shake and refute the correctness of the formula about the continuously progressing improvement. Furthermore, the strong emotional individual attachment which the patient develops towards the hypnotist is lacking. It remains to be seen whether any more is involved than a fleeting fascination of the individual reduced to the level of a particle in a mass, and whether the danger of defection is countered by sufficiently strong inhibitions.

Time alone will tell whether the crowds which flock to Coué will have enough inner cohesion to enable the individual successes achieved to endure for some time. The fascination of the crowd, as can be most clearly seen in America, has been largely responsible for making Couéism fashionable. It is very likely that its duration will be similarly shortlived. This is where its difference from psycho-analysis is most apparent. In the latter the emphasis is upon strict individuality, thorough working through, and considerable expenditure of time. This precludes its application to the great mass of people, which the prevalence of neuroses would make desirable. It remains, however, secure from the risk of becoming a fashionable money-making mass-movement, and does not expose people to the danger of being delivered up once again to their previous suffering after a brief spell of fascination.

INDEX

Abraham, Karl, *Selected Papers* 27, 47, 172
Abreaction
  cathartic 131
  of memories 19
  motor 62
Adaptation
  of thought to reality 89, 92
  neurotic's insufficient 112
Adler, Alfred
  and Freud's libido theory 312
  and importance of inferiority-feelings 313
  and 'The maculine protest' 313, 314
Agoraphobia 49
Aichhorn, August 303, 304
Amnesia, infantile and neurotic 111
Ambivalence
  of attitude towards paternal god 138
  of emotional impulses 111
  of inner drives 301
  of instinctual drives 323
  overcoming of 301
  present in Kolnidre 142
Amenhotep IV, (fourteenth cent. B.C.)
  a forerunner of Moses 275, 287
  Asiatic influence under 265
  branded a heretic 287
  changed his name to 273
  desires to rule through love 282
  exalted truth 283
  founded a new capital 273
  his great hymn 276
  planned a world religion 285
  prophet of monotheism 275
  rebellion against father 270
  removed name of Amon 273
  repression in instinctual life 265
  revolutionary changes 263
  similarity between Aton hymn and 104th Psalm 287
Analogies
  between childhood of individual and pre-history of mankind 132
  between dreams and myths 188
  between fire and life 175
  with the dream 173
  with obsessional neurosis 138
Analytical investigation 307
d'Annunzio, Gabriele 258
Anthropogeny, procreation of man—the basis of 199

Anxiety
  due to repression of instinct 242
  emotion transposed 199
  love-life may produce 94
Apple
  serpent and, in close proximity 195
  symbol for female fertility 167
Association
  – experiment 167
  method of free 117
Astasia and abasia 63
Atonement 137 ff
  deepest meaning of the Day of 147
Auto-erotic
  earliest impulses of sexuality 119
  gain in pleasure 318
  restriction 289
  wishful stimuli 242
Auto-suggestion
  a palliative 307
  by means of 308
  nature and mechanism of 319
  new form of 306
  stereotyped formula of 314
  suggestion cloaked in a magic formula 308
  unstable successes of 327

Bi-phasic actions 300
Bi-sexual disposition of human beings 223
Bleuler, Eugen 13, 169
Breasted, J. 262, 274, 276, 281, 283, 286, 290
Breuer, Joseph
  reawakening memories by hypnosis 116
  original discovery, importance of 121
  discovery 127
Breuer and Freud, *Studies on Hysteria* 19, 153, 179
Byron, Lord, example of true incest 27

Castration
  – complex 94
  – phantasy 93
  sort of 92
Catatonic hebephrenia 323
Cathexis, object – 105
Censorship
  circumventing the 196
  concept of 185
  conceals this design 70

328